ARDEN EARLY MODERN DRAMA

General Editors: Suzanne Gossett,
John Jowett and Gordon McMullan

EVERYMAN

and

MANKIND

ARDEN EARLY MODERN DRAMA

EVERYMAN

and

MANKIND

Edited by
DOUGLAS BRUSTER
and
ERIC RASMUSSEN

Bloomsbury Arden Shakespeare
An imprint of Bloomsbury Publishing Plc

BLOOMSBURY
LONDON · OXFORD · NEW YORK · NEW DELHI · SYDNEY

Bloomsbury Arden Shakespeare
An imprint of Bloomsbury Publishing Plc

Imprint previously known as Arden Shakespeare

50 Bedford Square	1385 Broadway
London	New York
WC1B 3DP	NY 10018
UK	USA

www.bloomsbury.com

BLOOMSBURY, THE ARDEN SHAKESPEARE and the Diana logo are
trademarks of Bloomsbury Publishing Plc

First published in 2009 by A & C Black Publishers Limited
Reprinted by Bloomsbury Arden Shakespeare 2015

British Library Cataloguing-in-Publication Data
A catalogue record for this book is available from the British Library.

ISBN: HB: 978-1-4081-1946-4
PB: 978-1-9042-7162-8

Library of Congress Cataloging-in-Publication Data
A catalog record for this book is available from the Library of Congress.

Series: Arden Early Modern Drama

Printed and bound in Great Britain

The Editors

Douglas Bruster is Professor of English at the University of Texas at Austin. He has edited *The Changeling* for *Thomas Middleton: The Collected Works* and has published on Shakespeare and early modern drama in *Drama and the Market in the Age of Shakespeare*, *Quoting Shakespeare*, *Shakespeare and the Question of Culture*, *To Be or Not To Be* and, with Robert Weimann, *Prologues to Shakespeare's Theatre* and *Shakespeare and the Power of Performance*. His essays have appeared in *Comparative Drama*, *Literature and History*, *Renaissance Drama* and *Shakespeare Quarterly*.

Eric Rasmussen is Chair and Professor of English at the University of Nevada. He has co-edited, with Jonathan Bate, the *Complete Works* of Shakespeare for the Royal Shakespeare Company. He is also co-editor of the *Norton Anthology of English Renaissance Drama*, *King Henry VI Part 3* in the Arden Shakespeare third series, *Doctor Faustus* in the Revels Plays Series, *Cynthia's Revels* in the *Cambridge Edition of the Works of Ben Jonson* and *The Two Noble Kinsmen* for the Malone Society. For over a decade he has written the annual review of editions and textual studies for *Shakespeare Survey*.

CONTENTS

LIST OF
ILLUSTRATIONS

Every effort has been made to contact the copyright holders of the illustrations included in this edition. The Publisher will be happy to agree an
appropriate permissions fee if necessary from any such holder who had
not responded to their inquiries by the time of publication.

GENERAL EDITORS' PREFACE

Arden Early Modern Drama (AEMD) is an expansion of the acclaimed Arden Shakespeare series to include the plays of other dramatists of the early modern period. The series publishes dramatic texts from the early modern period in the established tradition of the Arden Shakespeare, using a similar style of presentation and offering the same depth of information and high standards of scholarship. We define 'early modern drama' broadly, to encompass plays written and performed at any time from the late fifteenth to the late seventeenth century. The attractive and accessible format and well-informed editorial content are designed with particular regard to the needs of students studying literature and drama in the final years of secondary school and in colleges and universities. Texts are presented in modern spelling and punctuation; stage directions are expanded to clarify theatrical requirements and possibilities; and speech prefixes (the markers of identity at the beginning of each new speech) are regularized. Each volume contains about twenty illustrations both from the period and from later performance history; a full discussion of the current state of criticism of the play; and information about the textual and performance contexts from which the play first emerged. The goal of the series is to make these wonderful but sometimes neglected plays as intelligible as those of Shakespeare to twenty-first-century readers.

AEMD editors bring a high level of critical engagement and textual sophistication to their work. They provide guidance in assessing critical approaches to their play, developing arguments from the best scholarly work to date and generating new perspectives. A particular focus of an AEMD edition is the play as it was first performed in the theatre. The title-page of each volume normally displays the name of the company for which the play was written and the theatre at which it was first staged: in the Introduction the play is discussed as part of a company repertory as well as of an authorial canon. Finally, each edition presents a full scholarly discussion of the base text and other relevant materials as physical and social documents, and the Introduction describes issues arising in the early history of the publication and reception of the text.

Commentary notes, printed immediately below the playtext, offer compact but detailed exposition of the language, historical context and theatrical significance of the play. They explain textual ambiguities and, when an action may be interpreted in different ways, they summarize the arguments. Where appropriate they point the reader to fuller discussions in the Introduction.

CONVENTIONS

AEMD editions always include illustrations of pages from the early texts on which they are based. Comparison between these illustrations and the edited text immediately enables the reader to see clearly what a critical edition is and does. In summary, the main changes to the base text – that is, the early text, most often a quarto, that serves as the copy from which the editor works – are these: certain and probable errors in the base text are corrected; typography and spelling are brought into line with current usage; and speech prefixes and stage directions are modified to assist the reader in imagining the play in performance.

Significant changes introduced by editors are recorded in the textual notes at the foot of the page. These are an important cache of information, presented in as compact a form as is possible without forfeiting intelligibility. The standard form can be seen in the following example:

31 doing of] *Coxeter;* of doing *Q;* doing *Rawl*

The line reference ('31') and the reading quoted from the present editor's text ('doing of') are printed before the closing square bracket. After the bracket, the source of the reading, often the name of the editor who first made the change to the base text (*'Coxeter'*), appears, and then other readings are given, followed by their source ('of doing *Q;* doing *Rawl*'). Where there is more than one alternative reading, they are listed in chronological order; hence in the example the base text Q (= Quarto) is given first. Abbreviations used to identify early texts and later editions are listed in the Abbreviations and References section towards the end of the volume. Editorial emendations to the text are discussed in the main commentary, where notes on emendations are highlighted with an asterisk.

Emendation necessarily takes account of early texts other than the base text, as well as of the editorial tradition. The amount of attention paid to other texts depends on the editor's assessment of their origin and importance. Emendation aims to correct errors while respecting the integrity of different versions as they might have emerged through revision and adaptation.

Modernization of spelling and punctuation in AEMD texts is thorough, avoiding the kind of partial modernization that produces language from no known period of English. Generally modernization is routine, involving thousands of alterations of letters. As original grammar is preserved in AEMD editions, most modernizations are as trivial as altering 'booke' to 'book', and are unworthy of record. But where the modernization is unexpected or ambiguous the change is noted in the textual notes, using the following format:

   102 trolls] *(trowles)*

Speech prefixes are sometimes idiosyncratic and variable in the base texts, and almost always abbreviated. AEMD editions expand contractions, avoiding confusion of names that might be similarly abbreviated, such as Alonzo/Alsemero/Alibius from *The Changeling*. Preference is given to the verbal form that prevails in the base text, even if it identifies the role by type, such as 'Lady' or 'Clown', rather than by personal name. When an effect of standardization is to repress significant variations in the way that a role is conceptualized (in *Philaster*, for example, one text refers to a cross-dressed page as *Boy*, while another uses the character's assumed name), the issue is discussed in the Introduction.

Stage directions in early modern texts are often inconsistent, incomplete or unclear. They are preserved in the edition as far as is possible, but are expanded where necessary to ensure that the dramatic action is coherent and self-consistent. Square brackets are used to indicate editorial additions to stage directions. Directions that lend themselves to multiple staging possibilities, as well as the performance tradition of particular moments, may be discussed in the commentary.

Verse lineation sometimes goes astray in early modern playtexts, as does the distinction between verse and prose, especially where a wide manuscript layout has been transferred to the narrower measure of a printed page. AEMD editions correct such mistakes. Where a verse line is shared between more than one speaker, this series follows the usual modern practice of indenting the second and subsequent part-lines to make it clear that they belong to the same verse line.

The textual notes allow the reader to keep track of all these interventions. The notes use variations on the basic format described above to reflect the changes. In notes, '31 SD' indicates a stage direction in or immediately after line 31. Where there is more than one stage direction, they are identified as, for example, '31 SD1', '31 SD2'. The second line of a stage direction will be identified as, for instance, '31.2'. A forward slash / indicates a line-break in verse.

We hope that these conventions make as clear as possible the editor's engagement with and interventions in the text: our aim is to keep the reader fully informed of the editor's role without intruding unnecessarily on the flow of reading. Equally, we hope – since one of our aims is to encourage the performance of more plays from the early modern period beyond the Shakespeare canon – to provide texts which materially assist performers, as well as readers, of these plays.

PREFACE

Unlike Everyman, we have enjoyed the enduring fellowship of a large number of friends and colleagues who have come along with us and been our guides during the course of this six-year project. We are especially grateful for the good deeds of Donald L. Bailey, Richard Beadle, Daniel Birkholz, Mary Blockley, Anne Brannen, Thomas Cable, Rose Coyle, Julie Crosby, Elizabeth Cullingford, Arthur Evenchik, John Farrell, Arthur Freeman, Janet Ing Freeman, James Garrison, Ton Hoenselaars, Kelly Horton, Matthew Trey Jansen, Arthur Kincaid, Jonathan Lamb, Gary Lay, James Loehlin, John McKinnell, Gordon McMullan, James Mardock, Sonia Massai, Rick Michaelson, Douglas Morse, Tessa Musgrave, Stephen Orgel, Derek Pearsall, Suloni Robertson, Erin Salada, Tiffany Stern, Meg Twycross, and Kevin West. This project has been aided tremendously by the knowledge of Margaret Bartley, Suzanne Gossett, Jonathan Hope, John Jowett and Damian Love. And, finally, to our respective kindred, Elizabeth Scala, Madeleine Bruster and Claire Bruster, and Victoria Hines, Tristan Rasmussen and Arden Rasmussen, we are eternally grateful for both the time and space with which to finish this edition, and for their able assistance in making it whole and sound. To them we dedicate this fruit of our efforts.

INTRODUCTION

THE MORALITY PLAY

Imagine you have just a short while to live. You have been promised joy without end in another place, but to get there safely you
have to preserve your innermost being – your soul. Everywhere
are temptations that will damage your chances of attaining this
extended life. All around you, figures promise to help you by
taking this heavy burden from your shoulders. Listening to them
is easier than guarding your spirit, for their promises let you pay
attention to what you want right now. As you keep company with
these figures, however, you begin to see how thin their support
is, how weak you feel and how transitory all physical things are.
Friends, fine clothing, money, status, sex: these are attractive but
ephemeral pleasures. You realize that by indulging your body
you have endangered your soul. You may have lost everything
for an instant of pleasure. When you die, you will have nothing
and be alone.

To imagine this situation is to understand what happens in
morality plays, and why they were written. The English dramas
we call 'morality plays' can just as easily be called 'soul plays',
for they typically seek to teach the right way to live by showing
someone who gives in to the body's desires.[1] Seduced by the
forces of sin, this symbolic character – 'Mankind' in our first
play, 'Everyman' in the second – eventually learns the lesson of

---

1 For bibliography on the morality play in England, see Grantley; for an overview of
   scholarship, see Bevington, 'Castles'; for foundational critical treatments, see Potter,
   Feldman, Fifield, 'Community', Gilman and King. Godfrey argues that genre can
   lead us to define these plays 'in too narrow a way with regard to theme, character,
   and occasion' ('Forms', 39).

living rightly in the short term, on earth, so as to preserve the chance to live forever, in heaven. Morality plays are entertaining and instructive portrayals of a representative human figure who faces a choice between body and spirit, this world and the next. This choice is made more difficult by the competition for his soul between the parties of sin (the vices and devils) and redemption (the virtues and angels).

Mankind (1470s) and *Everyman* (*c.* 1518–19) are among the best surviving examples of a genre which flourished across Western Europe in the 1400s and 1500s and which remains one of this region's special contributions to world culture. Along with *Everyman*'s source – a Dutch drama called *Elckerlijc* – *Mankind* and *Everyman* plot a triangle that stretches from Antwerp in the Netherlands to London and from there to Bury St Edmunds in East Anglia (see Fig. 1). This geographical region had become wealthy from the cloth trade, and exchanged ideas and literary forms as well as citizens and commercial goods. Given the prosperity of this region, it is not surprising that the concept of 'reckoning' – of accounting for one's actions in relation to a judgement that seemed inevitable – came to stand at the centre of the dramatic morality.

Other instances of the morality play in England include *The Pride of Life* (1375–1400), *The Castle of Perseverance* (1405–25), *Wisdom* (1480–1500) and *Magnificence* (1515). Like these morality plays, *Mankind* and *Everyman* are strikingly *inclusive*: not only conscious that the audience exists and is watching the show, but dependent on that active relationship to get their messages and entertainment across. At various moments, each turns to the audience and includes it in the 'world' addressed by the dramatic story. Likewise, each uses humour for dramatic as well as thematic effect – sometimes, given the seriousness of their subjects, at moments and in relation to topics where we do not expect plays to make us laugh.

These two plays also have distinct differences. Some of their differences arise from their places of origin. *Everyman*, a printed

2

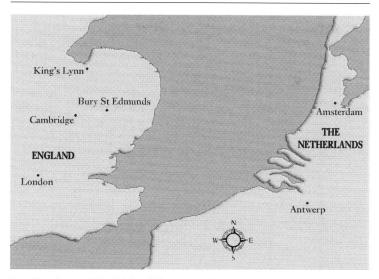

1. The places of *Mankind* and *Everyman* with attention to London and significant places in East Anglia and the Netherlands

playbook, was published in London at the beginning of that city's rise to national predominance in the early 1500s. *Mankind*, surviving in only a single manuscript, was most likely a product of the powerful Benedictine monastery at Bury St Edmunds in Suffolk. This was approximately sixty-two miles (one hundred kilometres) to the northeast of London in the theatrically vibrant region of East Anglia. *Mankind* is a 'regional' play, therefore, but only because London became a national centre that made other places, and dialects other than its Southern standard, seem marginal.

Neither draws directly upon classical drama, but *Mankind* will strike readers and audience members as being close to comedy. With the death of its protagonist, *Everyman* feels more like tragedy. *Mankind* is earthier, more at home with the body than *Everyman*, which largely distrusts the physical world. Correspondingly, *Mankind* is much more obviously a

3

theatrical script than *Everyman*, which may in fact never have been performed before its first recorded production in 1901. It is a paradox, given the uncertainty as to whether any early performance took place, that *Everyman* has been produced much more frequently than *Mankind* in modern times. *Everyman* can even be said to have ignited the twentieth century's interest in early English drama in performance.[1] Finally, *Mankind* is much more comfortable than *Everyman* in playing with religion. This is so much the case that we may be uncertain, if only for a while, whether it really wishes us to sacrifice our sense of humour and irreverence for the distant pay-off of salvation.

Both works exemplify qualities of the morality play genre that came to influence dramatic characterization in the English theatre. During the early 1590s, for instance, Christopher Marlowe and William Shakespeare would draw upon morality plays for works like *Doctor Faustus* and *Richard III*. The earlier form's influence can be seen not only in these plays' representations of sin and seduction, but also in their development of a newly deepened mode of characterization out of the morality's 'Vice' figure. As the shifty, self-confident Richard III describes himself in a gleeful aside to the audience: 'Thus, like the formal Vice, Iniquity, / I moralize two meanings in one word' (*R3* 3.1.82–3). In calling himself a 'formal Vice', Richard asks the audience to remember such plays as *Mankind*, where figures of sin called 'Vices' routinely spoke out of both sides of their mouths to fool spectators and protagonists alike.

Yet if this tradition proved highly influential, the time is long past when one could see *Mankind* and *Everyman* as merely prologues to Shakespeare's theatre.[2] Ongoing archival research has uncovered an astonishing variety of dramatic forms, venues and audiences in England in the centuries before the purpose-built

1 On the performance of medieval drama in modern times, see Sponsler, *Drama*, McKinnell and Elliott.
2 For an account of scholarship on medieval theatre emphasizing theatrical history's resistance to the evolutionary narrative, see Emmerson, 'History'.

theatres arose in Elizabethan London.[1] So while in retrospect it is possible to see the morality play as a kind of bridge between two periods, some caution is in order.[2] First, it goes without saying that the playwrights, actors and audiences connected with our two plays would have been unaware of and unconcerned over their place midway between what our own time would call the 'medieval' and 'early modern' eras. Next, to the extent that these period labels shed any light on our plays, we need to accord the medieval its due.[3] There was arguably more theatre, and were certainly more kinds of people involved in theatrical productions, before Shakespeare's time than after it. For these reasons and others, it will be important to focus not only on the specifics of these two plays' composition and structure, but also on those social and geographical contexts that we can determine for them.

Yet to resist a story of dramatic 'evolution' or 'progress' does not mean that we should give up all narratives about theatrical history. The morality play clearly recalls the intensively biblical nature of the medieval mystery cycles even as it anticipates the overwhelmingly secular dramas that would appear on the commercial stage during the time of Shakespeare and his contemporaries. *Mankind* and *Everyman* are part of a larger development in the English theatre. At its most basic, this development centred on both a change in the books used to make plays and on a subsequent, related alteration to the very identities of figures in these dramatic fictions.

In the fourteenth, fifteenth and sixteenth centuries, much of the drama performed in England was thoroughly religious.

---

1   Here we refer to the invaluable Records of Early English Drama (REED) project. For discussion of this project and its findings, see Douglas & MacLean, Klausner & Marsalek and Holland. Sponsler, 'Archives', explores the difficulties of connecting archival findings to performance.
2   On the morality play as a 'turning-point in dramatic history', see Wertz, 85.
3   The 'medieval' and the 'early modern' were overlapping, rather than distinct, eras. See Emmerson, 'Eliding', and White. As Lawrence Clopper has shown us, mystery plays were still being performed in Chester in 1575, only a year before James Burbage constructed the Theatre playhouse outside London (*Drama*, 293).

The mystery cycles were actually multiple plays that, together, sought to depict universal history. These plays typically began with the creation of the world and showed such familiar episodes as the temptation scene in the Garden of Eden, Noah's Flood, the birth of Christ and his ministry on earth (and, significantly, Satan's temptation of Christ in the wilderness), the Crucifixion, Resurrection, Harrowing of Hell and the Last Judgement. Because the great majority of the figures in these plays were scriptural, including God, Job, Moses, Christ and the Virgin Mary, among others, attending a play in medieval England usually meant watching entertaining performances of the Bible.

When the Reformation swept across Northern Europe in the early 1500s, severe tensions with the Roman Church made Christianity a battlefield. Arms and pens alike entered into fierce combat. Because staging scenes of a sacred nature seemed profane, extreme Protestants chose to see the mystery plays as dangerous. Eventually the English theatre ceased to represent figures on the upper rungs of the 'ladder of sanctity' – the scale of the sacred that had ordinary humans at its bottom and God, Christ, Mary and the Angels at its top.[1] Rather than showing sacred figures, drama developed characters from *this* world, secular personae such as Hieronymo, Shylock and the Duchess of Malfi. Instead of building their plays out of the Bible, playwrights constructed them by using various of the thousands of secular stories that poured out of the printing presses. Something important had changed in the relation of the Church and theatre. A century before Martin Luther nailed his religious protest to the door of the Castle Church in Wittenberg, Germany, on 31 October 1517, it would have been nearly impossible to imagine a serious play that did not draw on the Bible. Less than a century after Luther, there must have been avid English playgoers who had never seen sacred figures onstage.

1   On English biblical drama's gradual retreat down this 'ladder of sanctity', see Roston, 118, 120.

6

This profound reorientation of dramatic narrative – from sacred stories to secular ones – occurred during the rise of the morality play in England. It can be seen as well in the morality's emphasis on a spiritual struggle undergone not by a legendary or named individual, but by a representative human figure known merely as 'Mankind' or 'Everyman'. The morality play allowed the English theatre to imagine a pivotal figure – a character in the making – neither in terms of sacred, biblical precedent (Noah, Jesus, Pilate) nor secular, social specificity (Beatrice, Benedick, Dogberry), but as a kind of generalizing mirror. For over a century, this mirror reflected back to its audience members an image of what they shared with all human beings.

These plays' insistence on what we have in common leads us to ask whether the so-called birth of the modern age really separates us psychologically from the Middle Ages. We are used to hearing people identify Hamlet as a figure of the modern, as though today's individualism was invented only when Shakespeare's melancholy scholar stood centre stage at the Globe playhouse and delivered the 'To be or not to be' soliloquy. By presenting in fascinating detail the spiritual and psychological struggles that all individuals face, *Mankind* and *Everyman* remind us that *Hamlet* was hardly the first play to showcase the interior anxieties we feel in our private moments. These plays also show that, however sharply we may wish to define the advent of the 'early modern' era – with its great voyages of exploration, the rise of the printing press, Machiavellian political theory and new science – it is crucial not to think of morality plays as simple documents from a less complicated age.

Anyone reading *Mankind*, for instance, will realize that, like Chaucer's 'Miller's Tale', it is centuries 'ahead' of its time in its bluntness regarding sexuality and other bodily functions. The obscenity of its dirty 'Christmas song' (335–43) was impossible to perform upon the modern stage until the late 1960s, and is still a risky passage to read to public audiences expecting an older, 'religious' play to be serious and proper. Likewise the religious energies that lie behind the translation of *Everyman* – a conservative revision of the Protestant Dutch play *Elckerlijc* – seem strangely familiar in a time when religious fundamentalism has once more advanced itself, and when claims about the 'end of history' have themselves been ended by spiritual fervour.[1] *Everyman*'s tense spiritual dynamic is not something we can locate safely in the past. Finally, the fact that, during the past century, women have taken the lead roles in both *Mankind* and *Everyman* – plays written when the male gender seemed universal – testifies to both the flexibility of these dramas and the applicability of their lessons (see Fig. 2). These morality plays, then, are at one and the same time specifically late medieval, early modern and timeless. In treating the problems we all share, it might be argued, they could be nothing else.

MANKIND

Mankind *in brief*

Mankind, an anonymously authored morality play, is noisy, joyous, obscene and full of slapstick comedy. It was most likely written between 1471 and 1479 for performance by monks of the Benedictine monastery at Bury St Edmunds in East Anglia, then the virtual heart of theatrical activity in England. It may have been performed in a number of places, and for various kinds of audiences. The beginning of the play alludes to a mixed audience when it speaks of a division between those who will stand for the performance and those who are afforded the privilege of sitting down. Such playgoers may have included other monks and religious guild members, citizens from local towns and villages, and pilgrims travelling to religious shrines. The play's major themes are speech and the weakness of the flesh, with Mankind (its focal character) lured into a life of sin

---

1   In 1989, Francis Fukuyama published a controversial essay entitled 'The end of history?' widely taken to imply that the triumph of liberal democracy in the West had ushered in a comfortable era 'after' history.

2.   Edith Wynne Matthison as Everyman, 1903

before he finds forgiveness at the hands of a personified Mercy. The language of *Mankind* is divided between Mercy's aureate (that is, 'golden') style, a high level of speech marked by long Latinate words, and the simpler, native language of its comedic Vice figures. So engaging are *Mankind*'s comedic Vices, in fact, that, like Mankind himself, many readers and audiences members have found themselves drawn as much to the play's naughty games as to its moral messages. This seduction lies at the heart of *Mankind*, and reaches a climax when the Vices actually halt the play in order to gather money for the privilege of seeing Titivillus, the head devil. Whether or not we give money at this juncture, the play makes its point: we have lent the Vices our attention and laughter, and by so doing have shown the weakness of our bodies. In this way, *Mankind* uses our desire for theatrical pleasure to teach us about the dangers of desire itself.

Language, game and play in Mankind

The earnest farmer called Mankind appears in over half the action of the drama which takes his name. Given this title, however, we may be surprised to find out that Mankind speaks much less frequently than most of the play's cast. To think of *Mankind*, in fact, is to recall the play's *other* figures. And this is not merely because Mankind himself, in representing general humanity, lacks interesting detail. Instead, like the ingénue of a romantic comedy, his voice is often drowned out by a loud collection of speakers who, in competing for his soul, gain our own attention. These include: Vices named New-Guise, Nowadays and Nought (here called, for short, the 'Three Ns'); their immediate director, the aptly named Mischief; Titivillus, the lead devil who is summoned when the minor mischief makers fail in their attempt to pervert Mankind; and Mercy, the priest figure who struggles to keep Mankind on the straight and narrow.

While extremely entertaining, this competition of voices and beliefs reveals a key assumption that *Mankind* makes about life itself: our choice of *language* – who and what we listen to, as well as what and how we speak – is essentially a choice between sin and virtue, between being damned and being saved. Speech means salvation or sin.

10

The play opens and closes with speech that may sound peculiar. Mercy, the priest figure who works actively to safeguard Mankind's soul, speaks in a heavily Latinate form of English.[1] In the first four lines such words as 'creation', 'magnified', 'disobedience', 'indignation' and 'crucified' sound quite formal to our ears. The fact that these often fall at the end of lines, as in 'I beseech you heartily, have this premeditation' (44), only increases their formality. At the time, however, this register was quite common for prayers and sermons. Mercy's words are of a piece with the 'Parson's Prologue' in Chaucer's *Canterbury Tales*, for example, and sound like much of John Lydgate's writing.[2] The sermon, a popular form in the Middle Ages and later, seems to be Mercy's favourite form of communication.[3] But when magnified in and by his long speeches, the effect can verge on the comic.

The play's second speaker, in fact, gives us no choice but to laugh when he interrupts Mercy's formal language:

> I beseech you heartily, leave your calcation.
> Leave your chaff, leave your corn, leave your
>   dalliation.
> Your wit is little, your head is mickle, ye are full of
>   predication.
>   But, sir, I pray this question to clarify:
> Driff-draff, mish-mash,
> Some was corn and some was chaff,
> My dame said my name was Raff;
>   Unshut your lock and take an ha'penny.
>
>   (45–52)

Like students witnessing a spot-on imitation of a pompous teacher, we are likely to find Mischief's parody hilarious. He

---

1 Another aspect of Mercy's speech (and, for some of the play, Mankind's) is its four-stress rhythms. See Eccles, xli.
2 Cf. Chaucer, 'Parson's Prologue', 55–60; and, on Lydgate's aureation, Pearsall, 261–3.
3 For an analogue to *Mankind* from a fifteenth-century sermon, see Appendix 2.

has encountered Mercy winding up a sincere spiritual lesson by citing Matthew, 3.12 on the corn (i.e. the righteous) being saved, and the chaff (the sinners) burned. Quoting Mercy's own words back to him – 'I beseech you heartily' – Mischief proceeds to turn this spiritual message inside-out. He makes language a game.

With his closing lines here, Mischief also seems to be imitating a kind of game the play's original audience would have been familiar with. This was a popular form of entertainment called the 'mummers' play' – or 'plays' as Thomas Pettitt recommends we call them.[1] The word 'mumming' comes from a Dutch word for 'mask' or 'disguise' (*OED*). These mummers' plays comprised a simple form of interactive theatre staged by amateur players from small towns or villages, sometimes in group visitations to houses both great and small. Later mummers' plays would feature a mock killing and resurrection, much like the pretend beheading that Mischief performs upon Nought at 434–45. An important part of the mummers' plays was the *quête*, a ritual money-gathering like the group solicitation that the Vices practise at 457–74 before the entrance of Titivillus. A third aspect, as we will discuss below, was a big-headed clown or devil figure like Titivillus himself.

However much it may draw on mummings, the comedy in *Mankind* is also comparable to a Continental tradition of carnivalesque entertainment at Shrovetide. Shrovetide is the day before Ash Wednesday, which ushers in Lent, the period during which many Christians fast and pray. Shrovetide is traditionally marked by festivals of indulgence, as with the Mardi Gras celebrations familiar today. In Germany such Shrovetide carnival was known as the *Fastnachtspiel*, a boisterous and bawdy

1 On the mummers' play, see Pettitt, 'Pyramus', esp. 92 n.1; and Cass. For early reference to mummers' properties (including devils' heads) see Clopper, *Drama*, 300, entry 7.

12

genre which has been suggested as an analogue for *Mankind*'s comedy.[1]

Indulgence has its price, though. Whether we realize it at the moment, we become part of Mischief's world when we take his cue to laugh at Mercy. This 'booby-trap' structure is repeated throughout *Mankind*, and functions – along with the play's deep interest in language – as one of its most important features.[2] Again and again we are persuaded by *Mankind*'s fun to laugh ourselves away from spiritual foundations and towards the demands of the body. Sometimes this persuasion takes the form of trickery, as when we are seduced by the Three Ns into joining in with their 'Christmas song' (335–43): we are just into its second line before we realize that we have been conned into singing a very dirty little number. Likewise we are asked to engage in a devil's bargain when the players stop the action and make clear the contract: if we wish to see Titivillus, the head devil, we have to pay for the privilege. As New-Guise puts it with his blunt eloquence: 'We shall gather money unto, / Else there shall no man him see' (457–8).

When Titivillus finally arrives before us, he twice enlists our aid as he sets about to seduce Mankind. 'Whist! Peace! I shall go to his ear and tittle therein' (557), he says, promising to plant lies in Mankind's ear only if he first has our own. His next request makes the bargain absolutely explicit:

> An ever ye did, for me keep now your silence.
> Not a word, I charge you, pain of forty pence.
> A pretty game shall be showed you ere ye go hence.
> (589–91)

As Titivillus winks at us and asks for our sinning complicity in the seduction of Mankind, *Mankind* is showing how its performance is like life. By turning to its living audience for help with

---

1 See Pettitt, 'Early English'.
2 For this phrase see Denny, 263 n.16. On the dangers of audiences' engagement with stage Vices, see Jones.

13

the ongoing production, the morality play sutures us into its action. Just as there is no separation between the lively events of *Mankind* and the vital participation of the audience, no firm boundaries divide the 'life' of Mankind from our own.

The figures of Mankind

Who is Mankind? The contest for Mankind's soul led Dorothy Castle to call him 'the football that passes between Mercy and the Devil's helpers'.[1] In some ways the play is much like a match between the forces of good and evil. Listening to its comedy is to hear shrieks of merry excitement like 'Whoop! Ho!' (607), 'Whoop whoo!' (720), 'Hey, dog, hey!' (720) and 'Whoop how! Anow, anow, anow, anow!' (733). If Mankind is sometimes like a football jealously sought by rival teams, however, towards the end of the action he becomes a player himself.

That Mankind has the power to choose is foregrounded by the parodic 'swearing in' ceremony that the Three Ns stage at lines 702–17 to prove that he is, in the words of Nowadays, 'one of our men' (669). Like a conscript to an out-of-control military unit, Mankind must swear his commitment to a long list of transgressions, beginning with adulterous fornication and ending with robbing, stealing, killing and missing Mass. *Mankind* is convinced that not only is the body itself the site of a struggle between good and evil, devotion and temptation, but that individual bodies are soldiers. As Mercy puts it at 228, quoting Job from the Latin version of the Bible: '*Vita hominis est militia super terram*' ('The life of Man upon earth is a battle', Job, 7.1). Mercy goes on to urge Mankind: 'Oppress your ghostly enemy and be Christ's own knight. / Be never a coward again your adversary. / If ye will be crowned, ye must needs fight' (229–31). If he

---

1 Castle, *Game*, 37. We have chosen to refer to *Mankind*'s and *Everyman*'s dramatis personae as 'figures' rather than 'characters'. As Peter Meredith points out, morality play personae 'are not intended to be naturalistic human beings but rather to present elements of human character or of society or of theological doctrine and belief' (*Acting*, 14). Potter argues that the moralities present a 'functional scheme of characterization' in which what each figure is to do trumps abstraction (39; cf. 37–47). For further discussion, see Carpenter and Schmitt.

3. Medieval agricultural labourer, from Caxton, *Game and Playe of the Chesse* (1474)

sometimes seems a pawn manipulated by outside forces, then, Mankind is also portrayed as a figure possessed of free will, with the choice to enlist in one of two opposed armies. In this, his situation recalls the medieval *psychomachia*, the battle in which devils and angels struggle for one's soul.

Yet Mankind also bears some marks of a more specific identity, that of a farmer. Throughout *Mankind*, he is associated with the spade (see Fig. 3).[1] Early on, he devotes himself to digging as a way of avoiding the scoffing words spoken by New-Guise; as Mankind says, 'I hear a fellow speak; with him I will not mell. / This earth with my spade I shall assay to delve' (327–8). In their first interactions with Mankind, the Three Ns solidify this identity by derisively referring to his 'spade' (344), 'crop' (357), 'acres' (360), 'turn[ing] the earth up and down' (361), 'tilling' (363), 'good cart', 'harvest' and 'corn' (366), and

1   On the spade as a conventional property in this era's drama, see May.

'compost' (374). Nought's agricultural advice as to how a farmer may ensure a good crop allows him to mock Mankind's vocation: 'If he will have rain, he may over-piss it; / And if he will have compost, he may over-bless it / A little with his arse, like – [*Bends, as if to defecate*]' (373–5). Mankind is, in these Vices' eyes, a farmer: someone who, in stark contrast to them, labours for his bread.

To be a farmer in the literature of this period was to be identified with honest, straightforward work. Yet such an identity was far from simple. As their titles suggest, such popular works as William Langland's great poem, *Piers Plowman* (1380–1400) and the anonymous *Plowman's Tale* (1450–70), once ascribed to Chaucer, took farmers as their initiating figures. These figures anticipated Mankind in standing for humanity generally while drawing on the traditional, productive analogy between, on one hand, the life of the spirit, and, on the other, planting and harvesting. We have seen that Mercy is interrupted by Mischief at precisely the moment he turns to the biblical metaphor of the corn and the chaff, and that Mischief up-ends Mercy's sermon by saying 'Leave your chaff, leave your corn' (46).

Mankind follows *Piers Plowman* in giving its title figure an unusual ability: literacy in Latin.[1] Peter Meredith rightly cautions us from regarding Mankind *only* as a farmer: Mankind is, as his name tells us, a figure who stands for all, and he may signify Adam (the first digger, in Genesis) as well (*Acting*, 18–19). While we expect the priest figure Mercy to have Latin, it is – outside the literary tradition of the Christian Plowman – impossible to imagine an agricultural worker sitting down, as Mankind does, and composing a 'badge' for himself in that language (315–22). At 321 he paraphrases, as his motto, a passage connected with Ash Wednesday – Job, 34.15: 'Remember, Man, that you are dust, and that you will return to dust.'

---

1 For the relation of *Piers Plowman* to *Mankind*, see Keiller. Alford discusses the role of Latin quotations in *Piers Plowman*.

The Book of Job is significant to our understanding of *Mankind*, and not only because it is cited or mentioned at least seven times in the play.[1] This book tells of a righteous man who becomes the subject of a bet between God and the devil. The devil believes he can make Job renounce his faith by taking away all that Job has. When God agrees to the challenge, Job is deprived of his family and possessions, but – though suffering greatly – refuses to curse God. As Paula Neuss points out, 'the behaviour of Mercy and Mischief is comparable to that of God and Satan in the book of Job' (Neuss, 48).

Mercy offers up the proverbial patience of Job as an example for Mankind to follow:

> See the great patience of Job in tribulation;
> Like as the smith trieth iron in the fire,
> So was he tried by God's visitation.
>
> (286–8)

As though applying the text Mercy has set him, Mankind recalls an appropriate motto from the Book of Job to pin to his chest. Like a comic version of this biblical character, Mankind falls victim to the desires of devil figures in the world, and will seem to lose everything before he is restored to God's graces. We *hear* his degradation, in fact, when he stops speaking like Mercy and begins speaking like the Vices. In their company, he uses their characteristic tail–rhyme stanzas.[2]

Mercy is Mankind's guide and protector, and also guides us. His speech opens and closes *Mankind* in the manner of a formal presenter or chorus. While allegorical tradition had typically gendered Mercy as feminine, Mercy is represented as male in *Mankind*. This is most likely to support his priest-like function. As Sister Mary Philippa Coogan remarked, Mercy 'talks like a priest, acts like a priest, and is recognized as a priest by all the other characters in the play' (Coogan, 6). For most of the drama

1 In addition to 321, cf. 228, 233, 286–8, 292, 303, 830 and nn.
2 See 607ff. and cf. pp. 38–41.

17

Mercy has the power to instruct Mankind but not to control or shape his choices in any other way.

The play's Vices work from within a hierarchical structure of malice. Nought, Nowadays and New-Guise form a unit. Their names signal what they represent. Nought stands for both 'nothing' and 'naughtiness', and is often connected with defecation and the lower bodily stratum. He is the lowest of these three. Nowadays represents modern habits (as opposed to traditional, and good, manners). New-Guise stands for current fashions. Each of these Vices speaks some Latin in *Mankind*. Their immediate superior, as it were, is Mischief. The word 'mischief' was much stronger in the era of *Mankind* than today, and referred to malicious harm. Appropriately, Mischief is connected with the enticement to suicide in *Mankind*.[1]

When Mischief and the Three Ns fail to lead Mankind astray, they call in a more powerful figure still: Titivillus (see Fig. 4). The actor who plays Titivillus most likely dons a large devil's-head, mask or visor, for, as New-Guise puts it in the moment of money-gathering: 'We intend to gather money, if it please your negligence, / For a man with a head that is of great omnipotence' (460–1). The mummers' plays traditionally featured a big-headed clown, sometimes named Beelzebub, who 'captured the imagination and interest of the folk'.[2] Titivillus is a relatively minor devil in the theological tradition, but takes on supreme importance in *Mankind* because of his relationship to idle language.[3] He was known as a devil who gathered words that had gone astray, such as gossip or other malicious speech, and prayers which were mumbled or broken off. He triumphs, temporarily, when he tricks Mankind into forsaking his prayers and skipping Mass.

1 See Coogan, 59–61, who, citing Ramsay (*Magnyfycence*, xliii), compares the appearance of a 'Mischief' and 'Despair' in Skelton's *Magnyfycence* (60). See also Clopper, 'Audience'.
2 Brody, 60–1; quotation at 61. For reference to a devil's-mask as early as 1372, see Divett.
3 On Titivillus's reputation, see Ashley, Jennings and Cawsey.

4. Titivillus (Carl Heap) and an unsuspecting Mankind (Bridget Thornborrow), the Medieval Players' Tour, 1985

The places and people of Mankind

When was *Mankind* written and performed? And where? By whom was it acted, and for whom? Should we think of it as having been written by a single person, or is it more of a collaboration? Was it written all at once, or compiled from various scenes that had been performed for some time? We don't have solid answers to any of these questions, for no one in the late fifteenth century seems to have written down anything about

19

Mankind save for the words of the play itself. But while we lack external evidence for *Mankind*, these words give us some suggestive 'internal' evidence. Because they are recorded in a mysterious manuscript called the Macro collection, our investigation into the background of *Mankind* should start there.[1]

The Macro collection is a group of manuscript (handwritten) folio leaves currently residing in the Folger Shakespeare Library in Washington, D.C. It features three powerful morality plays written before *Everyman*: *The Castle of Perseverance*, *Wisdom* and *Mankind*.[2] Besides being morality plays, each of these fifteenth-century dramas is affiliated with the others geographically in drawing upon the form of the English language spoken and written, in the fifteenth century, in the East Midlands. Along with East Anglia, the East Midlands formed a large, vibrant region in which – partly owing to the area's booming cloth-making economy – England's theatrical tradition thrived in the Middle Ages. To the north of London, East Anglia encompassed such major counties as Norfolk and Suffolk on England's east coast, with parts of Cambridgeshire and Lincolnshire as well.

As much as its vocabulary, what helps us locate *Mankind* is how these words were written, for its manuscript features a number of spellings specific to East Anglia.[3] Where our modernized text has Mischief saying at line 55, for instance, 'And ye said the corn should be saved and the chaff should be fired', the manuscript of *Mankind* reads 'Ande ȝe sayde þe corn xulde be sauyde & þe chaff xulde be feryde'. Two of the unfamiliar letters here – the ȝ or 'yogh' and the þ or 'thorn' – are actually common ways of writing 'y' (for the initial position) and 'th' in Middle English, and as such do not tell us much about where *Mankind* may have been written or transcribed, or for whom. But the 'x-' for 'sh-' here in the two instances of 'xulde' (i.e. 'should')

---

1 'Macro' is conventionally pronounced '*May-crow*', after the family name of the Reverend Cox Macro, who later owned the manuscript collection.
2 Kelly examines these three plays in conjunction.
3 For further discussion of the *Mankind* manuscript, see pp. 34–6.

is much more revealing, for, like the manuscript's 'q-' for 'wh-' – in such words as 'Qwyll' for 'While' (543) and 'Qwyppe' for 'Whip' (795), among others – it is a regionalism common to East Anglia.[1]

We can also take confidence that *Mankind* has roots in East Anglia from its many references to specific locations (even real individuals) in Cambridgeshire, Norfolk and Suffolk. For example, as will be discussed later, when Titivillus drills his troops as to where they are to maraud, ten individuals from ten different locations across East Anglia come in for mention (see 502–15). This was clearly a way for whoever wrote *Mankind* to wink at its audiences, which may have included, at various times of performance, any or all of these people.

At 274 Nought brags that he has been for a long while 'with the common tapster of Bury', referring to a liaison with a barmaid in the town of Bury St Edmunds, in Suffolk. His casual reference is like the extended mention of the ten prominent men from East Anglia, but joins significantly with another connection to Bury St Edmunds in *Mankind*'s back story. At the end of the *Mankind* manuscript (just as at the end of the play *Wisdom*), a hand has written an identifying statement in Latin (see Fig. 9):

> *O liber si quis cui constas forte queretur*
> *Hynghamque monacho dices super omnia consto*
> (fol. 134)

[O book, if anyone shall perhaps ask to whom you
  belong,
you will say, 'I belong above everything to Hyngham,
  a monk']

Mark Eccles observed that a Thomas Hyngham wrote his name as the owner of a fifteenth-century Boethius manuscript

---

1 On the regional specificity of these spellings, which she calls 'Norfolk . . . shibbo-leths' (85), see L. Wright. On the potential value of spelling systems for determining a 'literary geography' of medieval drama, see Beadle, 'Prolegomena'; esp., in relation to these features of *Mankind*, 91–2. We should note that the second of the *Mankind* scribes prefers 'sch' where the main scribe uses 'x' (see p. 35).

5. The monastery of Bury St Edmunds and vicinity in the Middle Ages as imagined in the nineteenth century

formerly at Bury St Edmunds (now MS 601 in the Schøyen Collection, Oslo). Richard Beadle has recently argued that palaeographic evidence suggests that 'Hyngham himself, or someone who wrote very similarly' may have been the scribe as well as the owner of *Wisdom* and *Mankind*.[1] In addition, a sixteenth-century owner left the inscription '*Robertus olyuer est verus possessor hvius lybry*' ('Robert Oliver is the true owner of this book') on fol. 134 of *Mankind* and wrote various ciphers of his name in the manuscript of *Wisdom*. The identifier 'Rychard Cake of Bury' appears on folio leaves 105 (*Wisdom*) and 124 (*Mankind*) of the manuscript.

By the late fifteenth century, then, *Mankind* – transcribed in a form of English legible to those living in East Anglia – was clearly being performed for audiences familiar with Cambridgeshire, Suffolk and Norfolk. Its manuscript, further, appears to have been in possession of people associated with Bury St Edmunds, where it would remain until owned by the Bury resident, Reverend Cox Macro, in the eighteenth century. These are the solid facts concerning *Mankind*.

While we cannot know if a single person – whether Thomas Hyngham or someone else – was responsible for composing *Mankind*, Hyngham's autograph connects the play with the monastery of Bury St Edmunds. We might think of a medieval monastery as a secluded, inward-looking institution. But we would be mistaken to do so in this case. For, with nearly 80 monks and 200 servants and its 'virtual monopoly over every conceivable activity of the town of Bury', the Benedictine monastery at Bury St Edmunds was a massive, rich, powerful and sometimes aggressive corporation that dominated life in its part of East Anglia (see Figs 5 and 6).[2] This abbey was, in the words of Gail M. Gibson, 'a monastery of wealth and influence

---

1 See Beadle, 'Monk'. Eccles pointed to other possible contenders for 'Hyngham', including a Thomas Hengam of Norwich who owned two Latin manuscripts, and Richard Hengham, abbot of Bury St Edmunds from 1474–9.
2 Gibson, '*Wisdom*', 121. See also Bowers.

6. Bury St Edmunds Cathedral, with the ruins of the medieval monastery in the foreground

greater in the fifteenth century than most English cities' ('Bury', 76). Derek Pearsall suggests that 'it would be useful to think of Bury' in modern terms 'as a powerful business corporation' with assets running into the many millions and an annual income of over several million pounds.[1]

1 Pearsall wrote 'with assets running into millions and an annual income of about a quarter of a million pounds' (24). These computations were (a) done for the time of Lydgate (roughly a generation prior to *Mankind*) and (b) offered in currency values of 1970. Estimates for the 1470s, and in today's currency, would run to ten times Pearsall's figures.

The evidence suggests *Mankind* was probably written for and performed by highly talented, highly organized actors who happened to be monks at the abbey of St Edmund in Bury. We do not know whether most of the performances took place in Bury itself, or whether they took *Mankind* on tour in East Anglia or elsewhere. If Bury was a main site of performance, their audiences may have included some of the many thousands of pilgrims who came to Bury for its own shrine (of St Edmund) or passed through Bury on their way to the phenomenally popular shrine of the Virgin Mary at Walsingham.[1] There may have been connection to local religious guilds or other parish activities. Richard Beadle has long since established the participation of East Anglian monks in parish plays, specifically at a priory in Thetford, only about thirteen and a half miles (twenty-two kilometres) to the north of Bury St Edmunds. And Gail Gibson's argument for the *N-Town Cycle*'s origin in Bury St Edmunds leads her to suggest that these plays were fashioned in an environment that explains *Mankind* as well. These plays were, in Gibson's view, 'compiled by a rich and learned monastery for production not only in the borough of Bury itself but also in other parishes, both neighbouring and distant, that lay within the administrative and pastoral responsibility of the abbey' ('Bury', 75).

We can perhaps understand something about the play's original contexts by looking closely at the catalogue of ten citizens initiated by Titivillus at 502ff. Archival investigations have suggested that all of these names represent actual individuals in various East Anglian locales.[2] Moreover, the names Titivillus mentions demarcate two separate localities (see Fig. 7). The first is a King's Lynn group consisting of East Walton, Gayton, Massingham and Swaffham, all villages within walking distance of each other. None is more than approximately ten and a half miles (seventeen

---

1   For references in *Mankind* to the culture of religious pilgrimage (such as that which Chaucer describes in his portrait of the Wife of Bath in the 'General Prologue'), see 452 and n., 614 and n., and 628 and n. While 'Saint Patrick's way' (614) would have been familiar to many medieval Christians, it would have had special resonance for religious tourists.
2   See, for example, Brandl, xxvi, Smart, 'Continued' and 'Concluded' and Eccles, 222.

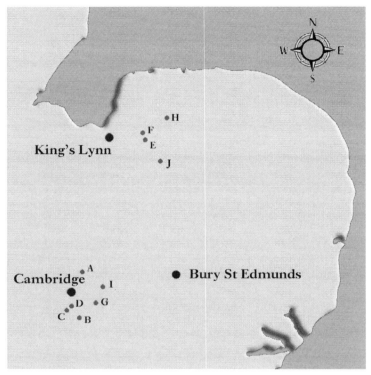

7. The East Anglia of *Mankind*. This map charts various places mentioned
    or alluded to in *Mankind*: (A) Waterbeach; (B) Sawston; (C) Hauxton; (D)
    Trumpington; (E) Walton; (F) Gayton; (G) Fulbourn; (H) Massingham;
    (I) Bottisham; (J) Swaffham. Beginning at 503, Titivillus says to take a man
    from A; New–Guise says he will visit B, C and D; Nowadays pledges to visit
    E and F but not G; Nought will go to H but not I or J

kilometres) from the others, and East Walton is less than six miles
(ten kilometres) from Massingham. The second sub-region suggested in the list circumscribes the East Cambridge villages of
Waterbeach,[1] Trumpington, Hauxton, Sawston, Fulbourn and

---

1   Waterbeach is not mentioned by name in *Mankind*, but Smart has connected the
    reference to 'William Fide' (503) with a family named Fide in that village. See
    'Continued', 55–6.

Bottisham, which are likewise within walking distance of each other. They also replicate the arrangement of the King's Lynn group in the oval-like shape they circumscribe.

Significantly, the abbey of St Edmund at Bury is equidistant from each of these clusters – the King's Lynn group of places is approximately thirty-five and a half miles (fifty-seven kilometres) distant, and the East Cambridge group twenty-seven and a half miles (forty-four kilometres). Shifting our geometric metaphor, we might say that Bury St Edmunds forms the third point of a triangle that reaches to King's Lynn and East Cambridge, encompassing in its references what appears to have been some of these localities' most influential citizens.[1] Such references were clearly designed to stimulate the audience members by including their lives and social awareness in the play's action. It is possible that these references were meant to flatter the very individuals so named. If, as was true in the coming years with certain plays in other East Anglian localities, *Mankind* was paid for in part by subscription, prominent mention of these citizens could have been a way to acknowledge their financial sponsorship as well as their social status (see R. Wright). This would make the catalogue of ten citizens something like the patron's portrait worked into a commissioned manuscript, or the wealthy parishioners' images painted or engraved into devotional icons in countless English churches of the time.

The date of Mankind

Mankind was almost certainly composed after 1464, when the coin known as the 'royal' (see 465) was introduced to England, and before 1479, when both William Allington and Alexander Wood, two of the men mentioned in the catalogue that Titivillus

---

1 Such people and places as those mentioned in lines 502–15 may conceivably have been 'swapped out' for others in other performances – as was the case with the well-known 'N-Town' cycle (where 'N' stands for the Latin *nomine*, or 'name', as in 'name to be supplied'). The similarity of many English place-names (e.g. '-ton', '-bury', etc.) could make for easy rhymes should such have been desired.

initiates (502ff.), died.[1] At least part of the play seems to have been written in or after 1471, the 'year of no king' in Nought's otherwise ridiculous court Latin (689–93). Nought's nonsense alludes to '*Edwardi nullateni*', or 'Edward the Nought', and thus punningly connects the nothingness of his own designation with the temporary nothingness of the off-again on-again English sovereign, Edward IV (1442–83). Edward ruled England from 4 March 1461 to his death on 9 April 1483. However, his reign was violently interrupted for over seven months when, from 2 October 1470 to 11 April 1471, a rebellion forced him to flee to the Continent, vacating the throne. This indeed rendered February 1471, as Nought puts it, '*Anno regni regis nulli*' (693), or 'the regnal year of no king'.

To English citizens of *Mankind*'s era, the phrase would be jarring: no year should be without a monarch. This allusion to a known historical episode, therefore, has tempted some scholars to zero in on specific years, even months and days, for the composition of *Mankind*.[2] Such certainty cannot be sustained by the available evidence. Hard-edged though it is, Nought's joke *about* Edward IV's absence from the throne by no means implies that *Mankind* was written or performed *during* that time. The satire could even be seen to gain from the perspective that a number of months or years would bring. The same could be said about the play's allusions to such things as Shrovetide, planting, winter weather, Christmas and football games: mention of them does not prove the play was written in any particular time of year. Arguments holding that *Mankind* was composed in the 1460s should not be dismissed out of hand, for part of the play may be that early: *Mankind* may have been 'in progress' for some time, and thus not (as many wish to believe) the product of a single

1 On the introduction of the royal, see Baker; for Allington and Wood, see Smart, 'Continued', 48–50.
2 See, for instance, Brantley & Fulton, who take such internal evidence to suggest 'the period around February 1471' (327).

month or year.[1] Until further research turns up new information (perhaps about the individuals named in Titivillus's catalogue), it seems safest to call *Mankind* a play of the 1470s.

Mankind *in performance*

Scholars have suggested a variety of spaces where *Mankind* may originally have been performed, from the halls of great houses to open air venues, even raised 'booth' stages in inn-yards. The variety of such arguments is surely the best support for Pamela King's insistence that *Mankind* is a drama 'of such evidently simple scenography that it can be played almost anywhere'.[2] The effect of *Mankind*'s action depends less on any particular acting space than upon the relation between its larger structure of repentance and the series of short games that make that repentance necessary in the first place. *Mankind*'s story is fairly simple: Mercy's protective instructions to Mankind are effective enough to protect Mankind from the lesser Vices (Mischief and the Three Ns) but not from the head devil, Titivillus, who perverts him from the path of righteous behaviour for a while until he can be rescued and forgiven by Mercy. Thus *Mankind* takes us from sermon to sin back to sermon again.

Along the way, however, the numerous short games played by the Vices are much more than distractions. The tension that many have felt over *Mankind* comes from the sheer enjoyment these games provide (see Fig. 8). This enjoyment is so prominent that it is not easily brushed aside with a moralistic explanation (such as, for instance, that we need to know how fallen we are

---

1 Composition in the 1460s is advanced, for instance, by Jambeck & Lee, who propose a date of 1464 based on reference to 'Pope Pocket' (144): a John Poket had been prior of Barnwell Abbey outside Cambridge (1444–64) as well as a papal representative, and died in 1464. Baker offers a date of 1466 on the basis of the play *not* mentioning, in its list of coins (464–5), the golden 'angel', a coin introduced in England between 1468 and 1470.

2 King, 247. Scholarly positions regarding *Mankind*'s original venue can be categorized according to the places hypothesized: indoor performance (Southern, 43; Eccles, xlii; Bevington, 'Popular', 97–8; Clopper, 'Audience'; Westfall, 54–5); outdoor or open air (Grantley, 224–5); inn-yard (Furnivall & Pollard, xv; Adams, 304; Tydeman, 31–52).

8. Nought (Clive Mendus), Nowadays (Roy Weskin) and New-Guise (Mark Saban) after Mankind (Bridget Thornborrow) has hit them with a spade (cf. ll. 380–90). The Medieval Players' Tour, 1985

in order to be saved). Although the Vices' misbehaviour often appears continuous, we might notice how the seemingly disparate episodes of mischief actually create a framework that provokes, sustains and mollifies Mercy's sermonizing. The physicality and broad comic potential of these episodes are typically revealed in performance and, because they are so enjoyable, they constitute much of the play's effect upon audiences and readers alike. It may say something about the limitations of speech alone, in fact, that Mercy finally rescues the title figure only upon threatening the Vices with his 'baleys' – most likely a staff or rod (805 SD).

Mercy's baleys is just one of many properties this play calls upon to further its physical comedy.[1] A richness of allegory and symbolism attaches itself to this range of objects, from Mankind's

---

1   For an abbreviated list, see Grantley, 225. Garner notes that 'much of the activity of the play's middle sequence centres around stage props, and that attention is repeatedly focused on the *materiality* of these props: a fake head's size, a shovel's weight, a board's thickness' (277).

spade to Mischief's fetters. Because they are employed with such efficient precision in the hurly-burly of its plot, we can guess that *Mankind* was the product *of* – as well as the script *for* – performance, a play moulded into an astonishingly consistent whole from numerous decades of skits, interludes and other successful 'games'. Although we do not know for certain that *Mankind* was performed in its own time, its quality as a script – including plot, language, figuration and comedic effects – suggests it may have been quite popular in performance.

The first mention of modern production consists of a theatre programme, since lost, with typescript annotation referring to a performance at the Hackett Theatre in Manhattan, 6 December 1910. Robert Potter surmises that this was a private performance, perhaps owing to the play's obscenity.[1] The first known public performance was staged in Toronto in 1966 by the Poculi Ludique Societas (Latin, 'cup and game society') or PLS, a group devoted to the study and performance of early plays. *Mankind* remained in regular rotation in the PLS repertoire thereafter, being revived in 1970, 1977 and 1995. The Cambridge Medieval Players produced the play in 1976, and in their subsequent incarnation as the Medieval Players mounted an impressive and influential production in 1982. The touring company's artistic director, Carl Heap, shared in his essay 'On Performing *Mankind*' what remains – along with Peter Meredith's invaluable acting edition – among the most extensive surveys of the play's performance dynamics.[2]

Crucial among Heap's numerous insights is the necessity of playing Mercy straight, rather than as an open figure of fun. Meredith concurs that 'Mercy in the end is the one you want to listen to' (*Acting*, 22). Experience in the late 1990s with a student production at Duquesne University led Anne Brannen

---

1 See Potter, 273 n.40. The Billy Rose Theatre Collection reports, in a private communication to the editors, that this programme has been missing since 1977.

2 See also Southern (21–45), Denny, Price, Tydeman (31–52) and Garner.

to confirm these positions: 'I did not know, with such absolute certainty, that the play does not make fun of Mercy, until I saw our version on the stage' (17–18). At the very least, these three theatrical participants have confirmed that Mercy makes little sense when played as a buffoon who does not deserve respect: a dignity in his lines and role provides both energy and meaning to the play.

More recently two other scholars have added to *Mankind*'s theatrical lineage through adaptation. In an abbreviated '(South) Africanisation' of the text, Margaret Mary Raftery employed English, Afrikaans and Sesotho for the lines of the trio of Vices.[1] In 2004, Julie Crosby updated the play by transforming it into a 'postmodern medieval musical'.[2] *Mankynde: The Musical* presented its title character as a young woman making her way through the decadent world of modern celebrity and pop culture.[3] In this way the satire of fifteenth-century fashion attached to the Three Ns has been shown to have modern application as well.

Mankind: *critical history*

The trajectory that *Mankind* has taken in the last century is well captured by the title of Anne Brannen's essay, '100 years of *Mankind* criticism: how a very bad play became good'. During the twentieth century *Mankind* indeed went from being a vulgar and obscene embarrassment to one of the most widely admired theatrical pieces in English prior to Shakespeare. As we have seen, many critics early on concerned themselves with establishing the text, date and provenance of *Mankind*, all of which seemed crucial to serious evaluation of the play. As we

1 For text and description, see Raftery.
2 *Mankynde: The Musical*, with book by Julie Crosby, music by Nancy Magarill, lyrics by Nancy Magarill and Julie Crosby; directed by Louis Scheeder at the Soho Playhouse, 15–26 August 2004.
3 According to the production's promotional materials, 'the original fifteenth-century drama is now a musical mix of boy band groove, troubadour lilt, and vaudeville hijinx, proving that the greatest cultural issues facing the world half a millennium ago still deserve ridicule today' (Press release dated 26/8/04, courtesy Julie Crosby).

have noted, too, performers had a great deal to do not only with elevating the status of *Mankind* but also with clarifying some of its principal themes and issues. John McKinnell reminds us that 'Early plays that have been poorly regarded by literary critics nearly always reveal unexpected subtlety, emotional depth and technical artistry when they are performed.'[1] Perhaps as much as with any early drama, *Mankind*'s critics have learned from modern performance.

Mankind was held to be crude and provincial by early critics and editors, who described it as 'degraded'.[2] Elbert Thompson spoke for many when he remarked that 'the moral tenor of the piece is submerged in the rude banter and the obscene jesting and song of the tavern and the market-place' (387). An early, positive and still foundational critical analysis, however, came with Sister Mary Philippa Coogan's dissertation, published in 1947 as *An Interpretation of the Moral Play, 'Mankind'*. Sceptical of the 'evolutionary theory of [English] drama' then in vogue, and persuaded that 'close investigations of individual plays' would provide a sounder basis for our evaluation of early English drama, Coogan interpreted *Mankind* as a Shrovetide play with a Lenten theme centring on the interventions of Mercy, whom she identified as a stage priest or friar. This identification not only makes sense of the absolution that Mercy offers Mankind (see 850–3 and n.) but was all the more crucial in light of the fact that such scholars as E.K. Chambers and B.J. Whiting did not realize the gender assigned to Mercy in the play, not to mention his status as a priest or friar.[3]

Subsequent studies have typically been more limited in scope. For Siegfried Wenzel, the key to *Mankind* is the theme of sloth (*Sloth*, 148–54); for Lorraine Stock, it is patience (406); whereas Dorothy Castle sees it as a rhetorically sophisticated struggle for 'sovereignty over the soul' of its title figure (*Game*, 45). The

1 McKinnell, 320.
2 See E.K. Chambers, *Medieval*, 62; and Furnivall & Pollard, xvii.
3 See E.K. Chambers, *Close*, 61; and Whiting, 73–5.

most prominent trend in recent studies, however, has been their attention to the importance of language and speech in *Mankind*, particularly the friction between Mercy's aureate style and the earthy colloquialism of the Vice figures. LynnDiane Beene notes how *Mankind*'s many references to language 'enhance the play's dramatic structure, individualize the characters, and emphasize the latter's relative positions' (25). Kathleen Ashley has explored the traditions associated with Titivillus as a gatherer of broken words, noting that he is 'logically cast as a star in a play concerned with the crucial distinction between God's word and the words of the Devil and the World' (129). In a foundational essay later expanded upon in a monograph, Janette Dillon has scrutinized the political valences of the play's deployment of English and Latin registers.[1] She argues that 'a simple lining up of Latin or pseudo-Latin with virtue and English with vice becomes unworkable' ('*Mankind*', 43). Relating the tension between these registers to contemporary debates about preaching, Lynn Forest-Hill suggests that the play endorses neither Latinate nor vulgar English for its own sake; instead, *Mankind* shows that 'the virtue of language . . . inheres in its use rather than simply in its form' (37).

Mankind: *textual introduction*

The text of *Mankind* is preserved in a unique manuscript, one of the three early dramatic manuscripts that make up the Macro codex now in the Folger Shakespeare Library (MS V.a.354). The *Mankind* manuscript consists of thirteen leaves, which measure 220 mm × 160 mm, beginning with a single leaf and followed by a quire of twelve leaves. It appears that the original second leaf has been lost, since the surviving leaves are numbered i, iii, iv, v, vi, vii, viii, ix, and x (with the last four leaves unnumbered) and there is an evident lacuna in the text (see 71 SDn.), and 'i' (containing lines 1–71) is an unpaired folio leaf. The pages were renumbered when *Mankind* was bound into a volume along with

---

1 See Dillon, '*Mankind*' and *Language*, esp. 53–79, 126–38.

Wisdom and *The Castle of Perseverance*; in this more modern numbering *Mankind* occupies fols 122–34. A glove (or gauntlet) and star watermark appears on the single leaf 122 and on the bifolios 124–33, 125–32 and 128–9; this watermark is similar but not identical to the hand and glove used in the Digby manuscript of *Wisdom*.

Mankind is the work of two scribes; the first, who may have been Thomas Hyngham, was responsible for fols 122–32^r; a second scribe wrote the last four pages, fols 132^v–4^r.[1] Since a number of marginal additions throughout appear to supply passages omitted in transcription, rather than representing authorial additions, it seems clear that the scribes were indeed transcribing an original rather than composing it. Although both wrote in a text-block of approximately 180 mm × 130 mm, the first scribe's work is notably more condensed, averaging thirty-nine lines per page, whereas the second writes only twenty-six or twenty-seven lines per page. Perhaps by the time the second scribe took over it was clear that there would be sufficient pages in the quire to hold the remainder of the text comfortably, so space-saving would no longer have been an issue. The first scribe transcribed the Macro manuscript of *Wisdom* as well,[2] although there the text is much less compressed throughout, with an average of twenty-five lines per page. The *Mankind* scribes are distinguished by the first's preference for 'Mankynde', 'xall' and 'xulde' compared to the second's preference for 'Mankend', 'schall' and 'schulde' (a distinction that is overlooked in Bevington's assertion (*Macro*, Bevington, xxiii) that 'the scribes use . . . *xall* or *xuld* for *shall* or *shuld*'). Both scribes follow the convention of separating speeches by a horizontal line across the page and of writing the speakers' names in the right margin; since stage directions

1 Furnivall & Pollard believed that the manuscript is in the hand of a single scribe but that the final four pages were written 'with a softer pen and different ink' (xxviii).
2 Although Bevington considered the scribes of *Mankind* and *Wisdom* to be different, and was supported in this by R.E. Alton, Eccles viewed the hands as the same (xvii), as did Norman Davis and Richard Beadle ('Monk').

are also placed to the right of the text, they occasionally get tangled with the speech prefixes (see Textual Notes on 478 SD, 482 SD and 486 SD).

Mankind: *editorial procedures*

Although there are a handful of difficult readings in the manuscript (see collations at 88, 96, 106, 309, 748, 834 and especially 394), the text of *Mankind* presents relatively few editorial challenges. The rhyme scheme is broken in places, suggesting that lines may have been lost at 153, 202 and 755; a word rhyming with 'ferthynge' and 'fyghtynge' is apparently missing at the end of 694; clauses are transposed at 844, and possibly at 49 (we emend the former but not the latter). A number of lines are inserted in the margins of the manuscript, usually in the same hand but in a different ink, indicating that the scribe proofread his original transcription and corrected his omissions; the added lines are 125–8, 130, 200–1, 238, 584–6); Manly and Brandl treated some of these added lines as notes and did not include them in the line numbering of their edited texts. It should be noted, however, that these two editors were operating under a disadvantage: the original manuscript having been 'temporarily mislaid' (Furnivall & Pollard, x–xi), they had to rely upon an inaccurate transcription of the manuscript undertaken by Eleanor Marx, daughter of Karl, in 1882. (This being the case, we have used the phrase '*MS as reported by*' in our textual notes when citing readings provided by Manly or Brandl from this transcript, which is no longer extant.)

One curious feature of the manuscript is that in several places another hand (not one of the two scribes) has added a different character's name after a speech prefix without deleting the original: 'new g' (for New-Guise) is written following the speech prefixes (SPs) for Titivillus at lines 555, 565 and 589; 'novad' or 'nowad' (for Nowadays) following the SPs for Mischief at 642, 664 and 670; and 'novght' following the SP for Mischief at 680. Since the roles of Titivillus and Mischief could be doubled by

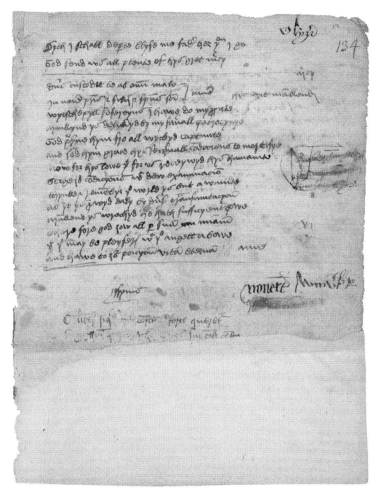

9. Final page of the *Mankind* MS with Latin ownership inscription at the foot

the same actor (see Appendix 1), these changes may reflect an attempt to redistribute their lines so as to facilitate the doubling, perhaps at a later date with a reduced cast. Because the alterations are of uncertain authority and do not seem to be appropriate attributions for any of the lines in question, they have been ignored by all modern editors. They may, however, be an early attempt to rearrange the parts and action of the play.

There are a few cancelled readings in the manuscript, one of which resulted in an interesting variant. At line 562, the scribe originally wrote, 'My bedys xall be here for who summ euer wyll ellys.' He then cancelled the line and rewrote it in its correct position at 564, but altered the final word to 'cumme', perhaps influenced by 'summ'. Since the tail-rhyme stanza requires that 564 rhyme with 560, which ends with *compels* ('compellys'), we follow Eccles in restoring the cancelled variant *else* ('ellys'). Another crux worth noting appears in line 665, where it is unclear whether 'Nowadays mak proclamaciyon', written to the right of the text box in the manuscript (see Fig. 10), should be treated as a stage direction (Manly, Lester) or as part of the dialogue (Eccles, *Macro*, Bevington). We conclude that the line represents an imperative that Mischief directs to Nowadays, coupled with 'do it' in the following line: 'Nowadays, make proclamation, / A' do it *sub forma juris*, dastard!' (665–6).

Save for the brackets that mark rhymed lines on fol. 132^v, stanzas are not marked or set off as such in the *Mankind* manuscript. Some editions of the play merely divide the text into stanzas without indenting the rhymed lines (e.g. Lester). The underlying stanzaic forms, however, play a central role in distinguishing characters in this and other early English dramatic texts – a role that can be underappreciated by students accustomed to the conventions of later drama. In plays such as *The Castle of Perseverance, Nature, The Four Elements, Wisdom* and *An Satire of the Three Estates*, virtuous characters tend to speak in eight-line stanzas (rhyming *abab bcbc*) whereas Vices characteristically employ tail-rhyme or *rime coueé* stanzas (*aaab cccb*).

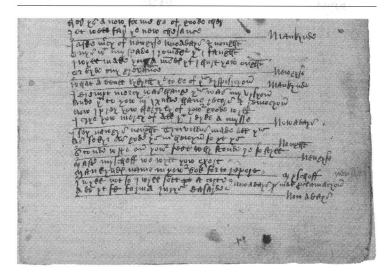

10. Detail of the *Mankind* MS showing line 665 'Nowadays mak proclamaci-
    yon' written to the right of the text box. Scholars are divided about whether
    this is a stage direction or part of the dialogue

Mankind further exploits the convention by having Mankind
speak in four-line stanzas (rhyming *abab*) in Mercy's presence
but employ tail-rhyme stanzas when under the Vices' influence.
Making the various stanzaic forms immediately apparent to the
modern reader is thus a prime task of a critical edition.

To this end – and following the examples of indentation
found in collections such as the Towneley plays, other parts of
the Macro manuscript and dramatic texts as late as Lindsay's
An Satire of the Three Estates (published in 1602) – we have
employed a system of progressive indention of rhyming lines
within each stanza, as illustrated by Mercy's opening speech:

The very founder and beginner of our first creation,	a
Among us sinful wretches he oweth to be magnified,	b
That for our disobedience he had none indignation	a

39

To send his own son to be torn and crucified.   b
Our obsequious service to him should be applied,   b
   Where he was Lord of all and made all thing of nought, c
For the sinful sinner, too, had him revived   b
   And for his redemption set his own son at nought.   c

                  (1–8)

The Vices' tail-rhyme stanzas are similarly indented, as in Mischief's first speech:

I beseech you heartily, leave your calcation.   a
Leave your chaff, leave your corn, leave your dalliation.   a
Your wit is little, your head is mickle, ye are full of
                  predication.   a
   But, sir, I pray this question to clarify: b
Driff-draff, mish-mash,   c
Some was corn and some was chaff,   c
My dame said my name was Raff;   c
   Unshut your lock and take an ha'penny.   b

               (45–52)

Sometimes stanzas are shared by several characters, and sometimes a stanza break occurs in the middle of a character's speech. Both of these features appear in the following passage:

MERCY
Nay, brother, I will not dance.   a
NEW-GUISE
If ye will, sir, my brother will make you to prance.   a
NOWADAYS
With all my heart, sir, if I may you advance.   a
   Ye may assay by a little trace.   b
NOUGHT
Yea, sir, will ye do well,   c
Trace not with them, by my counsel,   c
For I have traced somewhat too fell;   c
   I tell you, it is a narrow space.   b

40

But, sir, I trow of us three I heard you speak.	a

NEW–GUISE

Christ's curse have therefore, for I was in sleep.   a

NOWADAYS

A' I had the cup ready in my hand, ready to go to meat.   a

Therefore, sir, curtly, greet you well.   b

MERCY

Few words, few and well set!   c

NEW–GUISE

Sir, it is the new guise and the new jet.   c

Many words and shortly set,   c

This is the new guise, everydeal.   b

(90–105)

The textual arrangement not only makes it clear that the Vices work together as a stanza-sharing team but also reveals the way in which they hijack Mercy's lines and implicate him in their tail-rhymes. Thus, while the layout may be initially distracting to some readers, we trust that the benefit of a heightened awareness of the underlying stanzaic patterns will outweigh any initial difficulties caused by the unfamiliar format.

THE SUMMONING OF EVERYMAN

Everyman *in brief*

Everyman is an English morality play, most likely printed for the first time around 1518–19. Its emotional, continuous action shows the last hours of Everyman's life. The play's full title, *The Summoning of Everyman*, describes the moment when Death, acting at God's command, arrests the title figure, starting him on a rapid journey towards the grave. After trying to bargain his way out of dying, Everyman finds that his worldly associates and belongings abandon him. Their refusals add comedy to the first half of this play. *Everyman*'s second half commences when he discovers his Good Deeds, whom he finds lying immobile on the ground (she is too weak to move, as he has not done enough good in the world to give her the power to walk). The sister of Good Deeds, Knowledge, enters and acts as Everyman's guide. Together, they help Everyman make his way through major sacraments of the Catholic faith. Eventually, though, Everyman's bodily faculties desert him, leaving him to die with only his Good Deeds by his side. This moving story was actually not original with *Everyman*. It was translated from a Dutch original entitled *Elckerlijc* ('Everybody'), with both plays indebted to a tale that appears in Buddhist literature from the time before Christ.[1] Both versions parallel the popular genre of *ars moriendi* or 'Art of Dying' manuals in their focus on preparing their readers and audience members for death. Although it has strong connections to its own time, *Everyman* experienced a surprising rebirth in 1901, when a modern production met with an unprecedented level of success in Britain and the US, and led to a popular German version as well. The play's story of the brevity of life – and the need to live one's life rightly – has continued to resonate with readers and audiences during the twentieth and twenty-first centuries.

Everyman *and religious allegory*

Everyman is a dramatic allegory, a story in which things and ideas come to life as moving, speaking figures. Traditionally, audiences have found that it works like a theatrical picture, its various figures – including Death, Goods and Beauty, among others – being visually as well as rhetorically significant. Even those who only read *Everyman* can testify to the visual appeal of its story. When Death interrupts Everyman's walk to inform him that his life has ended, for instance, it is easy to imagine the scene: a masked or skeletal Death gloatingly calls to account someone blithely going about his day-to-day business. Likewise when Beauty refuses to go with Everyman into the grave, the forcefulness of the episode is only increased by the image of an

1 See Appendix 4 for the 'tale of the faithful friend'.

attractive woman too proud of her looks to voluntarily ruin them
with death.

Whether acted or read, *Everyman* depends heavily on its
iconography – its representation of persons, things and ideas
through visual images.[1] Prior to the Reformation's violent turn
against them, pictures of biblical stories and spiritual situations
were everywhere in the English church, and crucial to the lives of
ordinary Christians. A woodcut of the Last Judgement from the
late fifteenth century (Fig. 11) sets out in a single tableau many
of the themes, incidents and figures envisioned by *Everyman*.

Centred atop a rainbow is Jesus Christ sitting in the final
judgement on humanity, so that, as 2 Corinthians, 5.10 puts
it, 'euery man may receaue the workes of his bodie according
to that he hath done, whether it be good or bad.' Twin angels
trumpet doomsday in. Beneath the ground, surrounded by
various bones that will be reassembled for judgement, a worm
bores relentlessly through the winding sheet enclosing a corpse.
Immediately under Christ's feet, a grinning skeleton touches
a praying man with his dart – the implication being that, even
in prayer, one is not safe from Death's sting. On either side of
Death are the upper halves of men, as though rising out of the
ground; they appear alternately hopeful (on Christ's right – the
viewer's left) and despondent (on Christ's left) regarding the
particular judgement each will receive. Further to Christ's left
(our right), a wolfish devil holds in his outstretched palm a book
– almost certainly a register of the inadequate or sinful deeds
performed by the despondent figure nearest him.

This woodcut contains much of the story and thought behind
Everyman, and highlights the visual symbolism of the play's
many figures. Significantly, both works focus on the end of life.
In the play, the life is that of Everyman; in the woodcut it is that
of every man. Both works revolve around the certainty of the

---

1 A 1996 RSC production of *Everyman*, which downplayed the drama's traditional iconography, found little success; for discussion, see Billington, O'Connor, McKinnell,
316 and Godfrey, '*Everyman*', esp. 156, 166–7.

11.   The Last Judgement, fifteenth–century English woodcut

grave and of the judgement thereafter. The woodcut also has what looks to be an account book like that possessed by Good Deeds in *Everyman*. Figures of Death appear in both, and speak to the fifteenth- and sixteenth-century fascination with the *danse macabre* or Dance of Death. The Dance of Death was a gruesome but wildly popular series of images wherein Death (usually portrayed as a grinning skeleton or skeletons) escorts all ranks of men, women and children to the grave, often to their great surprise (see Fig. 12).[1]

This journey produced an important genre of publication in the fifteenth and sixteenth centuries, the *ars moriendi*, or 'Art of Dying' manual. One such manual, *The Art and Crafte to Knowe Well to Dye*, was published in the 1490s by both William Caxton and Richard Pynson, the latter of whom would go on to publish *Everyman*.[2] The *ars moriendi* manual saw death (one's own and others' alike) as so much a part of life that one should continually prepare for it through specific rituals and prayers.

This genre was the good twin of the Dance of Death, for both forms addressed the brevity of life and showed an uneasiness over the soul's eventual disposition. At this time an increased emphasis on God's particular judgement (i.e. judgement of the individual) as opposed to universal judgement of all humankind made for a 'deep uncertainty concerning individual salvation' (Duclow, 108). Structuring Everyman's last moments on earth, in fact, is the framework of rituals recommended by the *ars moriendi* manuals for the journey to the grave. We may therefore see *Everyman* as something like a dramatic *ars moriendi*, an 'art of dying' play that puts into motion the crucial last moments of its title figure's life.

---

1 On the Dance of Death, see Lydgate, *Dance* (esp. ix–xxxi), Clark, Anderson and Oosterwijk. For images, see Briesemeister. Puddephat discusses wall paintings illustrating this theme in the Guild Chapel of Stratford-upon-Avon.

2 See STC 789, 790. On the *ars moriendi* genre, see Beaty, Duclow and Moran. For a treatment of *Everyman*'s relation to the psychological stages surrounding death, see Goldhammer.

12. 'The Dance of Death' – Death leading an old man to the grave, woodcut
   c. 1538 after Hans Holbein the Younger

Coming and going in Everyman

Everyman is a play of coming and going. During his journey to
the grave, Everyman discovers to his horror that things he had
thought of as predictable if not stable – for instance, friends,
bodily senses, beauty and strength – are actually, like life itself,
always changing. The idea and vocabulary of movement in the
play thus remind us that nothing on earth stands still.

In portraying the final hours of Everyman's life as a kind of journey, *Everyman* relies on a longstanding analogy. Proverbs, metaphors and visual illustrations had traditionally set out life as a trip or pilgrimage. Works like *The Canterbury Tales* (*c.* 1385–1400) and *The Pilgrim's Progress* (1678) would put this analogy in motion. Dante's *Divine Comedy* (*c.* 1306–21), for its part, begins with the memorable phrase '*Nel mezzo del cammin di nostra vita*' ('In the middle of the journey of our life'). And if the sights and sounds that greet Dante's pilgrim unfold on an epic scale, *Everyman*'s more intimate story likewise uses the strangeness of travelling to new places to heighten its tension and effect.

We feel this sense of motion as early as the play's complete title: *The Summoning of Everyman*. An authoritative summoning is answered by a painful journey, all of which happens in a short period of time. As the preface spells things out:

> Here beginneth a treatise how the High Father of heaven sendeth Death to summon every creature to come and give account of their lives in this world, and is in manner of a moral play.

The play begins with a Messenger. Prologue-like, he prepares us for the words of the play's 'High Father'. God explains his displeasure with humanity, and summons Death – who is also described as a 'mighty messenger' (63) – to summon Everyman. This repetition of messengers and summoning reveals a great deal about the energy, ideas and implied distances of *Everyman*.

Childlike when we meet him, Everyman matures through symbolic movement that represents our common journey through life. Accordingly, *Everyman* emphasizes words of motion. The keyword 'come', for instance, appears twenty-seven times in various forms (including 'come', 'coming', 'comest' and 'came'). We sense its force early on when Everyman remarks to Death that 'thou comest when I had thee least in mind!' (119), and Death retorts: 'Come hence and not tarry' (130). The word 'come' is also noteworthy for its centrality to a thematic cluster of terms based on the 'com–' prefix: 'commandment' (and various forms of 'command'), 'comfort', 'complaint', 'commend' and 'commission'. Everyman's 'company' (that is, his associates) are also mentioned frequently.

Everyman sometimes flags this cluster by using several of its members in close conjunction. Everyman, for example, begs Fellowship to 'comfort me till I come without the town' (291). Likewise when he tells Confession that 'I am commanded a pilgrimage to take' (550), Confession replies 'Because with Knowledge ye come to me, / I will you comfort as well as I can' (555–6). This group finds its consummation, perhaps, in the Latin phrase that constitutes Everyman's last words on earth as he quotes Christ's words on the cross: '*commendo spiritum meum*' (888).

Something very similar occurs with 'go', which appears even more frequently in *Everyman* than 'come'. The keyword 'go' in its various forms (including 'goeth', 'going', 'gone') occurs sixty-seven times, solidifying our sense of movement and journey in the play. It sometimes appears with 'come', as when the Angel turns from Everyman to the audience at the drama's close:

> Come excellent elect spouse, to Jesu.
> Here above thou shalt go
> Because of thy singular virtue.
> Now the soul is taken the body fro,
> Thy reckoning is crystal clear.
> Now shalt thou into the heavenly sphere,
> Unto the which all ye shall come
> That liveth well before the day of doom.
> (895–902)

This short speech destabilizes our sense of place. Even as the soul is both leaving ('go') and arriving ('Come'), the space from which the Angel speaks ('Here') is both earth and heaven. Significantly, we hear 'Come' (895) and 'go' (896) at both the beginning of the speech and its end, where 'go' may be the understood first verb in the lines 'Now shalt thou [go/come] into the heavenly sphere, / Unto the which all ye shall come' (900–1).

Like 'come', the keyword 'go' also functions as the heart of an important cluster of keywords in *Everyman*.[1] The 'go' cluster divides into the positive ('God', 'good', 'Good Deeds' and 'good works') and negative ('Goods', 'goods' and 'gold'), with the terms for wealth hindering Everyman's choice of the right path.

Although the early texts have almost no stage directions, there are some clear cues for movement in *Everyman*. Death, for instance, hails an apparently distant Everyman at 85 and commands him 'Everyman, stand still!' Everyman may also need to move around the playing area to encounter Goods (393) and Good Deeds (486), and appears to lead a procession towards the grave at 788. Yet for most of a performance the actor portraying Everyman would most likely stand relatively still as he engages in dialogue. What these repeated verbs of movement do, then, is give dramatic life to the pilgrimage metaphor.

Everyman's journey divides in two. The first part, a doctrinal and emotional 'descent', comprises almost a third of the play, from lines 184 to 485 (Van Laan). The second half of Everyman's journey proceeds from his encounter with Good Deeds at 486, and leads inexorably to the grave. If *Everyman* feels like a tragedy by its end, the first half of the play offers a great deal of ironic comedy at the title figure's expense. Kindred and Cousin blithely decline to help Everyman, though Kindred offers to send his maid – on the condition that she and Everyman 'may agree' (364). Fellowship swears his fidelity to Everyman and offers his help seven times before Everyman makes clear the nature of his journey. Like the Vices of *Mankind*, Fellowship is ready to eat, drink and make merry, but not to die with Everyman. He responds to his fellow's request, in fact, with a humorously earnest counter-offer: 'Nay, in good faith, I will not

---

1   Sometimes the play appears to overuse the term, as at lines 316–17: 'For kind will creep where it may not go. / I will go say, for yonder I see them go.'

that way. / But, an thou will murder or any man kill, / In that I will help thee with a good will' (280–2).

Counting and reckoning in Everyman

The figure of Goods personifies money and property, and is pivotal in *Everyman* as its last figure of comedy. Goods may be present onstage from the beginning of the drama, a Jabba the Hutt figure immobile amongst a pile of moneybags (see Fig. 13). Responding diffidently to Everyman's call, he shows the consistency of the play's allegory. As property, that is, he is not easily movable:

> I lie here in corners, trussed and piled so high,
> And in chests I am locked so fast,
> Also sacked in bags. Thou mayst see with thine eye
> I cannot stir; in packs low I lie.
>
> (394–7)

Like Death's earlier scoffing, Goods's sardonic dialogue with Everyman soon reveals another consistency of allegory. As property, he has neither the ability nor the desire to help one who owns him only temporarily. As an earthly commodity, he will soon be owned by someone else.

But Goods is less than neutral. He actively tricks those who think that earthly wealth matters, or is even within human control:

> As for a while I was lent thee,
> A season thou hast had me in prosperity.
> My condition is man's soul to kill;
> If I save one, a thousand I do spill.
>
> (440–3)

Having exhausted his ties with Fellowship, and Kindred and Cousin, Everyman discovers to his great distress that 'his' Goods are neither his nor helpful. Goods ironically ends their

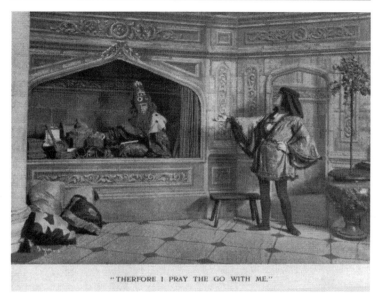

"THERFORE I PRAY THE GO WITH ME."

13.   Goods (left) and Everyman, US production, *c.* 1902

encounter, and Everyman's hopes of worldly help, with the taunting farewell, 'have good day' (462).

This exchange marks a turning point in the play. As readers and spectators, we have so far enjoyed 'discrepant awareness' over Everyman, possessing more knowledge than him of God's displeasure and Death's mission.[1] But our relation to him changes when he encounters a frail Good Deeds lying 'cold on the ground' (486). For all around her – she is the first of several female figures identified as such in this play – are scattered empty pages representing the single 'book' of Everyman's actions on earth:

> If ye had perfectly cheered me,
> Your book of account now full ready had be.

1   On 'discrepant awareness', see Evans.

51

Look, the books of your works and deeds eke:
Ah, see how they lie here under the feet
To your soul's heaviness.

(501–5)

Much as Dickens will have Ebenezer Scrooge confront what his life has added up to in the single night's action of *A Christmas Carol*, this simple tableau shows both us and Everyman the pages of a selfish life. The helplessness of Good Deeds on the ground testifies to his 'soul's heaviness' – here meaning the sadness and oppression that this brings to his soul, but hinting also at a worldly weight that may prevent it from rising to heaven.[1]

Midway through the play, then, we stop feeling superior to Everyman when we see, along with him, undeniable evidence of his paltry 'works and deeds'. From this moment on, there is little comedy in *Everyman*, and much seriousness. When we see the actual pages that Goods has claimed to have made 'blotted and blind' (419) – that is, illegible and hence unreadable – we feel for what is perhaps the first time the force of Everyman's predicament.

The play's original readers and audience members would have understood the accounting theme without a physical prompt. As we have seen, the summary prefixed to *Everyman* points to its importance: 'the High Father of heaven sendeth Death to summon every creature to *come and give account of their lives in this world*'. When we hear the phrase 'give an account of X', we are likely to forget the commercial basis of the metaphor. In contrast, when medieval and early modern readers came across a word like 'account' (as noun and verb), they would have been likely to feel its literal meaning: to reckon, enumerate, count. *Everyman* bases its spiritual message, in fact, on a series of terms that had a commercial as well as spiritual significance. The words

---

1 Ryan discusses Everyman's nurturing of Good Deeds. See Thundy on her relation to doctrine.

'count' and 'account' occur, in various forms, fourteen times in *Everyman*. The word 'reckoning' appears twenty-four times.

The source of the accounting theme (to which 'reckoning', as word and concept, contributes as well) is the Bible.[1] Throughout the New Testament we are reminded of a day of 'accounting' at which souls shall be judged, by God, for their behaviour while on earth. Matthew, Paul and Peter each refer to the certainty of such judgement.[2] The Book of Revelation sets it out as a dramatic scene:

> And I sawe the dead both great and small stand before God, and the bookes were opened: and another booke was opened, which is [the booke] of lyfe, and the dead were iudged of those thynges whiche were written in the bookes, accordyng to their deedes.
>
> (20.12)

The premise of *Everyman*, in short, is that God has sent an officer (Death) to summon Everyman to present his 'counting book' for audit. The stakes are between eternal life and everlasting death. Everyman realizes, to his horror, what the Puritan theologian William Perkins would note later in the century: in the eyes of God 'we are flat bankrupts.'[3] In contrast to the scene imagined by John in the Book of Revelation, *Everyman* is interested in the human story prior to the time of judgement. In this brief hour, Everyman faces up to his moral and spiritual bankruptcy as he both comes and goes to his grave.

The figures of Everyman

As its title suggests, Everyman is the chief figure of the drama.[4] During the past century, his 'name', such as it is, has become synonymous with 'The ordinary or typical human being' (*OED*).

1 On *Everyman*'s relation to the Parable of the Talents, see Kolve.
2 See Matthew, 12.36; Romans, 14.12; and 1 Peter, 4.5.
3 Perkins, 44. We are indebted to Ted Leinwand for this reference.
4 See p. 14n. on the distinction between 'figure' and 'character'; in specific reference to *Everyman*, see Van Dyke.

In *Everyman*, however, the title figure is characterized more specifically. The play may want us to imagine that he is well dressed: Death asks him 'Whither art thou going / Thus gaily?' (85–6). The word 'gaily' here could mean 'splendidly dressed' as well as 'airily', and may have implied both. Certainly his attempt to bribe Death with a 'thousand pound[s]' (122–3), and his exchange with Goods (392–462), whom he calls his 'goods and riches' (392), suggest that he is a wealthy man. He is intellectually uncomplicated, even childlike – continually surprised when things go against him, yet earnestly grateful to receive help. In the first half of the play, he confirms his importance by delivering four soliloquies after receiving bad news. Twice he produces humour by getting to false hope through a deceptively reassuring proverb (316, 412–13).

Everyman's other roles can be divided into three general categories, each of which relates to Everyman. These are: (1) authority figures who retain some distance from Everyman; (2) figures who hinder Everyman; and (3) figures who help Everyman.

The authority figures of *Everyman* participate largely at the beginning and end of its action. God resides at the centre of this group, and – depending on performance choices and venue – may sit on a raised throne observing the action throughout the entire production. Sorrowful and angry in his one and only speech, God is called various things in the play: 'the High Father of heaven' (0.1), 'the Lord heaven king' (84), 'thy maker' (86) – and even 'the high Judge, Adonai' (245), which reminds us of the judgement that awaits Everyman. The play understands Christ to be part of God, hence the lines 'shedding of my blood red. / I hanged between two, it cannot be denied; / To get them life, I suffered to be dead' (30–2).

As we have seen, God's power in the play is also shown in its sheer variety of servant and messenger figures – 'helpers', in a word – who draw upon his authority. Just as Mercy bookends *Mankind* with his speeches, *Everyman* begins with a Messenger's prologue and ends with a Doctor's epilogue. The Messenger, who is not in the Dutch source of *Everyman*, was presumably added to present God (it being potentially indecorous to have the supreme authority speak without an introduction). The Doctor is a figure of secular learning (more like a modern-day professor than a physician) and is actually preceded in his choric speech by the Angel's 'holy' epilogue. Yet God's most potent helper and messenger in *Everyman* is Death. Death was understood to touch humans with his 'dart' – a lance or spear – and thus end their lives, as he promises Everyman he will do to him (178–9). His sardonic dialogue with Everyman lends humour to the early part of the play.

The second major group consists of Everyman's false friends, those figures who appear to hinder him by refusing to help.[1] During the first half of the play, Everyman encounters four such false friends in three separate episodes. These include Fellowship, a boisterous figure of worldly and therefore false friendship; Kindred and Cousin, figures to whom Everyman is related by blood (both closely and distantly); and Goods, the mocking representative of wealth and property that, as we have seen, Everyman falsely understands to be under his control.

Everyman's helpers make up the play's third group of figures. Just as God is surrounded by helping messengers, these are figures who aid Everyman in his distress. The most important of these are the sisters, Good Deeds and Knowledge.

Good Deeds is a female figure representing virtuous acts of kindness and charity.[2] She acts as a book-keeper, quite literally a figure who holds the account 'book' (perhaps only loose pages) that records his acts of faithful kindness and generosity on earth

---

1   For an excerpt from a sermon story of the 'faithful friend', see Appendix 4.
2   Good deeds and good works were held to be spurred in humanity by Christ and scripture for the glory of God. Although serving as evidence of faith at the day of judgement, they are not enough for salvation: both faith and works are needed. See, for representative references in the Bible, Hebrews, 6.10; Philippians, 1.11; 2 Timothy, 3.16–17; and James, 2.14–26.

(see Fig. 14). She is paralysed with weakness when Everyman first encounters her, as his good deeds have been eclipsed by his interest in his worldly goods. Only when Everyman undergoes the process of penance and contrition, confessing, praying and mortifying his flesh does Good Deeds become 'whole and sound, / Going upright upon the ground' (625–6).

Her sister Knowledge is one of the key figures in *Everyman*. Knowledge represents understanding and religious learning.[1] As her name suggests, she knows what Everyman does not, and functions, as she promises in words that have become the play's most famous, as his counsellor and guide: 'Everyman, I will go with thee and be thy guide, / In thy most need to go by thy side' (522–3).[2] She directs Everyman to Confession in the 'house of salvation' (535–44), and hands him the scourge of penance by which he can mortify, or punish, his flesh (605). While Knowledge knows that she cannot go with Everyman into his grave – as Good Deeds can, and does – she keeps her promise to accompany him there, and even delivers a kind of epilogue before those of the Angel and Doctor, respectively (889–94).

In addition to Good Deeds, Knowledge and Confession, Everyman is temporarily helped by four bodily aspects, represented by Beauty, Strength, Discretion and Five Wits. Each member of this group swears earnestly on a cross to go with Everyman to the grave (778–88). Just as we invariably lose such bodily faculties as we age, however, Everyman finds these figures abandoning him one by one. *Everyman* has them depart in the order they leave us in life: Beauty goes first, then Strength, Discretion (that is, practical judgement) and last of all the Five Wits (our senses of sight, hearing, taste, smell and touch). In this, they are like the false friends who abandon Everyman. Yet they are closer to him, and escort him further, because they are temporarily part of who he is.

1   See Thomas and Warren.
2   These lines became the motto of the 'Everyman's Library' series in the early twentieth century.

14. Everyman (Paul Barry) and Good Deeds (Lindsay Rae Taylor, holding the book of account), from the Douglas Morse film *The Summoning of Everyman* (2008)

Woodcut representations of some of these figures appeared in early quartos of *Everyman*.[1] On the title-pages of Q3 and Q4, for instance, we see a richly attired figure (labelled 'Eueryman' in one panel of Q4), with a rotting corpse representing Death

---

1 For further discussion of *Everyman*'s early texts, see pp. 76–83. On the woodcuts of *Everyman*, see Davidson, 'Woodcut', Cuda and Driver.

in another. Death stands amongst bones in a graveyard, holding a coffin and pointing a finger of warning towards Everyman
(see Fig. 15). On the other side of this title-page in Q4 only, six
figures appear, labelled 'Felawshyp', 'Eueryman' (duplicated
from the title-page), 'Beauty', 'Dyscrecyo[n]', 'Strengthe' and
'Kysne' (that is, 'Cousin') (see Fig. 16). These woodcuts imitate
those made for Antoine Verard's French translation of Terence,
printed in Paris *c*. 1500, and copied in Pynson's 1506 *Kalender of
shepherdes* (STC 22408) after Verard reused the originals in his
1503 English *Kalendayr* (STC 22407).[1] As Martha Driver has
shown, the 'Everyman' image appears with incredible frequency
in early printed books (55–65). Many books from the time use
this figure to stand for a character in their pages. For this reason,
perhaps, we are justified in thinking of it *as* Everyman: its ability to stand for so many identities in early books does what the
morality play asks 'Everyman' to do.

Because their presentation of various of *Everyman*'s figures
must have affected how some of this text's original readers
understood the play, its woodcuts are worth taking seriously.
We could notice that these woodcuts portray Everyman and
Fellowship as wealthy townsmen in fine clothing.[2] Far from
the 'man in the street' associated with the term in our own day,
'Everyman' is here (and in the play) a wealthy man. This might
be taken, however, not as something that separates him from the
ordinary viewer or reader, but rather as an exaggeration of the
possessiveness we all share. Robert Potter (40, 42) dissuades us
from interpreting morality plays with any populist sentiment by
reminding us that in the first English morality play, *The Pride of
Life* (also known as *The King of Life*), the principal figure is not
only not middle–class but indeed a king.

1 See Davidson, 'Woodcut'.
2 Such finery also appears in a woodcut illustration to the Vorsterman *Elckerlijc*
   (1518–25), which shows Death piercing the breast of an attractively garbed man. For
   a reproduction, see Meier, 17. On the moral significance of similar clothing in East
   Anglian art, see Nichols, 309–11.

Here begynneth a treatyse how the hye fader of heuen sendeth dethe to somon euery creature to come and gyue a counte of theyr lyues in this worlde/and is in maner of a morall playe.

15. Title-page of Q3 *Everyman* with woodcut of Death and a coffin

59

16.   Verso of Q4 title-page of *Everyman* with woodcut illustrations of six figures

The Pride of Life also sheds light upon another aspect of *Everyman*'s woodcuts, for while one of these woodcuts portrays Strength as male, the text of *Everyman* uses a female pronoun to describe this figure: 'He that trusteth in his Strength / She him deceiveth at the length' (828–9). Lester points out that Strength is a knight in *The Pride of Life*.[1] Modern productions invariably portray Strength as a burly male, sometimes in the tradition of the circus strong-man. We cannot know for certain which portrayal is accurate, or even if 'accurate' applies here. Perhaps the very desire to pin down a gender for Strength may be a function of our own time rather than of the original text's, for allegorical literature was much more comfortable mixing gender than literature written in the wake of the realist tradition.[2]

The places and people of Everyman

Everyman has often been called one of the great English plays, but in one sense it is not really English. It is a translation, with some changes, of a Dutch play, *Elckerlijc*. This can be pronounced *El-kehr-leek*, and renders literally as 'like' (*-lijc*) 'each' or 'all' (*Elcker-*), or, more simply, 'Everybody'.[3] It was most likely composed in the 1480s or 1490s. Like *Everyman*, this play has a longer full title: *Den Spyeghel der Salicheyt van Elckerlijc*, or *The Mirror of Everyman's Salvation*.

It will help us to understand *Everyman*'s relation to *Elckerlijc* if we begin by recognizing the proximity of the Low Countries to England. Geographically, the Low Countries (also known as 'the Netherlands', and, somewhat less precisely, 'Holland') were just a short voyage from the end of the Thames. Culturally, the population of the Netherlands was markedly industrious, wealthy and literate. Thomas More's *Utopia* – written in 1516, just prior to the likely date of *Everyman*'s issuance – was partly the result

1 Lester, 828n.: 'Strength in *Everyman* is feminine, and was probably more of an abstraction.'
2 On the malleability of gender in religious representations of the Middle Ages, see Bynum. Riggio explores the function of gender identity in the figures of *Wisdom* (39–47).
3 Translation in *Mirror of Salvation*, 92.

61

of that writer's experience of Antwerp and its wealth while on a diplomatic mission.[1] The Dutch were especially skilled in textiles and in the related industries of printing and engraving, with Antwerp an international printing centre and business hub. The cultural advancement of the Low Countries can be seen in the fact that, between 1485 and 1525, approximately eight times as many books were printed in the Netherlands as in England.[2] The two languages, Dutch and English, shared many words and grammatical structures; that Queen Elizabeth spoke Dutch suggests the utility as well as the proximity of that language for sixteenth-century English citizens.

Two phenomena particular to the Low Countries lent *Elckerlijc* its shape. The first of these is religious, the second civic. From the late 1300s and continuing through to the 1600s, the Low Countries experienced the *Devotio Moderna*, or 'Modern Devotion'. This was a religious movement which saw individuals actively seeking, and practising, a more personal and intense spiritual life than was currently afforded by the Catholic Church.[3] A work essential to the Modern Devotion, and representative of this movement's character, was Thomas à Kempis's *The Imitation of Christ*, a manual of spirituality that stressed (as its title indicates) patterning one's life on Christ's through self-renunciation, reflection and rejection of this world.

The second major influence on *Elckerlijc* were the so-called 'chambers of rhetoric' in the cities and towns of the Low Countries. These chambers can be understood as civic guilds or fraternities dedicated to the production of intelligent, verbally sophisticated citizens.[4] Even as the practitioners of the

1 See Wojciehowski, who, in an essay exploring the influence of Antwerp upon *Utopia*, points out that, 'At the time of More's visit, Antwerp was the merchant's emporium *par excellence*' (3).
2 Parsons, 4. On the Low Countries' relation to England at this time, see, in addition to Parsons, Murray.
3 On the *Devotio Moderna*, see Weiler, Post and Mertens.
4 On the chambers, see Waite, van Dixhoorn and Schenkeveld, 11–22; on the role of drama in the chambers, see Waite, Van Bruaene and Hummelen, 'Drama' and 'Boundaries'.

Modern Devotion banded together in new religious houses to perfect their faith, the *rederijkers*, or 'rhetoricians', associated with these urban chambers joined with one another to refine their skills in language through poetry, speech-making and writing plays. So active and ambitious were these chambers that eventually a tradition of contests arose, whereby new works by various chambers of rhetoric would be judged against one another in annual competition. *Elckerlijc* was reported to have won such a prize in a play competition in Antwerp, perhaps in 1496. The same source identifies its author as one 'Petrus' (i.e. Peter) of Diest.[1]

Elckerlijc reads so much like *Everyman* that it is clear one translates the other. For the first half of the twentieth century scholars argued as to which play came first.[2] E.R. Tigg finally laid the question to rest with convincing evidence from the two plays themselves. He showed that remnants of rhyming pairs from *Elckerlijc* were actually buried within *Everyman*'s dialogue. Where *Elckerlijc*, for example, reads

> *Hier in desen aertschen leven.*
> *Die Heylighe Sacramenten seven:*

> [here, in this earthly life.
> The Seven Holy Sacraments:]
>   (675–6; 677–8)

the corresponding lines in *Everyman* read

> Here in this transitory **life**, for thee and me,
> The blessed sacraments **seven** there be:
>   (721–2)

---

1 Christian Stercke identified *Elckerlijc* as a prize-winning play in the preface to his own Latin translation of *Elckerlijc* in 1536, titled *Homulus*. For transcription and discussion of the evidence, see Parker, 24. Four early texts of *Elckerlijc* are known: printed editions of *c*. 1496 (Delft), *c*. 1501 (Antwerp), *c*. 1518–25 (Antwerp), and a manuscript from *c*. 1593–4. In addition to these, R. Vos ('*Elckerlijc*') has argued that as many as five versions earlier than the 1496 edition were produced. See Vos and Streitman, 113, for an English summary of Vos's argument.

2 See, for sample positions, Manly, Wood, de Vocht and Zandvoort.

As Tigg pointed out, *Everyman* translates the Dutch rhyme words '*leven*' and '*seven*' as 'life' and 'seven', respectively. Then, because these words do not rhyme in English, *Everyman* is forced to produce a rhyme pair of its own ('me' and 'be'). Such embedded rhymes from the Dutch occur frequently in *Everyman*.

Adding to the evidence of *Elckerlijc*'s priority are instances in which the play's translator clearly misunderstood the Dutch. To provide only one example, *Everyman* takes *Elckerlijc*'s 'O Godlic Wesen' (586) 'as 'O goodly vision' (582) rather than 'O Divine Being' (a more accurate translation of the Dutch *Wesen*). At numerous other moments the English translator appears to have guessed at a Dutch word based on its sound.[1]

Although *Elckerlijc* and *Everyman* have a great deal in common, there are differences between the two versions. Most noticeably, *Everyman* adds a prologue to its action. We have seen that it appears to do this out of decorum – so that God, that is, who speaks first in *Elckerlijc*, won't go unannounced. Other changes seem like this in general motivation. Overall, *Everyman* softens what is sometimes, in *Elckerlijc*, material potentially critical of the Catholic faith. During its title figure's absence from the stage from 686 to 730, for instance, *Elckerlijc* has the Five Senses (*Vijf Sinnen*) and Knowledge (*Kennisse*) engage in a sobering dispute about the worthiness of priests.[2] Five Senses praises the representative priest as an agent of God who, because he 'binds and looses all bonds / in Heaven and on earth' (698–9), is 'placed above the angels' (707). Knowledge retorts, sharply, that such is true 'for those who stay unblemished', then goes on to indict those priests who 'buy or sell God' (i.e. through peddling pardons or indulgences), have children and even 'live with women' (715, 718–19). All Five Senses can answer is 'I hope, God willing, that none do this' (721), a very lukewarm declaration.

---

1   In addition to Tigg's work, see Conley, 'Aural'.
2   On this digression, see McRae.

Everyman changes this scenario in seemingly small ways, but ways that shed light on the play's thoughts about the Church. Where *Elckerlijc* allows its title figure the freedom to exit the stage during this debate, *Everyman* adds a personal address near the end of Five Wits's speech praising priesthood – 'Everyman, God gave priests that dignity' (747) – which makes it necessary for Everyman to remain in place for the duration of Five Wits's speech. Free to exit after the speech of praise, he misses Knowledge's indictment. *Everyman* thus has its main figure present for the praise of priests, whereas his counterpart in *Elckerlijc* does not seem to hear this. Likewise, *Everyman* translates *Elckerlijc*'s tepid line – 'I hope, God willing, that none do this' – with a more confident, and more faithful, endorsement of priesthood: 'I trust to God no such may we find' (764).

Similarly, *Everyman* translates *Elckerlijc*'s figure *Duecht* not as 'Virtue' (the meaning of the Dutch) but rather as 'Good Deeds'. This is important because good deeds had long been a part of medieval Christianity's structure. Such actions as charitable deeds and gifts, fasting, pilgrimages and reciting the rosary, for instance, were thought to contribute to the merit of the individual who performed them. During the fifteenth and sixteenth centuries, however – and especially as the Reformation began unfolding – dissatisfaction with the apparently mechanical nature of this system led many theologians and believers to stress a Christian's justification by 'faith alone' ('solifidianism', as it was known in England). To be sure, both *Elckerlijc* and *Everyman* significantly feature an account book by which their principal figures' actions on earth are recorded for judgement. But *Everyman* translates *Elckerlijc*'s singular, generalized and humanistic figure of 'Virtue' into a plural, more doctrinal and conventionally Catholic 'Good Deeds'.

Likewise *Everyman* masculinizes *Elckerlijc*'s feminine figure of Confession. *Elckerlijc* clearly makes Confession ('*Biechte*') female, employing half a dozen female pronouns to describe her: 'Everyman, this is Confession; fall at her feet. / She is very dear and precious to God' (494–5). In contrast, *Everyman* chooses to alter its source so as to present Confession as a priest figure. It refers to Confession as 'that holy man' and 'him' before Knowledge says 'Lo, this is Confession. Kneel down and ask mercy, / For he is in good conceit with God almighty' (543–4).[1]

Elckerlijc tells a strong story of faith, then, but does so in a way that appears to have made the *Everyman* translator uncomfortable. Why so? Perhaps it was in part the Dutch play's freer approach to questions of faith, and its willingness to identify resources for salvation outside the official agents of the Church. The roots of this approach may be traced not only to the *Devotio Moderna* but also to the ancient sources of its plot. *Elckerlijc*'s story of the false friends who abandon a central figure in his time of need, for instance, had a long lineage. It is found in many medieval sermon collections, exists in both Arabic and Oriental forerunners, and may come ultimately from a Christianized parable of Buddhist origins (see Appendix 4 for one analogue). A.C. Cawley thus puts his finger on the hybrid appeal of *Elckerlijc* when he describes it as an 'amalgam': 'its teaching is a product of Western Christendom, its fable a product of the Buddhist East' (xv–xvi).

Who translated *Everyman*? None of the early texts mentions an author or translator, and differences of spelling among the quartos suggest that various individuals may have adapted it at various times. More's experiences in Antwerp just prior to writing *Utopia* testify to the constant stream of exchange between the two regions. More's interest in answering challenges to Catholic orthodoxy also helps to frame the goals of the English translation. Cawley advanced Laurence Andrewe as a candidate (Cawley, xiii). Andrewe worked as a bookseller and printer in London during the 1520s, and was known to have translated other books from Dutch to English at this time. One

---

1 Note, however, that *Everyman* keeps *Elckerlijc*'s reference to 'Shrift, mother of salvation' (552).

such translation, *The vertuose boke of distyllacyon of the waters of all maner of herbes* by Hieronymus Brunschwig (STC 13436), shares a number of words and phrases with Q3 *Everyman*, nearly a hundred of them spelled identically.[1] While this is unsatisfying as an indicator of collaborative agency, more research into the vocabulary of the *Everyman* quartos may help us come closer to identifying the individuals involved in their translation.

Everyman *in performance*

Everyman's performance history begins, as far as we can be certain, in 1901, when an astonishingly successful production opened the floodgates to its modern popularity. Since that time, *Everyman* has been successfully staged countless times, committed to film on multiple occasions, adapted in many languages (most notably in the German *Jedermann*) and served as the basis of cantatas and operas. Notably, it has given its title as a word and concept to the English language. The word 'Everyman' has been used as the name of a periodical, a publishing series, various theatres, acting companies, cinemas and business concerns. It has also come to describe not only a representative figure with whom readers and audiences can easily identify, but also, and more specifically, male film stars who seem unpretentious and likeable.[2] How did the morality play Everyman, a figure judged as being too at home in the secular world, become a populist hero of that world itself?

We could begin our answer by noticing that performance is an open question in the text of *Everyman*. Its translator labels it a 'treatise . . . *in manner of* a moral play' (0.1–0.3, emphasis added), and as originally published its two stage directions – 'God speketh' and 'Felawshyp speketh' – seem almost an afterthought.[3] Yet too much in the play seems based in theatrical performance for it to be *only* a treatise. There are, first of all, a

---

1 Such spellings include words like *mynysshe*, *lytell*, *incontinent*, *medycyne(s)* and *condycyon*, among others.
2 See, for only two instances of this widespread appellation, Natale and Schwartz.
3 At 22 and 206, respectively. See Textual Notes.

great many references to distance and movement in the text. Bob Godfrey ('*Everyman*', 162–3) points out that the play's frequent use of 'yonder' and 'Where?' implies both real space and movement. To Suzanne Westfall, this movement takes place 'from station to station' as Everyman encounters various figures who help and hinder him (Westfall, 178). Godfrey draws the parallel to the stations of the cross in Catholic tradition.[1]

Other modern interpreters have seen the possibility of a locus/platea structure for staging the play. 'Locus' and 'platea' are conventional terms for describing, respectively, a fixed locale onstage (the 'locus'), a position of authority or stability contrasted with a relatively free area of movement (the 'platea').[2] In *Everyman*, the locus would be represented by God's throne upon a raised scaffold, under which a space (perhaps with a trap door or other opening) could afford the play Everyman's grave. The typically unlocalized platea area might be anchored, in various places, by a seated Goods and a prone Good Deeds, but would be otherwise available for some of the walking implied in the text's dialogue.[3] Just such an arrangement characterized early twentieth-century productions of *Everyman*.

In July 1901 the innovative theatrical manager William Poel staged a production of *Everyman* in the courtyard of the Charterhouse in London.[4] A former monastery, the

---

1 See Westfall, 178 and Godfrey, '*Everyman*', 162–3. To Frost, the play's 'heavy cueing' of entrances' and 'lengthy exits' suggests that '"off-stage" in the playwright's conception was some distance away from the main playing area' (42–3). See also Harkness on departure in the play.

2 On 'locus' and 'platea' in early English theatre, see Dillon, *Early*, 4–16. See Cawley, xxix–xxx for discussion of staging possibilities. Godfrey, '*Everyman*' and Frost provide the fullest discussions of performance issues. See Schreiber and Isaac for the play's performance history.

3 E.g. at 85–9 (Death hailing Everyman) and 788ff. (Everyman leading his group towards the grave).

4 Information on early productions of *Everyman* in the following paragraphs draws on Isaac, 75–85, and Elliott, 42–4. Poel's promptbook (currently in the Victoria and Albert Museum) reveals cuts to the description of the Crucifixion in God's opening speech; likewise Five Wits's digression on priesthood and Knowledge's retort about priests' 'lechery' were deleted as well (Elliott, 43).

Charterhouse lent an appropriate gravity to the production, and the play became a commercial and critical sensation – not only in London, but in Oxford and on tour across Britain. Allegedly impatient with the play's theology, Poel sold the rights of the production to the actor and director Ben Greet, who in 1902 took it to the US. Greet's production enjoyed so much success that he was ultimately able to split his company in two and perform in numerous venues across the US, often on college campuses or other sites where appropriately 'classical' architecture magnified the play's historical resonance. Greet's productions continued in the US well on through the 1920s and into the 1930s.

These early productions employed the historical distance of *Everyman*'s script to their advantage. Flowing costumes that seemed suitable to the formality of a religious scene were patterned after Holbein. Space was liberally used: Goods and Confession often resided in stage alcoves or 'houses' (see Figs 13 and 17). Organ music accompanied parts of the performance, and some church architecture was imported for the action. To avoid offending religious sensibilities, God was referred to in the programmes as 'Adonai' (cf. 245). Indeed, the startling fact and nature of God's appearance on a raised throne, in 'a red robe trimmed with silver, whiskers and full beard', often came in for special mention, as few playgoers of the time had ever seen God represented onstage before. To imitate what they felt was historical practice, the actors of these early productions delivered their lines in a near chant.

In a move that would become customary, Greet cast a woman as Everyman: the talented and well-known actress Edith Wynne Mathison (see Fig. 18, and Mateer). Mathison's 'tender and beautiful' performance – the contemporary description hints at a vulnerability she brought to the production – came in for special note, and she continued in the role for over a decade. Other actresses of the period who played Everyman include May Douglas Reynolds and Sybil Thorndike.

17. Everyman descending into the grave, US production, *c.* 1902

18.   Tita Brand (left) as Knowledge and Edith Wynne Matthison as Everyman,
      c. 1902

An important line of *Everyman*'s busy theatrical life in the
twentieth century sprang from Hugo von Hofmannsthal's
German-language translation of 1911, *Jedermann* ('Everyman').
This version has arguably introduced as many people to the
Everyman story as the English *Everyman*. This is in part

71

because of Hofmannsthal's skilful modern adaptation, and in part because of *Jedermann*'s place in the Salzburg Festival (Austria), where it has become a cultural mainstay, having been performed annually in Cathedral Square since 1920 (see Fig. 19). Max Reinhardt staged an extravagant version of the Salzburg *Everyman* at the Hollywood Bowl (Los Angeles) in 1936; its 'not-so-spiritual angels singing as Jedermann enters the grave' appeared to be 'gaudily attired Busby Berkeley dancers' (Schreiber, 101).

Everyman also appealed to audiences outside the theatre. It was broadcast successfully on US radio in both 1926 and 1938, and televised with a jazz score by the BBC in 1960 (Schreiber, 100). Also noteworthy among such adaptations are a spoken-word recording of 1955 with Burgess Meredith as Everyman and Darren McGavin as Fellowship, and Charles Wilson's 1972 opera, *The Summoning of Everyman*. In addition to these, *Everyman* has been filmed numerous times since 1913.[1] Three filmed productions merit special mention. A version presented in period costume and recovering some of the earlier productions' staging was directed by Bob Morris in 1991 and distributed through an academic film library. John Farrell's film presents a modernized *Everyman* in New England in the 1980s; it features Death in a suit and sunglasses and, eerily, an early personal computer as Goods.

An especially impressive film version is Douglas Morse's *The Summoning of Everyman* (2008), shot in Cambridge, England, and the Greenwood Cemetery in Brooklyn, New York. Its talented cast of theatre professionals manages to capture not only the personal journey of Everyman (performed by Paul Barry as a man advanced in years), but also the iconographical force of the play's supporting cast. For instance, Lindsay Rae Taylor, as Good Deeds, bears a

1 For a review of the 1913 *Everyman* film, apparently based closely on the English-language text, see Bush. For information on Jos Stalling's 1975 film of *Elckerlijc* in the Netherlands, see Harty, 80.

19.   Death (Clemens Schick) claims Everyman/Jedermann (Peter Simonischek) in the Salzburg *Jedermann* (2007)

large, bound volume in her arms as the 'account book' of Everyman's virtuous actions (see Fig. 14). Sally Conway is fittingly cast as Beauty, with Grace Zandarski (as a thoughtful Knowledge) and Uma Incrocci (as an earnest Five Wits) appropriate to their figures as well. Collectively, these various adaptations confirm what the first readers and audience members of both *Elckerlijc* and *Everyman* surely recognized: the story of our short time on earth, and of the ephemeral nature of most of our attachments, translates easily across various times and media alike.

Everyman: critical history

Much of *Everyman*'s early critical history hinged on its relationship to the Dutch play *Elckerlijc*. Such critical attention as there has been outside the limited scope of this debate has returned again and again to the significant differences between these apparently similar texts.

Most commentators agree that *Everyman* is more conservative than *Elckerlijc*, with Christopher Wortham holding the two plays 'polemical'; in his view, *Everyman* is an orthodox retort to Luther: '*Elckerlijc* is *ante*-Reformation; *Everyman* is *anti*-Reformation' (Wortham, 23). For Jacqueline Vanhoutte, however, the major differences between the two plays derive from the movement away from performance (*Elckerlijc* considered as a virtual script) and towards print (*Everyman* seen as a doctrinal text). This movement has an ideological component, with the shift from outdoor, public play to document for private reading working to eclipse *Elckerlijc*'s commitment to social responsibility. David Mills qualifies this dichotomy, however, and provides a thoughtful discussion of the possible social contexts for each work by locating *Elckerlijc* in relation to the popular genre of realist painting in the Netherlands and speculating that *Everyman* may have found multiple kinds of readers. These include readers who took it to be a treatise; those able 'to translate the text into their own imagined theatre, based upon experience of performances in England'; and those for whom it may have been 'an acting text for practical performance'.[1]

Everyman's religious content has long dominated critical discussion.[2] John Conley points out the two elements of Catholic faith greatly emphasized in the play: the necessity of good works for salvation; and the certainty of divine judgement after death (Conley, 'Doctrine'). The play's interest in the Parable of the Talents (found in Matthew, 25.14–30) forms the centrepiece of V.A. Kolve's argument in an influential essay that explores the nexus of commercial and spiritual ideas in the play.[3] Phoebe Spinrad concentrates on what she sees as the little-noticed trick ending in *Everyman*. The play seems to begin again at 649ff. when Everyman resumes his journey to the grave, pridefully confident with a new set of companions (Beauty, Strength, et al.) who will abandon him just as surely as the false friends he had earlier encountered.[4]

This collusion of form and doctrine in *Everyman* has been accepted since the publication of a foundational essay by Thomas Van Laan. Van Laan discerns a 'two-part, descent-ascent structural pattern as the basic principle of the play's organization', and sees this structural pattern as the engine of its profound emotional effects as well (Van Laan, 466). Refining this model, Richard Hillman has noted the play's 'ultimate loyalty' to 'opposing the complacency of its audience' (Hillman, 212). *Everyman*'s supposed lack of humour has been refuted by Ron Tanner, who explores the comedy in the play's first half, relating much of the comic business with Fellowship, Kindred and Cousin to the joking irreverence of the traditional stage Vices (Tanner, 156–7). As we have seen, Everyman's repeated

1 Mills, 'Anglo-Dutch', 88. See also Mills, 'Theaters'.
2 See, for commentary on *Everyman* and religion, Conley, 'Doctrine', Cunningham, Rendall, Bacquet, Best, Peek and Cooper & Wortham.
3 See Harper & Mize for a reconsideration of Kolve's thesis; they argue the play is more 'engaged with the discourse of social complaint' than previously realized (266). On 'mercantile salvation' in *Everyman*, see Ladd.
4 On this desertion, see also Johnson.

moments of surprise when the reality of his situation sinks in also provide laughter in the play.

Everyman: *date and textual introduction*

With four early quarto editions, all of which are undated, and two of which survive only in fragments, *Everyman* presents some unique editorial challenges. However, typographic analysis undertaken for this edition has helped us to narrow the range of *termini a quo* and *ad quem* for each quarto. The first, Q1 (STC 10604), was printed by Richard Pynson, whose colophon appears on the final page: 'Imprynted at London in Fletestrete at the Sygne of the George by Rycharde Pynson prynter unto the Kyngs noble grace' (see Fig. 20). Pynson, who was active between 1491 and 1528, resided in Fleet Street from 1500 onwards, and was made the King's printer in May 1508. Analysis of Pynson's black-letter pilcrows (¶), the sign standardly used to signal the beginning of each new speech in early English printed drama, indicates that the text was printed *c.* 1518–19.

Q1 survives in two fragments: four leaves, comprising the whole of signature C (lines 684–922), recovered out of the binding of a book, were bequeathed by Francis Douce to the Bodleian Library in 1834 and are sometimes referred to as the Douce fragment. A second fragment of two leaves, unsigned but apparently comprising sigs B3–4 (lines 429–552), was part of the Bulkeley Bandinel library auctioned by Sotheby's in 1861 (lot 461) but unknown to scholars and editors until it was rediscovered at the beginning of the twenty-first century; it is now in the private collection of Arthur and Janet Ing Freeman (see Fig. 21). Following Freeman's lead, we will refer to this as the Bandinel fragment.

A second quarto, Q2 (STC 10604.5), also printed by Pynson, can be dated between 1525 and 1528; the sole extant copy of this edition is a fragment of ten leaves, comprising the whole of sigs B and C (lines 305–922), that Thomas Astle gave to David

Unto the whiche all ye than come
That lyueth well after the daye of dome
Th... morpall men maye haue in mynde
ye here... take it aworthe olde and yonge
And forsake pryde for he deceyues you in the ende
And remembre beaute.v. wytt strength & discrecion
They all at last do euery man forsake
Saue his good dedes there do he take
But beware for and they be small
Before god he hathe no helpe at all
None excuse may be there for euery man
Alas howe shall he do than
For after deth amendes may no man make
For than mercy and pyte dothe hym forsake
If his rekenynge be not clere whan he do come
God wyll say ite maledicti in ignem eternum.
And he that hath his accounte hole and founde
Hye in heuen he shall be crounde
Unto whiche please god brynge vs all the...
That we may lyue body and soule togyder
Therto helpe the trinyte
Amen saye ye for saynt charyte.
Finis.
Impzynted at London in Fletestrete at the
Sygne of the George by Rycharde Pynson
pzynter vnto the kyngs noble grace.

20. Final page with colophon from the Douce fragment of Q1 *Everyman*

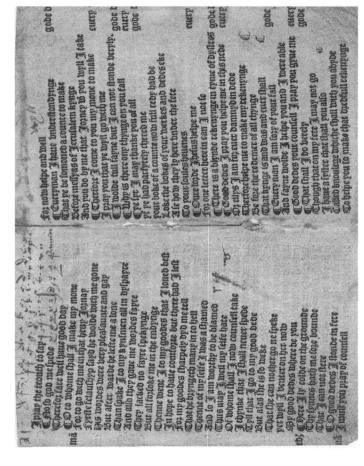

21. The newly discovered Bandinel fragment of Q1 *Everyman*

Garrick in 1763, and which is now in the British Library.[1] Both Q1 and Q2 have thirty-one lines of type per page (although six lines were cut off from the top of each page in the Douce fragment, presumably when it was trimmed for use as binding material). Pynson's black–letter font used for the two quartos did not have an upper-case 'Y'. It would appear that Q2 is a page-for-page reprint of Q1, although it adds the signature-title (the shortened version of the title that appears at the foot of most recto pages), 'Every man', and differs from Q1 in certain other formal respects – speech prefixes in Q2 are set in smaller type and some Latin phrases near the end of the play are in roman – and it introduces a host of verbal variants.

Another quarto, Q3 (STC 10606), now in the Huntington Library, has the colophon 'Imprynted at London in Poules chyrch yarde by me John Skot' (see Fig. 22). Skot was active between 1521 and 1537; analysis of the progressive damage to the woodcuts used in this quarto and in other datable books published by Skot suggests that it was printed between 1521 and 1528; it is here termed 'Q3' for convenience, although it may have predated Q2. Q3 is a complete text, collating $A^4 B^8 C^4$, with a title-page illustrated with woodcuts of Everyman and Death with a coffin (see Fig. 15, p. 59), and the signature-title 'The Som' throughout. Q3 has thirty-two lines per page. It exhibits orthographic patterns not found in the previous two editions, employing the spellings 'hyder', 'thyder', 'whyder', 'togyder' where Q1 and Q2 use 'hether', 'thether', 'whether', 'together'.

A fourth quarto, Q4 (STC 10606.5), now in the British Library, was also printed by Skot, probably between 1528 and 1531. It, too, is a complete text, with the same title-page

---

1   W.W. Greg incorrectly asserts that Q2 'does not form part of the collection of plays bequeathed to the Museum by David Garrick' (Greg, 35). In *The Garrick Collection of Old English Plays*, George Kahrl lists it as item 406 and notes that 'this was one of the items in the volume which Thomas Astle gave to Garrick in July, 1763, and which had previously been in Bishop Percy's possession' (Kahrl, 20–1). In 1765, Thomas Percy observed that 'in Mr Garrick's collection is an imperfect copy of the same play' (*Reliques*, 2.105).

22.   Final page of Q3 *Everyman* with John Skot's colophon

illustrations as Q3 supplemented on the verso by six additional woodcuts representing characters from the play (see Fig. 16, p. 60). Q4 has thirty-two lines per page and appears to be a page-for-page reprint of Q3, although it is differently collated – $A^6 B^6 D^4$ (omitting C) – and has the signature-title 'The summenynge'.

Everyman: *editorial procedures*

Greg maintained that, of the extant editions, the 'very accurately printed' Q1 was 'almost certainly' the earliest, but concluded that the fuller Q3 'appears to offer somewhat the more satisfactory text' (Greg, 61, 69). All twentieth-century editors followed Greg's advice and chose Q3 as their control text. But given that, with the Douce fragment supplemented by the Bandinel fragment, we now have a text of Q1 for just over one third of the play, the present edition breaks with tradition and uses the first quarto as control text where it is available; that is, the two leaves of the Bandinel fragment provide the base text for lines 429–552; the four leaves of the Douce fragment (bearing in mind that the top six lines are missing from every page) provide the base text for lines 684–707, 714–38, 745–69, 776–800, 807–31, 838–62, 869–94 and 901–22.

This editorial procedure raises the question of which later quarto should be used as control text where there are lacunae in Q1. Q2's apparent bibliographical links to Q1 make it a prime contender. However, Q2 is, in fact, the most variant of the four early editions. Q2's individuality is well illustrated by lines 828–31: the text of this passage is identical in Q1, Q3 and Q4, but Q2 offers at least one substantive variant in every line:

He [Q2: **But I se well he**] that trusteth in his Strength
She him [Q2: **Is greatly**] deceiveth at the length.
Both [Q2: **For**] Strength and Beauty **forsaketh** [Q2: **hath forsaken**] me,
Yet they promised me **fair and lovingly** [Q2: **stedfast to be**].

(828–31)

81

Greg proposed an elaborate textual stemma in which a lost edition or manuscript 'Y' served as the source of Q1 and Q2, a lost 'X' was the source of Q3 and Q4, and a lost 'Z' was the source of Q4 and 'Y'. Thus the Pynson quartos and the Skot quartos were each viewed as a set of twins with only a vaguely distant relation to the other set.

Our analysis suggests that the situation is somewhat less complex. Although Q2 derives from Q1, the Q2 text does not appear to have influenced the later quartos. On the other hand, Q3 – which may in fact predate Q2 – tends to follow Q1 much more closely than does Q2 (in addition to the above examples from 828–31, see the textual notes at lines 432, 433, 445, 451, 455, 464, 470, 473, 474, 489, 508, 812, 822, 839 and 841). Q4 generally follows Q3; the very few instances of textual agreement between Q1/Q4 against Q3 (such as 507) suggest coincidence rather than influence.

We are gratified that Arthur Freeman's recent re-analysis of the variants, occasioned by his discovery of the Bandinel fragment, is in substantial agreement with our revised stemma. Freeman argues that 'Q2 is a textual dead end in the surviving quarto tradition'; that 'insofar as we can judge from the surviving text of Q1, Q3 seems largely to depend upon it'; and that Q4 'is simply a modernized, very slightly corrected and sometimes dumbed-down version of Q3, which shows no sign of direct contact with Q1 or Q2' (Freeman, 426–7). The presumed stemma divides after Q1, with one branch leading to Q2 and another to Q3 followed by Q4. It is possible, however, that the compositors in Pynson's shop had access to a variant manuscript version of the play that they may have consulted when setting Q2.

We use Q3 as control text for those sections of the play that are not present in Q1: 1–428, 553–683, 708–13, 739–44, 770–5, 801–6, 832–7, 863–8 and 895–900. We realize that it is unusual, although not unprecedented,[1] to have multiple control texts in a

---

1   An analogous situation arises with editing Shakespeare's *1 Henry IV*. Most recent editions take the oddly named 'Q0' – a fragment of four leaves recovered by Halliwell 'some years' prior to 1867 from the binding of a copy of William Thomas's *Rules of the Italian Grammar* (1567) – as control text from 1.3.201 to 2.2.105, using Q1 for the rest of the play.

critical edition of an early modern play. To aid users in keeping track of the underlying text, we include in the Textual Notes indications of each point at which the control text shifts from Q1 to Q3 and back again.

This edition of *Everyman* – the first to be prepared since the discovery of the Bandinel fragment, and the first to use Q1 as control text – restores some significant original readings, such as Q1's 'wash from me the spots and vices clean' (546) where all previous editors have followed Qq3–4's 'wash from me the spots of vice unclean'. A fidelity to Q1 means that our text differs from previous editions in a number of readings: 'forsook' for 'forsake' (471); 'ne' for 'nor' (483); 'cold on the ground' (where Good Deeds lies) rather than 'in the ground' (486); 'herein can I' for 'here I can' (507); 'there were' for 'were there' (537); 'Repent' for 'Redempt' (549); 'gave he us' for 'he gave' (752); 'and hie' for 'fro me' (807). We have not slavishly followed Q1 when it is clearly in error, as in 'lyberacion' for 'deliberation' (691), or when its readings make only a kind of sense, as in 'a grete countes' for 'great accounts' in 'And great accounts before God to make' (551). But we have trusted Q1's readings when they can be defended, as in 'God's body in flesh and blood to take' (738); although all other editors follow Qq3–4's 'make', the Q1 reading can certainly be defended, and perhaps even preferred, in a passage about the consecration of the Eucharist.

MANKIND

LIST OF ROLES

MERCY
MISCHIEF
NEW–GUISE
NOUGHT
NOWADAYS 5
MANKIND
TITIVILLUS

LIST OF ROLES: This list is based on the figures' order of appearance. For discussion of casting possibilities, see Appendix 1.

1 MERCY As the priest figure who guides Mankind, Mercy stands for the compassion shown to humanity by a forgiving God. Mercy was one of the Christian graces: see e.g. Matthew, 5.7 and Luke, 6.36. As an abstraction, mercy was conventionally understood to be female; cf. 840–1n. It is most likely that Mercy is male in *Mankind* so that, as a priest, he can receive Mankind's confession and say 'go and sin no more': only priests have the ability on earth to grant mercy (i.e. to absolve from sin), through the power lent to the Church by Christ (see 850–3 and n.). Meredith discusses the implications of clothing Mercy as friar, monk or priest, respectively, and notes his unusual moments of overpoliteness toward the audience (Meredith, *Acting*, 21, 23, 35). Mercy typically speaks in stanzas of eight or four lines, rhyming *ababbcbc* and *abab*, respectively.

2 MISCHIEF Mercy's antagonist, Mischief leads New-Guise, Nowadays and Nought – the trio of Vices referred to in these notes as the 'Three Ns' – against Mankind. A more serious word in the fifteenth century than today, 'mischief' appears frequently in translations of the Hebrew Bible, where it typically betokens both aggressive malice hidden from view, and, as in Psalms, 10.7, dangerously loose speech (a central theme in *Mankind*): 'His mouth is full of cursing, and of deceate, and of fraude: vnder his tongue is labour and mischiefe.' Coogan sees Mischief as an agent of suicide in the play (Coogan, 60–1). Mischief speaks in the Vices' tail-rhyme stanza rhyming *aaabcccb*.

3 NEW-GUISE a name emphasizing prideful devotion to fashion, practice, habit or custom (*OED* 2). In Lydgate, *Fall of Princes*, Death deploys this as a familiar notion: 'Commeth forth Syr Squyer, right fresh of your araye, /

That conne of daunces al the new[e] guise' ('The Daunce of Machabree', ll. 47–8). In *Robin Conscience*, 234, one 'Mother Newgise' revels in the luxury of her apparel: 'What, thovgh the people doo raile and rage, / And say, that I goe painted vp like bvtter-flyes, / I will haue my clothes made of the new gise' (ll. 112–14). Heap points out that New-Guise often takes the lead among the Three Ns, is frequently connected with the gallows and seems to take pains to protect his groin from assault (Heap, 97). New-Guise speaks in the Vices' tail-rhyme stanza rhyming *aaabcccb*.

4 NOUGHT Literally 'nothing', the name *Nought* here signifies (1) 'A person or thing of no worth or consequence; a mere nothing' (*OED sb.* 2); and (2) 'Wickedness, evil, moral wrong – (also) promiscuity, indecency' (*OED sb.* 3b). This sense survives in our word 'naughty', to which 'nought' is related. Nought, the butt of the other Vices' jokes, is typically connected with defecation. Heap calls him 'the useless one . . . in sum, a loser' (Heap, 97). Nought speaks in the Vices' tail-rhyme stanza rhyming *aaabcccb*.

5 NOWADAYS a name suggesting the sin of living for this moment, according to (fallen) modes of behaviour. The devil Belial uses the term in *Conversion*, 17–18: 'Thowgh on hath dyssayvyd vs, yet nowadays / Twenti doyth gladly folow oure layes: / Some by Pryde, some thorowgh Envye; / Ther rayneth thorow my myght so moch dysobedyaunce, / Ther was neuer among Crystyans less charyte / Than ys at this howre.' Nowadays speaks in the Vices' tail-rhyme stanza rhyming *aaabcccb*.

6 MANKIND the play's *human genus* figure, a representative of humanity generally. Mankind is identified more specifically as a farmer. Perhaps as an effect of *Piers Plowman*, he is also shown to be literate and able to write biblical Latin. See 315–22. The word –*kind* in his

LIST OF ROLES] *Manly subst.*

name affords the play conventional puns on *unkind* as meaning both 'unnatural' and 'hurtful' or 'wicked' (cf. 742 and n.). Dorothy Castle aptly describes Mankind as 'the football that passes between Mercy and the Devil's helpers' (Castle, *Game*, 37). In Mercy's presence, Mankind typically speaks in a four-line stanza rhyming *abab*; under the Vices' influence, he employs their tail-rhyme stanza.

7 TITIVILLUS Originally a minor fiend, Titivillus may be made synonymous with 'the' devil in *Mankind* because of this play's interest in speech. Since at least the fourteenth century, Titivillus had been identified as a gatherer of words pronounced poorly (or not at all) during religious services – and, by extension, of any sinfully loose talk. He may come onstage wearing a devil's mask or grotesquely oversized head. Meredith notes that Titivillus is 'in a constant teasing relationship with the audience, taking them into his confidence, enlisting their aid, implicating them imaginatively with his invisibility, promising them entertainment – and, in a sense, damning them' (Meredith, *Acting*, 14). Titivillus employs the widest variety of stanzaic forms in the play, from the couplet through to a twelve-line stanza.

MANKIND

[*Enter* MERCY.]

MERCY

The very founder and beginner of our first creation,
　Among us sinful wretches he oweth to be magnified,
That for our disobedience he had none indignation
　To send his own son to be torn and crucified.
Our obsequious service to him should be applied,　　　5
　Where he was Lord of all and made all thing of
　　　　nought,
For the sinful sinner, too, had him revived
　And for his redemption set his own son at nought.

It may be said and verified, Mankind was dear bought.

0 SD *Enter* MERCY Mercy delivers a traditional prologue to the audience, even as he will deliver a traditional epilogue, similarly alone onstage, at 903–14. Religiously as well as theatrically authoritative, he most likely wears the garments of a priest; see 88n., 209n. and Coogan, 1–7.

1 **very** true; ultimately from Latin *verus*, 'true' (cf. modern French *vrai*)
　founder and beginner i.e. God. Mercy's redundancy, drawn in part from biblical formula, signals the high register of sermonic discourse: cf. *sinful sinner* (7), *humility and reverence* (14) and 'my name and my denomination' (122).

2 **oweth . . . magnified** ought to be praised. Cf. Psalms, 70.4: 'let all such as delight in thy saluation say alway, the Lorde be magnified.'

3 **for** despite
　none no
　indignation anger (at what is unworthy or wrongful; *OED* 2); cf. Psalms,

6.1: 'O God rebuke me not in thine indignation: neither chasten me in thy wrath.' This polysyllabic rhyme-word confirms Mercy's Latinate register.

5 **obsequious** submissive, dutiful; here without the modern sense of falsity. Cf. *Ham*1.2.91–2:'In filial obligation . . . To do obsequious sorrow'.

6 **Where** it being the case that (*OED adv.* and *conj.* 12a; 'chiefly in legal and other formal documents')
　thing things; see *MED sb.* 2g, citing *Antichrist*: 'All thinge I made thrugh my myght, son and mone, day and nyght.'

8 **set . . . nought** valued him at nothing (i.e. and thus gave him over to death). A proleptic pun on 'Nought'; cf. 98n.
　own son i.e. Jesus Christ

9 **dear bought** redeemed (from death) at a high price. A common metaphor in the Christian Bible likened Christ's sacrifice to economic exchange; cf. 1 Corinthians, 6.20: 'For ye are dearely bought: therefore glorifie God in your

0 SD] SCENE I *Eccles* SD] *Manly* 7 too] *(to)*

By the piteous death of Jesu he had his remedy.   10
He was purged of his default, that wretchedly had
                        wrought,
By his glorious passion, that blessed lavatory.
O sovereigns, I beseech you your conditions to rectify
And with humility and reverence to have a
                        remotion
To this blessed prince that our nature doth glorify,   15
That ye may be participable of his retribution.

I have be the very mean for your restitution.
Mercy is my name, that mourneth for your offence.
Divert not yourself in time of temptation,
That ye may be acceptable to God at your going
                        hence.   20
The great mercy of God, that is of most preeminence,
By mediation of our Lady that is ever abundant

body and in your spirite, which are Gods.' This idea contributes to an oath repeated by Mercy at 116 and 255, Mischief at 415 and New-Guise at 614.

11 **default** failure, neglect of duty
12 **his** i.e. Christ's
lavatory bath, purifying wash – i.e. the blood of Christ. Cf. lines from '*Hostis Herodes impie*': '*Lavachra puri gurgitis Cælestis Agnus attigit*' (Latin, 'the Heavenly Lamb made Baths from pure waters'), where *Baths* suggests baptismal fonts. Cited in Gray, 83, 131–3.
13 **sovereigns** lords, masters (i.e. those who are allowed to make decisions for themselves). Mercy flatters the audience with conventional address; cf. the Epilogue to *Brome Play*, 56: 'Lo! sovereyns and sorys, now haue we schewyd, / Thys solom story to gret and smale' (ll. 435–6) and the Poet in the Epilogue to *Killing of Children*, 114: 'Honorable souereignes, thus we conclude / Oure matere that

we haue shewid here in your presens' (ll. 551–2). Mercy will use *sovereigns* at 25, 29 and in his epilogue at 903.
conditions states of being
14 **remotion** inclination. Mankind uses this word at 656.
15 **blessed prince** Christ. A biblical metaphor; cf. Revelation, 1.5: 'prince of kingis of the erthe' (Wycliffe) and Acts, 3.15, 5.31.
our ... glorify uplifts our fallen state (i.e. through his sacrifice on the cross)
16 **participable ... retribution** able to participate in the reward he has earned; like *obsequious* (5), *retribution* has a positive sense here (pertaining to recompense for merit or service).
17 **be** been
mean means
18 **that** who
19 **Divert not yourself** Do not lose your way.
20 **going hence** i.e. death
22 ***mediation** intervention, action. For this theological sense, see *MED*

To the sinful creature that will repent his negligence.
I pray God at your most need that Mercy be your
defendant.

In good works I advise you, sovereigns, to be
                                        perseverant   25
To purify your souls that they be not corrupt;
For your ghostly enemy will make his avaunt,
Your good conditions if he may interrupt.
O ye sovereigns that sit and ye brethren that stand
                        right up,
Prick not your felicities in things transitory.   30
Behold not the earth, but lift your eye up.
See how the head the members daily do magnify.
Who is the head? Forsooth, I shall you certify:

mediacioun 1c. MS *medytacyon* is most likely a scribal misreading.

our Lady Mary (Jesus' mother), who was especially linked to the forgiveness of sins

abundant overflowing, more than sufficient

24 **pray** ask
defendant defender, protector (*OED a.* and *sb.*, B.1a, describing a now obsolete sense it first records from *c.* 1533). Like *Everyman*, *Mankind* makes frequent recourse to the metaphor, drawn from the legal system, of the trial that will determine humanity's salvation or damnation.

25 **good works** In later medieval theology, Christians were instructed to gain salvation by demonstrating their obedience to the Church through acts of penance, submission and technical observance. Cf. the sequence of contrition in *Everyman* (543–650), which includes confession and scourging the flesh.
be perseverant persevere, keep doing

26 **that** so that
27 **ghostly enemy** (1) enemy of your spirit, or 'ghost'; (2) enemy in the shape of a spirit. Both readings centre on the devil. The phrase is repeated at 837 (by Mankind) and 855 (by Mercy). Medwall uses this phrase in his contemporaneous play, *Nature* (ll. 1258, 1455).
avaunt boast
28 **interrupt** pervert, corrupt
29 Mercy distinguishes socially superior men, *sovereigns*, who possess (by rank and/or wealth) the right to sit, from men of the lower orders, *brethren*, who stand during the performance. See 13n. On the staging of *Mankind*, see pp. 29–32 and Appendix 1.
30 **Prick** place
felicities happiness
31 **eye up** eyes upwards (i.e. as towards heaven)
32 **members** limbs; cf. 1 Corinthians, 12.27: 'Ye are the body of Christe, and members one of another.'
33 **certify** inform certainly

22+ By] *(Be) throughout as indicated by meaning* 22 mediation] *Manly subst.;* medytacyon *MS* 27 avaunt] *Manly subst.;* a vaunce *MS* 29 brethren] *(brothern)*

I mean our saviour, that was likened to a lamb;
And his saints be the members that daily he doth
                                        satisfy   35
With the precious river that runneth from his womb.

There is none such food, by water nor by land,
   So precious, so glorious, so needful to our intent,
For it hath dissolved Mankind from the bitter bond
   Of the mortal enemy, that venomous serpent,   40
From the which God preserve you all at the last
                                        judgement!
For, sickerly, there shall be a strait examination,
'The corn shall be saved, the chaff shall be brent.'
I beseech you heartily, have this premeditation.

[*Enter* MISCHIEF.]

34 **likened . . . lamb** as in John, 1.29: 'The next day, Iohn seeth Iesus comming vnto hym, and saith, beholde the lambe of God, which taketh away the sinne of the worlde.'
35 **satisfy** i.e. through his nourishing blood
36 **womb** abdomen (*OED sb.* 1a). The reference is to the blood (*precious river*) that trickled from the wounds Christ endured on the cross. See Revelation, 7.9–17.
37 **food** i.e. Christ's body, especially his blood, which is represented by wine at the sacrament of communion; cf. John, 6.35: 'And Iesus sayde vnto them, I am the bread of lyfe: He that cometh to me, shall not hunger: and he that beleueth on me, shall neuer thirst.'
38 **intent** purpose
39 **dissolved** freed
   bond i.e. of death
40 **venomous serpent** Satan takes the form of a serpent to tempt Eve in Genesis, 3.1–14.
41 **last judgement** the judging that

will occur at the end of the world; see Matthew, 10.15: 'For we must all appeare before the iudgement seate of Christe, that euery man may receaue the workes of his bodie according to that he hath done, whether it be good or bad.'
42 **sickerly** surely
   *strait examination strict measuring (of souls). See 41 and n., and cf. Edmund Bunny's *Christian Exercise* (1584) on the judgement that the soul (assigned a feminine pronoun) must face: 'the terror of Gods presence; the strait examination she must abide; and the like' (Bunny, 42). We emend MS *strerat* to 'strait'.
43 Cf. Matthew, 3.12: 'he will throughly purge his floor, and gather his wheat into the garner; but he will burn up the chaff with unquenchable fire.' Like good grain separated from inedible husks and stalks, those who have lived properly will be saved, while the sinful will be discarded into hellfire. Cf. also Luke, 3.17, Mischief at 54–63, and Mercy at 180 and 185.
44 **premeditation** forethought

42 there] *Manly;* þe *MS*   strait] *Furnivall & Pollard;* strerat *MS*   44 SD] *Manly*

MISCHIEF

I beseech you heartily, leave your calcation.   45

Leave your chaff, leave your corn, leave your dalliation.

Your wit is little, your head is mickle, ye are full of

predication.

But, sir, I pray this question to clarify:

Driff–draff, mish–mash,

Some was corn and some was chaff,   50

My dame said my name was Raff;

Unshut your lock and take an ha'penny.

45 **I . . . heartily** Mischief enters quoting Mercy's words at 44.
calcation threshing or trampling under foot (the implication being that Mercy struts around the playing space). See *OED* calcation *sb.*, calcate *v.*, and calcatory *sb.*; this last ('A winepress, where the grapes are trodden') occurs in a work from *c.* 1420. Another possible reading is 'calculation', for which the MS form may be an intentional debasement (i.e. on the part of Mischief) or a scribal error. The meaning is clouded by Mischief's rude parody of Mercy's Latinate speech.

46 **chaff . . . corn** as in Mercy's biblical image at 43
dalliation dalliance, empty talk

47 **mickle** much, huge. Proverbial: 'Great (Mickle) head little wit' (cf. Dent, H245)
predication preaching, sermonizing; see Prologue to Chaucer's 'Pardoner's Tale': 'And in Latyn I speke a wordes fewe / To saffron with my predicacioun / And for to stire hem to devocioun' (344–6).

48 **question** an intellectual problem or puzzle; cf. *MED* questioun *sb.* 2a ('A philosophical or theological problem or topic') and 3a ('A difficulty, an obscurity').

49–52 Satirizing a formal *question* (perhaps theological or academic in nature; see 48n.), Mischief changes Mercy's vocabulary, shortens the verse lines and structurally parodies the high–register redundancies of Mercy's opening speech by invoking the nonsense rhymes of childhood.

49 **draff** worthless stuff; cf. *MED* draf *sb.*, where sense 1a encompasses 'Refuse of grain, chaff, husks', citing the Prologue to Chaucer's 'Parson's Tale': 'Why shoolde I sowen draf out of my fest, / Whan I may sowen whete, if that me lest?' (35–6). The phrase *Driff–draff* plays on 'riff–raff': 'persons of a disreputable character or belonging to the lowest class of a community' (*OED* 1).

51 **Raff** perhaps drawing on 'raff', meaning 'Worthless material, trash, rubbish, refuse' (*OED* 3a). The citation there, *Palladius on Husbandry* (*c.* 1420), confirms the agricultural context Mercy has established at 43: 'Take chaf & raf And ley hit on thy lond . . . And when thou sist the myst, let brenne vp chaf And raf' (1.827). *Raff* may have been pronounced like 'Rafe', a conventional, low comic name; cf. the title character in *Ralph Roister Doister*.

52 Open your door and take/give a half-penny. The verb *take* here is ambiguous, and could mean either 'take' (*OED* 12) or 'give' (*MED* taken *v.* 31a.b). The former would

49] Mysse-masche, dryff-draff *Eccles*

MERCY

Why come ye hither, brother? Ye were not desired.

MISCHIEF

For a winter-corn thresher, sir, I have hired,

And ye said the corn should be saved and the chaff

should be fired,   55

And he proveth nay, as it showeth by this verse:

'Corn *servit bredibus*, chaff *horsibus*, straw *firibusque*.'

This is as much to say, to your lewd understanding,

As the corn shall serve to bread at the next baking.

'Chaff *horsibus et reliqua*',   60

The chaff to horse shall be good provent,

When a man is for-cold the straw may be brent,

And so forth, *et cetera*.

have Mischief mocking priests by pretending to give Mercy a kind of 'alms-penny': cf. *OED* alms 4b, and Peele, 392: 'Father, here is an Almes pennie for mee' (line 148). The 'give' sense would have Mischief performing a kind of festival utterance chanted by those who knock at successive doors in a village or town; cf. the refrain from *Guisers'*, 93: 'If you haven't got a penny a ha'penny will do / If you haven't got a ha'penny God bless you.' Either reading has this line anticipating the money collection of 459–74.

53 **brother** Mercy speaks down or laterally to Mischief (cf. the contrast between *sovereigns* and *brethren* at 29).

54 **winter-corn** grain planted in autumn or winter
thresher one who separates the grain from the straw (as at 43)
sir Mischief answers Mercy's *brother* (53) with an ironically deferential honorific. Although *sir* had a specific valence for priests and other clergy (*MED* sire *sb.* 1b), it is used as

a default greeting throughout the play.
hired been hired, hired myself out

55 **fired** burnt (cf. *brent* at 43)

56 **he** i.e. the one who wrote the following *verse*

57 mock Latin: 'Corn serves (is good for) bread, chaff horses, and straw fire.' The *–ibus* ending (plural Latin ablative) seems particularly adapted to comedy in this play: see 398–9, 446, 680–1.

58 **lewd** unlearned; see *OED a.* 2: this word had yet to acquire any erotic connotation. Obnoxiously switching roles with Mercy, Mischief interprets his own nonsense Latin line (57) in the manner of a medieval preacher performing exegesis of a biblical passage. Such exegesis (here parodied by Mischief) involves interpreting a difficult text by explaining its various words and phrases with reference to other Bible passages and moral situations.

60 *et reliqua* Latin: 'and the remainder'

61 **provent** feed, supply

62 **for-cold** thoroughly chilled, freezing (see *OED* for– prefix 1)

63 *et cetera*] *(& c)*

MERCY

>Avoid, good brother! Ye been culpable
>To interrupt thus my talking delectable. 65

MISCHIEF

>Sir, I have neither horse nor saddle,
>>Therefore I may not ride.

MERCY

>Hie you forth on foot, brother, in God's name!

MISCHIEF

>I say, sir, I am come hither to make you game.
>Yet bade ye me not go out in the devil's name 70
>>And I will abide.

MERCY ...

Here a leaf is missing from the unique manuscript of the play. From context as well as the existing leaves, we can guess that this leaf contained – on its front and back – approximately 70 lines of dialogue and several lines of stage directions.

[*Enter* NEW-GUISE, NOWADAYS *and* NOUGHT, *as minstrels.*]

64 **Avoid** go away
been are (probably pronounced with two syllables)
culpable blameworthy, guilty
68 **Hie** go
69 **make you game** (1) play, perform for you; (2) make you the object of my game. For the former, cf. *MED* game *sb.* 2a.b, citing Chaucer's 'Sir Thopas': 'His myrie men commanded he / To make hym bothe game and glee' (839–40); for the second, transitive sense, see *MED* 2a.a, 'make fun (of *sb.*)'.
70–1 Because you did not invoke the devil's name when you asked me to leave, I will stay. Mischief indicates that he takes his orders not from God

(cf. Mercy's *in God's name*, 68) but from the devil. Stage imps would commonly display this devotion to the bureaucracy of hell. Cf. Mephistopheles in *Faustus*: 'I am servant to great Lucifer / And may not follow thee without his leave. / No more than he commands must we perform' (1.3.40–2, A-text).
71 SD During this gap in the text, at least two things happen: (1) New-Guise, Nowadays and Nought enter, presumably in a noisy, physical fashion; (2) Mischief exits (perhaps after calling for the Three Ns and observing their entrance and subsequent actions). In addition, it seems likely that, prior to Mischief's exit, Mercy has remarked

71+ SP] *MS, followed by a missing leaf* 71 SD] *this edn*

NEW-GUISE

And ho, minstrels, play the common trace!

[*to Nowadays*] Lay on with thy baleys till his belly burst!

[*Nowadays urges Nought on.*]

NOUGHT

I put case I break my neck: how then?

NEW-GUISE

I give no force, by Saint Tanne!   75

NOWADAYS

Leap about lively! Thou art a wight man.

disparagingly on the harms that *new guise* has brought about *nowadays* – unwittingly summoning, in this way, the personified trio of Vice figures (he has mentioned *nought* twice already: see 98n.). For an abbreviated reconstruction of the missing material, see Meredith, *Acting*, 98–9.

72 **minstrels** performers, including such entertainers as musicians, story-tellers, mimes, actors, jugglers and dancers (*MED* minstral *sb.* 1). New-Guise, Nowadays and Nought certainly dance; they may sing (or, in Nought's case, play an instrument) as well. These Vices will put their heads together with Mischief and summon a greater *minstrel* at 451–74.

common trace familiar footsteps (of a dance). Although *MED* (trace *sb.* 1, 3a, citing this passage) suggests this is also 'the music for a dance', Titivillus's 'I shall make him to dance another trace' (528) makes the 'step' interpretation more likely. Cf. also 93n.

73 New-Guise urges Nowadays to drive Nought to dance ever faster. Nowadays may flog Nought, or play an instrument with increasing energy and tempo. Meredith sees *baleys* as a metaphor for 'drum-stick' and *belly* referring to the skin of a drum (Meredith, *Acting*, 22).

Lay on apply, swing. Cf. *Mac* 5.8.33:

'lay on, Macduff.'

thy New-Guise uses the singular and more familiar *thy* for the first time in the play. To this point, Mercy and Mischief have both exchanged the plural and more deferential *you* and *ye*.

baleys a rod or bundle of twigs used to flog (*MED* baleis *sb.* 2). Chambers identifies the *baleys* as an instrument of spiritual discipline and correction, and suggests it may have a special tradition of deployment in East Anglia (Chambers, M., 5).

belly burst Note the potential parody of alliterative verse in this line's repeated 'b' sounds. Shakespeare parodies this kind of poetry as late as *MND*, where the Prologue to the play-within-the-play notes how Pyramus 'bravely broach'd his boiling bloody breast' (5.1.146). With *burst*, cf. 616.

74 **I put case** suppose

75 **give no force** don't care

Saint Tanne St Anne, mother of the Virgin Mary (a common oath: see *Everyman* 353). The spelling here conveys the Vices' slangy prounciation. Cf. *Saint Denny* at 487 and, for reduplication similar to *Saint Tanne*, the phrase *an napple* at 427.

76 **Leap about lively** Nowadays may torment Nought with his *baleys*.

wight nimble, flexible

72 SP] *Furnivall & Pollard (Manly)*; not in *MS*   73 SD1] *Lester* burst] (breste)   SD2] *this edn*; *whipping him to make him dance* | *Lester at 71*   75 Saint Tanne] *MS* (sent tanne); Saint Anne *Lester*

Let us be merry while we be here!

NOUGHT

Shall I break my neck to show you sport?

NOWADAYS

Therefore ever beware of thy report.

NOUGHT

I beshrew ye all! Here is a shrewd sort. 80

Have thereat then with a merry cheer!

Here they dance. Mercy sayeth:

MERCY

Do way, do way this revel, sirs! Do way!

NOWADAYS

Do way, good Adam? Do way?

This is no part of thy play.

NOUGHT

Yes, marry, I pray you, for I love not this revelling. 85

Come forth, good father, I you pray!

By a little ye may assay.

Anon off with your clothes, if ye will play.

78 i.e. do we have to go so far as breaking my neck for you to be entertained?

79 i.e. so always be careful of what you say. Perhaps Nowadays's admonition puns on some stage business involving music, belching or flatulence.

80 **beshrew** curse, indict
shrewd sort sorry lot

81 **Have thereat** let's proceed

82 **Do way** cease, end this
revel game, festivity

83 **good Adam** i.e. old man. A generic label, sometimes implying rusticity as well; cf. *AYL* 2.6.18.

84 Nowadays teases Mercy by claiming that the latter's phrase (*Do way*) should not be in Mercy's performance. Because the word *part* puns on an actor's 'part' or 'role', Nowadays can

be seen as mawkishly implying that the script is being performed for Mercy's own benefit (*thy play*).

85 **marry** a mild oath, collapsing 'by the Virgin Mary'

86 **good father** a generic name for an older man; cf. *MED* fader *sb.* 10, and Nought's *good father* to Mankind at 356. The word *father* will come, in this play, to have its religious sense of a spiritual guide (*MED* 4) and, more specifically, a priest or monk (see *MED* 8).

87 You may try (*assay*) this without much effort. In the following line, Nought suggests it will be easier for Mercy to *dance* (see 90) if he wears fewer clothes.

88 **Anon** quickly
clothes Mercy may be clothed in

77 while] *(wyll)*   82 SP] *Manly*   88 play] *MS as read by Eccles;* pray *MS as reported by Manly*

Go to, for I have had a pretty scuttling.

MERCY

Nay, brother, I will not dance.   90

NEW-GUISE

If ye will, sir, my brother will make you to prance.

NOWADAYS

With all my heart, sir, if I may you advance.

Ye may assay by a little trace.

NOUGHT

Yea, sir, will ye do well,

Trace not with them, by my counsel,   95

For I have traced somewhat too fell;

I tell you, it is a narrow space.

But, sir, I trow of us three I heard you speak.

NEW-GUISE

Christ's curse have therefore, for I was in sleep.

religious robes; see 0 SDn. The Vices apparently try to disrobe Mercy to humiliate him; they will succeed in doing so to Mankind at 671–719.

89 **pretty scuttling** fine dancing (ironic)

91 **my brother** New-Guise refers to Nowadays, who may flog Nought in order to keep him dancing.

92 **advance** playing on both 'help' and 'propel forward' (i.e. by flogging)

93 **trace** dance. Cf. 72 and n.

94 Indeed, sir, if you wish to do well

95 **counsel** advice

96 **fell** dangerously

97 I declare, it is indeed a narrow place in which to dance. Like 84, this line has a metatheatrical awareness: this *space* is at one and the same time the imagined space within the play and the physical space in which the play is being performed.

*you There appears to be a word missing from MS; 'you' was first

suggested by Manly. For *tell you* see 299, 345, 587, 870, the last two instances offering *I tell you*.

98 Nought indicates that he has heard Mercy invoke their names, and will repeat this observation at 111. Mercy uses the word *nought* twice (in its general sense) in his opening speech (6, 8), and perhaps included a similarly incidental rebuke of the Three Ns' attributes (i.e. that which is variously *nought*, popular *nowadays*, or concerned with *new guise*) during dialogue with Mischief that has been lost with the second MS leaf.

trow trust, believe

99 **Christ's curse** This strong and earthy insult is ironic because, while Christ's curse of a fig tree is recalled in Mark, 11.21, he is more commonly known as one who redeemed humanity from the curse of original sin.

in sleep New-Guise's *sleep* connects

92 advance| *(a vaunce)* 96 fell| *MS as read by Eccles, with* fylde *cancelled;* fylde fell *MS as reported by Manly* 97 you| *Manly subst.; not in MS* 99 have| *Manly (Kittredge);* hade *MS*

NOWADAYS

A' I had the cup ready in my hand, ready to go to meat.   100
Therefore, sir, curtly, greet you well.

MERCY

Few words, few and well set!

NEW-GUISE

Sir, it is the new guise and the new jet.
Many words and shortly set,
This is the new guise, everydeal.   105

MERCY

Lady, help! How wretches delight in their simple ways!

NOWADAYS

Say nought again the new guise nowadays!

---

him with the sin of sloth. See Proverbs, 19.15: 'Slouthfulnesse bryngeth sleepe, and a soule accustomed with craft, shall suffer hunger.' In *Faustus*, the personified Sloth comes onstage with a similar story (2.3.147–50, A-text).

100 **A'** and. Cf. 524, 611, 666, 678 and 712.
to meat i.e. eat. Nowadays's *cup* and *meat* connect him with the sin of gluttony. See 99n., and cf. the personified Gluttony in *Faustus* (2.3.134–46, A-text).

101 **A curtly** both 'briefly, without delay' (*MED* courtli *adv.*, citing this passage alone), and (as pun) 'courtly'. 'Court' could be spelled 'curt' at this time. Cf. Dunbar, 204, 'The tua mariit wemen and the wedo' : 'Alse curtly of his clething, and kemmyng of his haris' (line 182), where 'curtly' = 'courtly'.
greet you well greetings. Nowadays perhaps bows or performs some other fashionable (i.e. 'courtly') gesture of greeting. Context suggests these words (as well as any gesture) are ironically delivered. Cf. Oswald's courtly, laconic superiority and 'roundest manner' in *KL* 1.4.45, 52–3, 77–83.

102 **set** put, said (for which *set* is homonymic). Probably ironic, for Nowadays's greeting is rude in its brevity.

103 **new guise** new fashion, custom, habit or practice (*OED* 2) – the source of his name: see List of Roles 3n.
jet fashion. Chaucer's Pardoner 'thoughte he rood al of the newe jet' ('General Prologue', 682).

104 a large vocabulary, but curt sentences. A version of the comic contrast in Mischief's 'Your wit is little, your head is mickle' (47)

105 **everydeal** through and through, totally (see *OED* everydeal (as *adv.*) 2)

106 **Lady** Mercy invokes the Virgin Mary for assistance. Cf. 22–3.
simple ignorant, foolish. See *MED* simple *adj.* 5. MS appears to offer *sympull* but has been read as *synnfull* (Manly) and *synfull* (Eccles).

107 Nowadays invokes all three of the Vices in this retort.
***nought** MS reads *not*. Nowadays collocates the Three Ns by name: see 114 and n.
again against

---

106 simple] *(sympull)*; synnfull *MS as reported by Manly;* synfull *Eccles*   107 nought] *Manly;* not *MS*

Thou shall find us shrewish at all assays.
Beware! Ye may soon lick a buffet.

MERCY

He was well occupied that brought you, brethren.   110

NOUGHT

I heard you call 'New-Guise, Nowadays, Nought' all
these three together.
If ye say that I lie, I shall make you to slither.
Lo, take you here a trippet!   [*Trips Mercy.*]

MERCY

Say me your names, I know you not.

NEW-GUISE

New-Guise, I.

NOWADAYS   I, Nowadays.

NOUGHT   I, Nought.   115

MERCY

By Jesu Christ that me dear bought,
Ye betray many men.

NEW-GUISE

Betray? Nay, nay, sir, nay, nay!

108 **shrewish** obnoxious, quarrelsome
assays i.e. in every aspect or endeavour
109 **lick a buffet** taste a blow. Eccles
compares *Noah and his Sons* in
Towneley, 41: 'Ye shal lik on the whyp'
(line 546).
110 Mercy ironically praises whoever
led these brothers (*brethren*) in his
presence; he doesn't realize (as Nought
insists in the following line) that he,
Mercy, has summoned them himself.
112 **say . . . lie** deny you called us. See
114n.
slither crawl on the ground (like a
snake). Cf. 40, and see Genesis, 3.14,
where the serpent receives a similar
punishment.

113 **take . . . trippet** Trip there for your
pains.
114 Although the three have punned
on their names (95, 103, 107), and
although Nought has declared both
that Mercy spoke of them (98) and
that Mercy has called *'New-Guise,
Nowadays, Nought'* (111), to this point
neither Mercy nor the audience has
been told explicitly who the three are.
See also 182n.
Say tell
115 ***SP2, SP3** MS offers these names
and personal pronouns on a single line
attributed to New-Guise, though with
separate underscoring that suggests
this is a space-saving gesture.

108 shrewish] *Manly subst.;* schewys *MS*   113 SD] *Bevington subst.*   115 SP NOWADAYS] *Manly
subst.; not in MS*   SP NOUGHT] *Manly subst.; not in MS*

We make them both fresh and gay.
But of your name, sir, I you pray,   120
   That we may you ken.

MERCY

Mercy is my name and my denomination.
I conceive ye have but a little favour in my
                communication.

NEW-GUISE

Ay, ay! Your body is full of English Latin.
   I am afeared it will burst.   125
'*Pravo te*', quod the butcher unto me
   When I stole a leg o'mutton.
Ye are a strong cunning clerk.

NOWADAYS

I pray you heartily, worshipful clerk,

119 **fresh and gay** i.e. fashionably, attractively apparelled. Cf. *Everyman*: 'Also thou delightest to go gay and fresh' (614).
121 **ken** know
122 **my denomination** what I am called (i.e. *my name*). On Mercy's redundancy, see 1 and n.
123 **ye . . . communication** both 'what I profess pertains little to you' and 'you little like what I say'. Mercy's *communication* encompasses not only what he says but what he stands for, as in 1 Kings, 9.11: 'Ye knowe what maner of man it is, and what his communication is.'
124 **body** In contrast to Mercy's emphasis on spiritual matters, New-Guise stresses Mercy's physical being.
English Latin (overly) Latinized English words. Mercy uses polysyllabic words drawn from Latin throughout the play, often in the rhyming position at a line's end. Cf. *denomination* and *communication*

(122–3), and see pp. 11–12, 34.
125 **afeared** afraid
126–7 The first instance (of two) of a longstanding figure of speech, later called a 'Wellerism' after Sam Weller and his father in Charles Dickens's *Pickwick Papers*: 'a form of comparison in which a familiar saying or proverb is identified, often punningly, with what was said by someone in a specified but humorously inapposite situation' (*OED*). Cf. 618 and n.
126 *Pravo te* 'I curse you' (Latin). Eccles cites the *Ortus Vocabulorum* (1500), which translates this verb (*pravo*) as 'to shrew'. Cf. Nought's 'I beshrew ye all' (80).
128 **strong cunning** very intelligent
clerk cleric, student (and thus one who is learned in Latin). New-Guise addresses Mercy directly again.
129 Nowadays effectively extends the game of insult by taking up New-Guise's *clerk*.

122 and my] *cancelled and by interlined*   125–8] *Eccles; opp. 130 and followed by* I prey &c *MS; treated as a note by Manly, Brandl*   126 Pravo te] *MS as read by Eccles*   128] *assigned to Nowadays* | *Bevington*

To have this English made in Latin: 130

'I have eaten a dishful of curds,
And I have shitten your mouth full of turds.'
Now open your satchel with Latin words
    And say me this in clerical manner!
Also I have a wife, her name is Rachel;   135
Betwixt her and me was a great battle;
And fain of you I would hear tell
    Who was the most master.

NOUGHT

Thy wife Rachel, I dare lay twenty lice.

NOWADAYS

Who spake to thee, fool? Thou art not wise!   140
Go and do that longeth to thine office:
    Osculare fundamentum!

NOUGHT

Lo, master, lo, here is a pardon belly-met.

---

130 **made in** made into (i.e. translated). The first of two problems or riddles Nowadays poses to Mercy. Cf. 137–8.

132 **shitten** defecated in; the first of the play's many scatological jokes

133 **satchel . . . words** Nowadays pretends that Mercy's Latin is like money or other objects kept in a purse or peddler's pack for disbursement.

134 **this** i.e. the preceding rhyme at 131–2
clerical manner i.e. in a manner characteristic of the clergy; *MED* (clerical *adj.*), citing this passage alone, suggests this means 'in Latin', i.e. the language of the learned.

135 **her . . . Rachel** an unexpected biographical detail that lends realism to these otherwise allegorical figures. The name also suggests the resourceful biblical figure whose story is told in Genesis, 29–35.

137–8 Nowadays poses a second riddle for Mercy to solve. Cf. 130 and n.

137 **fain** gladly

139 **twenty lice** Nought offers worthless stakes to a wager. Walker, though, suggests the possibility of 'twenty *li*'s', i.e. the abbreviation for *librae* or 'pounds' (See *OED* li, from 1450). Perhaps also a pun on 'lies'.

141 **longeth** which belongs
office state, condition

142 *Osculare fundamentum* Latin: kiss [my/his] arse (US ass) (there is no pronoun)

143–4 Nought may pick Mercy's pocket, pretending to discover a *pardon*, a document granting a pardon or indulgence for sin. The sale of such official forgiveness, a focus of Chaucer's 'Pardoner's Tale', became extremely controversial in the Middle Ages.

130] *Eccles; opp. 129 MS; treated as a note by Manly, Brandl*

It is granted of Pope Pocket.

If ye will put your nose in his wife's socket,   145

Ye shall have forty days of pardon.

MERCY

This idle language ye shall repent.

Out of this place I would ye went.

NEW-GUISE

Go we hence all three with one assent.

My father is irk of our eloquence.   150

Therefore I will no longer tarry.

God bring you, master, and blessed Mary

To the number of the demonical friary!

NOWADAYS

Come wind, come rain,

143 **belly-met** of measure large enough to fill the belly (thus satisfying or meet for a belly). On *met* see *OED* met *sb.*[1] I.1a, b. and i-met, and cf. Matthew, 7.2: 'And with what measure ye meate, it shalbe measured to you agayne.' Coogan suggests a pun on the technical expression 'by limit' (Coogan, 6).

144 **Pope Pocket** an ambiguous reference; some possibilities include (1) one's pocket or purse considered as a *Pope* able to dispense a *pardon* (143); (2) such a *pardon* itself (considered a 'Pope'), produced on demand from one's pocket (cf. the *satchel* of 133); (3) a topical reference to John Poket, onetime prior of Barnwell Abbey near the place where *Mankind* may have been acted. See Jambeck & Lee, and p. 29, n. 1. Along with *belly-met* (143) and *socket* (145), Nought's *Pocket* may coincide with a comically obscene gesture or series of gestures relating to his and/or Mercy's lower body.

145 **socket** vagina

146 **forty days** a conventional unit of time in the Bible; cf. Genesis, 7.4 and

Matthew, 4.2.

148 **would ye went** wish you would go

149 **with . . . assent** i.e. all agreed

150 **My** i.e. this

father (1) old man; (2) priestly figure. Cf. 86n.

irk of irked by, annoyed by

eloquence fine talking (ironic)

151 **tarry** linger

152–3 May God and the blessed (Virgin) Mary bring you into the company of the devil's agents. Here New-Guise *beshrew*[s] (80) – i.e. curses – Mercy by calling upon the latter's *Lady* (106). The *demonical friary* has been seen as an allusion to Dominican friars (those of the order of St Dominic), as in *Ypocresye*: 'ffryer Domynike And ffreyer Demonyke' (ll. 2205–6).

154–7 Nowadays's appeal to the wind, the rain and the devil has the cadence of folk verse. Cf. the four-beat line of the witches in *Mac* 1.1.1–11, 1.3.14–37. For similarly worded lines, cf. *Mundus et Infans*: 'come wynde and rayne, / God let hym neuer come here agayne!' (ll. 491–2).

Though I come never again!   155
   The devil put out both your eyn!
      Fellows, go we hence tight.
NOUGHT
   Go we hence a devil way!
   Here is the door, here is the way.
   Farewell, gentle Geoffrey,   160
      I pray God give you good night!

                              Let them go out together, singing.

MERCY
   Thanked be God, we have a fair deliverance
      Of these three unthrifty guests.
   They know full little what is their ordinance.
   I prove by reason they be worse than beasts: 165

   A beast doth after his natural institution;

---

156 **The . . . out** may the devil put out
   eyn eyes
157 **tight** together, in a group
158 **a devil way** a traditional curse; cf.
   Chaucer's Harry Bailly to the Miller:
   'Tel on, a devel wey!' ('Miller's
   Prologue', 3134).
159 Nought perhaps leads the trio
   offstage.
160 **gentle Geoffrey** proverbial for a
   gentle, even overly meek person. Cf.
   Dent, G81.
161 **I pray God** Nought parodies a phrase
   Mercy has used early in the play (24),
   and which Mankind will similarly use
   at 330.
161 SD No tune is specified; the Three
   Ns may reprise a melody that one or
   more of them could have sung during
   their *revelling* (85) at 72ff. Their music
   here anticipates the 'Christmas song'
   (see 332n.).
163 **Of** from
   unthrifty wasteful. Mercy (164–85)

will characterize the trio as *wanton*
types (181) who will rue wasting their
time when the great *account* is reckoned
at the Last Judgement (174–7). The
dangers of loose talking are a recurrent
theme; see 173 and n., and p. 18.
guests visitors
164 **ordinance** what has been ordained
   for them by God (*OED sb.* 3a). Cf.
   1 Peter, 2.13: 'Submit youre selves
   vnto all manner ordinaunce of man
   for the lordes sake whether it be vnto
   the kynge as vnto the chefe heed'
   (Tyndale).
165–81 Mercy constructs a formal 'proof'
   that the play's audience might have
   associated with the pulpit. His argument
   begins with the generally accepted
   fact that animals behave according to
   their nature (166) and proceeds to the
   more specific instance of the Three
   Ns' behaviour (167–9), ending with the
   certainty of their *sad*[ness] at the Last
   Judgement (175–81).

161 SD] *(Exiant simul cantent)*

Ye may conceive by their disport and behaviour,
Their joy and delight is in derision
    Of their own Christ to his dishonour.

This condition of living, it is prejudicial;   170
    Beware thereof, it is worse than any felony or treason.
How may it be excused before the Justice of all
    When for every idle word we must yield a reason?

They have great ease, therefore they will take no thought.
    But how then when the angel of heaven shall blow
                    the trump   175
And say to the transgressors that wickedly hath wrought,
    'Come forth unto your Judge and yield your account'?

Then shall I, Mercy, begin sore to weep;
    Neither comfort nor counsel there shall none be had;
But such as they have sown, such shall they reap.   180
    They be wanton now, but then shall they be sad.

---

169 **their own Christ** Christ considered as a personal saviour owing to his sacrifice for all
170 **prejudicial** bad, harmful
172 **Justice of all** God
173 Mercy explains how the Three Ns are *unthrifty* (163): they routinely utter *idle word*[s]. His rhetorical question here draws upon Matthew, 12.36–7: 'But I say vnto you, of euery idell worde that men shall speake, they shall geue accompt therof, in the day of iudgment. For of thy wordes, thou shalt be iustified: and of thy wordes, thou shalt be condemned.'
reason account
174 **They** New-Guise, Nowadays and Nought
175 **angel . . . trump** See Revelation, 10.7: 'But in the dayes of the voyce of the seuenth Angel, when he shall begyn to blowe, euen the misterie of God shalbe finished.'
177 Mercy calls upon a familiar analogy: our deeds (good and bad) are recorded in an account-book that will be scrutinized at the Last Judgement. Cf. *Everyman*, where such a book appears as a stage property (502–5), and see Fig. 14.
179 **Neither . . . none** The double negative here reinforces the sense rather than negating it: there shall be no comfort or counsel at all for these transgressors.
180 Cf. Galatians, 6.8: 'For he that soweth into his flesshe, shal of the flesshe reape corruption: But he that soweth into the spirite, shall of the spirite reape lyfe euerlastyng.'

169 their] *Manly subst.;* her *MS*

182 *Mankind*

The good new guise nowadays I will not disallow.
I discommend the vicious guise; I pray have me
excused,
I need not to speak of it, your reason will tell it you.
Take that is to be taken and leave that is to be refused. 185

[*Enter* MANKIND.]

MANKIND

Of the earth and of the clay we have our propagation.
By the providence of God thus be we derivate,
To whose mercy I recommend this whole congregation:
I hope unto his bliss ye be all predestinate.

Every man for his degree I trust shall be participate,   190
If we will mortify our carnal condition
And our voluntary desires, that ever be perversionate,
To renounce them and yield us under God's provision.

182–5 Wrapping up a miniature sermon, Mercy qualifies his remarks by saying: 'I do not dislike all new fashions, only the evil ones; in fact, I ask your pardon for mentioning what could have gone unsaid (because your reason would have led you to see it). Take what's lawful to take up, and don't touch what you're forbidden to have.' Meredith attributes Mercy's loss of focus here to his catching sight of an approaching Mankind (Meredith, *Acting*, 23).
182 **new guise . . . not** In this line Mercy unwittingly invokes the Three Ns: *new guise*, *nowadays* and *not* (i.e. 'Nought'). See 107 and n., and 114 and n.
186 Adam was made from 'dust' (Genesis, 2.7). Note that Mankind enters speaking the Latinate language with which Mercy opened the play: 'propagation . . . derivate . . . congregation . . . predestinate' (186–9). See pp. 11–12.

187 **derivate** derived
188 **congregation** Mankind presumably speaks to and about the audience.
189 **predestinate** predestined
190 **Every . . . degree** (each and) every man, in relation to his own social or official rank, grade, order, estate or station
shall be participate shall participate in, share (i.e. God's *bliss*, 189)
191 **mortify . . . condition** tame (*mortify*) our bodily appetites. See *OED* mortify *v.* 4a, and cf. Romans, 8.13: 'For if ye liue after ye fleshe, ye shall dye: But if ye through the spirite, do mortifie the deedes of the body, ye shall lyue.'
192 **voluntary** wilful
perversionate perverted, wicked (*OED*, citing this passage uniquely)
193 **under** to
God's provision that which has been provided, laid up for, by God. Cf. 2

185 SD] *Manly*

106

My name is Mankind. I have my composition
   Of a body and of a soul, of condition contrary.   195
Betwixt them twain is a great division;
   He that should be subject, now he hath the victory.

This is to me a lamentable story
   To see my flesh of my soul to have governance.
Where the goodwife is master, the goodman may be sorry.   200
   I may both sigh and sob, this is a piteous
             remembrance.

O thou my soul, so subtle in thy substance,
Alas, what was thy fortune and thy chance
   To be associate with my flesh, that stinking dunghill?

Lady, help! Sovereigns, it doth my soul much ill   205
   To see the flesh prosperous and the soul trodden
             under foot.

Corinthians, 8.21: 'and therfore make provision for honest thynges not in the sight of god only but also in the sight of men' (Tyndale).

194 **My . . . Mankind** Like Mercy (18), Mankind proudly identifies himself.
I . . . composition I am composed, made up

195 **condition contrary** The struggle between the body and the soul, the flesh and the spirit, is one of the foundational metaphors of Christianity. Cf. Matthew, 26.41: 'Watche, and praye, that ye enter not into temptation: The spirite in deede is wyllyng, but the fleshe is weake.' See 897n.

196 **them twain** the two of them

197 The part (*He*) that should be controlled (i.e. the body) is actually in charge (i.e. of the soul).

199 **of . . . governance** rule my soul

200 Mankind calls upon an analogy that seems commonsensical to him: when wives rule their husbands, the world is similarly upside-down. Cf. Nowadays's query at 137–8.
goodwife the mistress of a house

201 **piteous** sad, sorrowful
remembrance thought, realization

202–3 A line may have dropped out between the present 202 and 203, leaving this unmatched three-line stanza. If so, its final word would have rhymed with *dunghill* (204).

202 **subtle . . . substance** intricate in your composition

204 **associate** associated

205 **Lady . . . Sovereigns** Mankind's closeness to Mercy is suggested by the repetition of vocatives that the latter has already employed; cf. *Lady, help!* (106) and 'ye sovereigns that sit' (29).

201–2] *Eccles; added opp. 203 MS*   201 sigh] *(syth)*

I shall go to yonder man and assay him I will.
I trust of ghostly solace he will be my boot.

[*to Mercy*] All hail, seemly father! Ye be welcome to
this house.
Of the very wisdom ye have participation.   210
My body with my soul is ever querulous.
I pray you, for saint charity, of your supportation.
[*Kneels.*]

I beseech you heartily of your ghostly comfort.
I am unsteadfast in living; my name is Mankind.
My ghostly enemy, the devil, will have a great disport   215
In sinful guiding if he may see me end.

MERCY
Christ send you good comfort! Ye be welcome,
my friend.
Stand up on your feet, I pray you arise.
[*Mankind rises.*]
My name is Mercy; ye be to me full hend.

208 **ghostly** spiritual (cf. 27n.)
boot aid, help
209 **All hail** a deferential or respectful
greeting; cf. *R2* 4.1.170: 'Did they not
sometime cry "All hail!" to me?'
seemly playing on both 'handsome, well-
proportioned' (*OED a.* 1), and 'apparent'
(i.e. from his apparel; *OED a.* 5). Along
with *father*, this second sense and the
following line suggest that Mercy wears
the garments of a priest. See 0 SDn.
212 **saint charity** Although 'Saint Charity'
enjoyed a feast day (1 August) in the
church calendar, here (as in *Everyman*
148, 290, 344, 922) the impersonal sense
of 'sacred charity' (cf. French *seint*)
seems the primary meaning.

supportation assistance, support
(*OED* 1a), often used 'in formulae of
supplication or submission' (1b)
215 **great disport** much enjoyment,
gaiety. Chaucer's Prioress is 'of greet
desport' ('General Prologue', 137).
216 ***sinful guiding** leading me into
sin. MS appears to read *sympull* (cf.
106 and n.); here emended owing to
context: throughout *Mankind*, the
devil is portrayed as cunning (the
opposite of 'simple').
see me end see my death
219 **full hend** pleasing to the sight,
welcome. Cf. Wisdom in the morality
play *Wisdom*: 'To all clene sowlys I am
full hende' (line 45).

209 SD] *Manly subst.*   212 SD] *Adams after 208*   216 sinful] *Manly subst.; Eccles maintains MS*
sympull *was corrected to* synfull   218 SD] *this edn*

To eschew vice I will you advise.   220

MANKIND

O Mercy, of all grace and virtue ye are the well.
I have heard tell of right worshipful clerks
Ye be approximate to God and near of his counsel.
He hath institute you above all his works.

O, your lovely words to my soul are sweeter than honey.   225
MERCY

The temptation of the flesh ye must resist like a man,
For there is ever a battle betwixt the soul and the body:
'*Vita hominis est militia super terram.*'

Oppress your ghostly enemy and be Christ's own
                                   knight.
Be never a coward again your adversary.   230
If ye will be crowned, ye must needs fight.

---

221 **well** i.e. font, source. Cf. Revelation, 21.6: 'And he sayde vnto me, it is done, I am Alpha and Omega, the begynnyng and the ende: I wyll geue to hym that is a thirst of the well of the water of lyfe freely.'

222 **of . . . clerks** either 'I have heard *from* distinguished clerks' or 'I have heard that, of (all) distinguished clerks'. See *OED* worshipful *a. (sb., adv.)* 3a, for 'right' with secular applications. This latter sense would have the virtue of implying that Mankind, in contrast to the Vices' negative characterizations at 128 and 129, respects Mercy as a learned man or *clerk*.

223 **approximate . . . counsel** next to God, and privy to his intent

224 **institute** placed
works creation. Cf. also 231n.

225 **to . . . honey** Cf. Psalms, 119.103: 'Howe sweete are thy wordes vnto my

throte: truely [they be sweeter] then hony is to my mouth.'

226 **like a man** playing on (1) with manly resolve; (2) according to your nature (as at 166: *natural institution*); cf. 280n.

228 'The life of Man upon earth is a battle' (Latin). Cf. Job, 7.1: 'Is not the life off ma[n] vpon earth a very batayll?' (Coverdale).

229 **Oppress** subdue, overcome (in the '*militia*' or 'battle' of life, 228)
ghostly enemy Cf. 27n.
Christ's own knight a warrior for Christ (like Redcrosse Knight, the model Christian novice, in Bk 1 of *FQ*)

230 **again** against (i.e. when confronted by)

231 **crowned** i.e. with the glory and honour of spiritual victory over your *ghostly enemy* (229). Cf. Hebrews, 2.7,

---

228 *militia*] *MS (milicia) as reported by Manly; nnilicia MS as read by Furnivall & Pollard*

Intend well and God will be your adjutory.

Remember, my friend, the time of continuance.
  So help me God, it is but a cherry-time.
Spend it well; serve God with heart's affiance.   235
  Distemper not your brain with good ale nor with
                              wine.
'Measure is treasure.' I forbid you not the use.
  Measure yourself ever; beware of excess.
The superfluous guise I will that ye refuse,
  When nature is sufficed, anon that ye cease.   240

If a man have an horse and keep him not too high,
  He may then rule him at his own desire.

of Man: 'Thou madest hym for a litle whyle lower then the Angels, thou hast crowned him with glorie and honour, and hast set hym aboue the workes of thy handes.' This verse's 'workes' (Wycliffe: 'werkis') may also have influenced *works* at 224.

232 **Intend well** have pure intentions, goals
  adjutory helper. Cf. *Monarche*, 384: 'Tharfor, cal god to be thi adiutory' (line 6270).

233 **time of continuance** lifespan (i.e. your *continuance* upon this earth). Cf. Job, 14.1: 'Man that is borne of woman, is of short continuance, and full of trouble' (Geneva).

234 **cherry-time** i.e. brief season. The time of cherry harvest and any subsequent festival or 'fair' is proverbially brief. Cf. *Confessio Amantis*: 'Al is bot a chirie feire' (Prologue, 454), and the lyric 'Farewell, this World is but a Cherry Fair' (*c.* 1500).

235 **it** i.e. your time on earth (as at 233)
  affiance faithfulness, warm trust. Cf. *Paraphrase of Erasmus*: 'Puttyng his affyaunce in God' (*Hebrews*, 11:24).

237 **Measure is treasure** proverbial, invoking the golden mean: 'to do things moderately is best' (cf. Dent, M461). John Skelton repeats this commonplace in *Magnificence*, Neuss: 'Where measure is ruler, there is nothynge amysse; / Measure is treasure: howe say ye, is it not this?' (ll. 125–6).
  use i.e. of *good ale* or *wine* (236). The implication is that these items should be used moderately.

238 **Measure yourself** live moderately (i.e. in a *measure*[d] way)

239 **superfluous guise** excessive, immoderate way of living (with a glance at the theme of fashion announced in *New-Guise*)
  will ... refuse want you to turn down

240 **nature is sufficed** your bodily needs (*nature*) are satisfied (*sufficed*)

241 **keep ... high** feed him only moderately. In Rolle's *Treatise of Ghostly Battle*, the body is compared to a horse that must be restrained by the bridle of Abstinence (cited in Smart, 'Concluded', 294).

232 your] *Knittel & Fattic subst.;* yow *MS*   237–8] *one line MS, with 238 perhaps added in margin*

If he be fed overwell he will disobey
And in hap cast his master in the mire.

NEW-GUISE [*from offstage*]
Ye say true, sir, ye are no faitour. 245
I have fed my wife so well till she is my master.
I have a great wound on my head, lo! And thereon lieth
a plaster,
And another there I piss my peson.
An my wife were your horse, she would you all to-ban.
Ye feed your horse in measure, ye are a wise man. 250
I trow, an ye were the king's palfreyman,
A good horse should be geason.

MANKIND
Where speaks this fellow? Will he not come near?

243 **he** the horse (241)
244 **in hap** perhaps
245–52 New-Guise begins a series of 'cat-call' harangues out of Mercy and Mankind's sight (cf. 261–8, 269–76), but the Three Ns may be visible to the audience the whole time. Having left the playing space in noisy triumph over Mercy at 161, they now seem unwilling or unable to share the same space as Mercy and Mankind. The implication is that by elevating the moral tone of the playing space, Mercy's sober counselling has temporarily buffered it from evil.
245 **faitour** impostor or cheat; 'esp. a vagrant who shams illness or pretends to tell fortunes' (*OED*). This insult appears over a dozen times in the York plays and survives in Pistol's 'Down, down, dogs! Down, faitors!' (*2H4* 2.4.155–6).
247 **lo** i.e. behold. Here New-Guise presumably refers to his wound, a gesture that would be irrelevant if the audience did not see him. See 245–52n.

plaster bandage (often applied with adhesive mixture or material)
248 **another** i.e. plaster or wound
there where
peson A *peson* was a balance or scale that employed a staff with balls as counterweights (*OED sb.*); this would suggest the penis and testicles.
249 **all to-ban** curse to pieces, thoroughly; *ban* = curse (*OED v.* II.2a, b). Cf. Suffolk in *2H6* 3.2.319: 'every joint should seem to curse and ban.' For the 'all to-[verb]' construction, repeated at 422, see *OED* 'to–', *prefix*[2], headnote. See also 773.
251 **palfreyman** one who holds or otherwise tends to a horse
252 **should be** i.e. would be
geason rare, scarce; cf. *Wounds*: 'friends are geason nowadays' (1.1).
253 Mankind's question implies that New-Guise has addressed his lines largely to the audience, and out of Mankind's sight. Cf. 245 SD.

245 SD] *this edn; speaks from behind* | *Adams; New-Guise, Nowadays, and Nought, who have been eavesdropping, speak from backstage or from some concealed position* | *Bevington; Enter* Newguise, Nowadays *and* Nought *at a distance* | *Lester* 249 An] *(And)*

MERCY

> All too soon, my brother, I fear me, for you.
> He was here right now, by him that bought me dear,   255
> With other of his fellows; they can much sorrow.
>
> They will be here right soon, if I out depart.
> Think on my doctrine; it shall be your defence.
> Learn while I am here, set my words in heart.
> Within a short space I must needs hence.   260

NOWADAYS [*from offstage*]

> The sooner the liefer, an it be even anon!
> I trow your name is Do Little, ye be so long from home.
> If ye would go hence, we shall come every one,
> More than a good sort.
> Ye have leave, I dare well say.   265
> When ye will, go forth your way.
> Men have little dainty of your play
> Because ye make no sport.

254 i.e. he will arrive sooner than you might wish. Mercy perhaps delivers this as an aside.

255 **by . . . dear** i.e. by our saviour (Jesus Christ), who paid for our sins (*bought me*) with his invaluable (*dear*) sacrifice; cf. 9 and n., 116.

256 **can** are able to cause, perform. Used elliptically, with the verb implied from context. See *OED* can *v.*[1] B.II.8, and cf. 520 (*con*) and 619 (*could*).

257 **out depart** leave this place

258 **doctrine** teaching, advice (begun at 220 and continuing 226–44)

260 **space** time

261 **liefer** better
  even anon right away. Cf. *Mary Magdalene*, 86: 'Ye shall be there even anon' (line 1885).

262 **Do Little** lazy loafer. See *Cobbler's*

Prophecy: 'And shall I warrant yee to your cost my Lady do-little' (D4ʳ). Eccles notes that Dolittle is found as an English surname from the year 1204 onwards.
  from home i.e. away from your residence

264 **good sort** large number. Cf. *Conflict*: 'For heere be a good sort I believe in this company' (2.1).

265 **leave** permission

267 **dainty of** liking of
  play activity. Here used generally, though Nowadays points to *play's* recreational meaning in the following line.

268 **make no sport** provide no fun (i.e. for others). Cf. *LLL* 4.1.98–9: 'one that makes sport / To the Prince'. Mercy has refused to *dance* for them at 90.

261, 269 SD] *this edn; speaks from behind* | Adams; *unseen* | Bevington   263+ every one] (euery chon)   264 More than] MS (Mo þen); Me thynk Manly (Kittredge)

NOUGHT [*from offstage*]

Your pottage shall be for-cold, sir; when will ye go dine?

I have seen a man lost twenty nobles in as little time;   270

Yet it was not I, by Saint Quentin,

For I was never worth a potful o'worts sithen I
was born.

My name is Nought. I love well to make merry.

I have be sithen with the common tapster of Bury

A' played so long the fool that I am even very weary.   275

Yet shall I be there again tomorn.

MERCY

I have much care for you, my own friend.

Your enemies will be here anon, they make their
avaunt.

Think well in your heart, your name is Mankind;

269 **pottage** a thick soup or stew; here used generally for 'food'. The word *pottage* would have been familiar from the cautionary tale in Genesis, 25.34, in which Esau trades his birthright for 'pottage'.

270 **twenty nobles** A noble was a gold coin worth 6*s.* 8*d.*; 'twenty nobles' was a commonplace phrase. Cf. the Hostess in *2H4* 2.1.151–2: 'Pray thee, Sir John, let it be but twenty nobles.'

271 **Saint Quentin** a legendary saint, reputed to have preached in Picardy, whose life was remembered in the calendars of many medieval English monasteries. Merry Report swears by St Quentin in Heywood, *Weather* (line 852), as does Drede in Skelton, *Bowge* (27, line 511).

272 **worts** cabbage, often used in a general sense for pottage. A 'potful of worts' would be almost worthless.
sithen since

274 **sithen** continuously; Nought oddly

uses *sithen* in two different senses in the space of three lines.
common . . . Bury a server of beer (typically female) in Bury St Edmunds, a town in Suffolk in the East of England. It is not certain that Nought refers to a real individual; more likely, perhaps, he means to lend detail to his story of debauchery. See 135 and n. Smart points to a 1465 order at Lynn to expel 'eny common Tapster . . . which is knowen for a misgoverned woman' (Smart, 'Concluded', 294).

276 ***tomorn** tomorrow (MS *to morow*). Emended by Manly to rhyme with *born* at 272.

277–309 Castle notes that in addressing Mankind in this speech, Mercy reveals 'an increasing tenderness and devotion' (Castle, *Game*, 89): *my own friend* (277), *my own sweet son* (290), *Good son* (297), *my dear darling* (307).

278 **avaunt** boast

274 sithen] *MS* (sethen*) as read by Furnivall & Pollard;* sechen *MS as reported by Manly*   275 very weary] *(*wery wery*)*   276 tomorn] *Manly subst.;* to morow *MS*

Be not unkind to God, I pray you be his servant.   280

Be steadfast in condition; see ye be not variant.
Lose not through folly that is bought so dear.
God will prove you soon; and if that ye be constant,
Of his bliss perpetual ye shall be partner.

Ye may not have your intent at your first desire.   285
See the great patience of Job in tribulation;
Like as the smith trieth iron in the fire,
So was he tried by God's visitation.

He was of your nature and of your fragility;
Follow the steps of him, my own sweet son,   290
And say as he said in your trouble and adversity:
'*Dominus dedit, Dominus abstulit; sicut sibi placuit,
    ita factum est; sit nomen Domini benedictum!*'

---

280 **Be not unkind** playing on (1) do not act out of your natural identity as 'Mankind' (with play on un/mankind) (279); (2) act not cruelly. This duality of 'kind' glances backward at the word's roots (for which cf. the terms 'kin' and 'kindred') and forward to our modern sense of polite, generous behaviour. Cf. Hamlet's pun 'more than kin, and less than kind' (*Ham* 1.2.65).
281 **condition** morals, character, disposition
variant changeful, inconstant
282 **that is** that which has been
283 **prove** test, make trial of
284 **partner** sharer or partaker of (*OED* I.1, citing this passage)
285 **your intent** i.e. what you wish; your pleasure, desire
286 **Job** the biblical figure whose sufferings and patience became

proverbial. Cf. Aylett: 'But none for Patience like to Job is known' (2.4). On the significance of the Job story and theme, see pp. 16–17.
287–8 **trieth . . . tried** A blacksmith 'tries' – refines, removes the impurities of – metal by melting it with fire. Cf. Job, 23.10: 'But as for my way, he knoweth it, and tryeth me, that as the gold I may come foorth.'
288 **visitation** the act of God (or other supernatural power) coming to, or exerting power over, a person or persons for some end (*OED* B.II)
289 **He** i.e. *Job* (286)
292 'The Lord gave, and the Lord took away: as it pleased Him thus was it done. Blessed be the name of the Lord' (Latin). An elaboration of Job, 1.21 from the Vulgate, which reads: '*Dominus dedit Dominus abstulit sit nomen Domini benedictum.*'

286 in] *Manly;* & *MS*   292 *ita factum est*] *Eccles; opp. 290 in a different hand,* ita *also written above* placuit *and cancelled MS*

114

Moreover, in special I give you in charge,
  Beware of New-Guise, Nowadays and Nought.
Nice in their array, in language they be large;   295
  To pervert your conditions all the means shall be
                            sought.

Good son, intromit not yourself in their company.
  They heard not a mass this twelvemonth, I dare well
                            say.
Give them none audience; they will tell you many a lie.
  Do truly your labour and keep your holy day.   300

Beware of Titivillus, for he loseth no way,
  That goeth invisible and will not be seen.
He will round in your ear and cast a net before your eye.

293 **in special . . . charge** both 'I charge you to especially' and 'I especially charge you to'
295 **Nice . . . array** They are dressed fashionably.
  large immoderate, vulgar
296 They will stop at nothing to lead you astray. For *conditions* see 281n.
  ***your** MS *per*. Mercy's sermon centres on the harm the Vices direct towards Mankind.
297 **intromit** insert, place (cf. *OED* 1, whose first entry for a transitive sense postdates *Mankind*)
299 **Give . . . audience** i.e. do not listen to them at all.
300 **keep . . . day** Remember to observe the Sabbath. The Fourth Commandment; cf. Deuteronomy, 5.12: 'Kepe the Sabbath day, that thou sanctifie it as the Lorde thy God hath commaunded thee.'
301 **Titivillus** a devil, known for collecting fragments of words dropped, skipped or mumbled in the recitation of divine service before carry-

ing them to hell, where they were registered against the offender (*OED* titivil 1). Central in this play, Titivillus is elsewhere a minor devil; Eccles cites *Mirror of Our Lady*, 54: 'I am a poure dyuel, and my name ys Tytyuyllus'. This devil's name was applied to scoundrels and others of ill repute, especially mischievous tale-bearers. See p. 18.
  loseth no way i.e. never loses his course of action (*OED* way *sb.*[1] 7g); never loses a way of tempting, etc.
303 **round . . . ear** whisper, speak privately to; this will come to pass at 593–4 in nearly identical words. For whispering in the ear by an invisible spirit, see Job, 4.12: 'Nowe a thing was secretly brought to me, and mine eare receiued a litle thereof' (KJV).
  cast a net Sin was sometimes portrayed as a net to snare humankind. Cf. Psalms, 10.9, on the ungodly: 'he doth carry away violentlye the afflicted, in halyng hym into his net.'

296 your] *Manly subst.;* Þer *MS*   the] *Eccles subst.;* Þer *MS*   298 this] *Manly subst.;* Þi *MS*   301 for] *MS as reported by Manly;* fo *MS as read by Eccles*   303 eye] *Manly;* eyn *MS*

He is worst of them all; God let him never theen!

If ye displease God, ask mercy anon,   305
   Else Mischief will be ready to brace you in his bridle.
Kiss me now, my dear darling. God shield you from
                                           your fon!
   Do truly your labour and be never idle.
The blessing of God be with you and with all these
                                worshipful men!   [*Exit.*]

MANKIND
Amen, for saint charity, amen!   310

Now blessed be Jesu, my soul is well satiate
   With the mellifluous doctrine of this worshipful man.
The rebellion of my flesh now it is superate,
   Thanking be God of the cunning that I can.

---

304 **theen** prosper, thrive (*OED* thee $v.^1$; dialectal)
306 **brace . . . bridle** grip you in his harness
307 **Kiss . . . darling** The phrasing and request allude not only to the 'kiss of peace' in Christian ritual, but to Mercy's allegorical basis in affectionate compassion. On the kiss of peace, cf. 1 Peter, 5.14: 'Greete ye one another with the kysse of loue. Peace be with you all which are in Christe Iesus. Amen.' Cf. Mischief's *ba me* at 430.
fon foes
309 **The . . . God** Mercy concludes his exhortative sermon with a standard benediction.
310 **Amen** Mankind offers the conventional and solemn expression of consent.
311 **satiate** satisfied. Cf. Proverbs, 12.14: 'man shalbe satiate with good things by the fruite of his mouth' (Geneva).
312 **mellifluous** sweet, honey-sounding.

Cf. *Mary Magdalene*, 73: 'O Jhesu, thi mellyfluos name / Mott be worcheppyd with reverens!' (ll. 1446–7).
313 **rebellion . . . flesh** a commonplace. Cf. Matthew, 26.41: 'The spirite in deede is wyllyng, but the fleshe is weake.'
superate overcome, conquered (*OED pa. pple.*, citing this line)
314 **Thanking be** thanks be to
*cunning . . . can** knowledge that I have. MS reads 'cōmynge þat I kam', which may have been an error of reading or transcription ('m' for 'n' or 'nn') on the scribe's part. In support of emendation here, cf. *Killing of Children*, 114: 'For after the sympylle cunnyng that we can' (line 556). 'Conning' is an obsolete form of 'cunning' (see *OED* conning *vbl. sb.*¹), with both words related to *can*: see *OED* can $v.^1$ B.1–8. Mankind is thankful for his *cunning*, which at this time possessed a positive sense describing learning and skills;

---

304 theen] (then)   309 these] *MS* (þes); yower *MS as reported by Manly*   SD] *Adams*   314 cunning . . . can] *Manly subst.*; cōmynge þat I kam *MS*

Here will I sit and title in this paper   [*Sits and writes.*]   315
The incomparable estate of my promition.
[*to the audience*] Worshipful sovereigns, I have written
here
The glorious remembrance of my noble condition.

To have remorse and memory of myself thus written it is,
To defend me from all superstitious charms: 320
'*Memento, homo, quod cinis es et in cinerem reverteris.*'
[*Pins it to his chest.*]
Lo, I bear on my breast the badge of mine arms.

[*Enter* NEW-GUISE.]

see *OED sb.* 1–3, and cf. 128. *Can* meant 'to know or have learned (a thing); to have practical knowledge of (a language, art, etc.)' (*OED* can *v.*[1] B.1b), and rhymes here with *man* (312). Note that Mankind puts his *cunning* to immediate use in the following lines by writing Latin – an unusual skill for a simple farmer. See p. 16.

315 **title** write down, make a list of

316 **estate** state, general condition (*OED sb.* I.1a, b); perhaps with a hint of the sense, obtaining briefly in the late 1400s, of a more formal inventory of goods or particulars (see *OED sb.* I.1f) **promition** what has been promised (to me). Coined to rhyme with *condition* (318), and modelled on 'promise' (*sb.* 1, 2) and Latin forms of *promittere*, to promise. It seems to have been used nowhere else.

318 **remembrance** record of, memorandum (*OED* 7a, 8a). Mankind's eagerness anticipates Hamlet's vow to 'set . . . down' what the Ghost has revealed (*Ham* 1.5.107).

319 **remorse** perhaps pronounced

'remos', as in MS; cf. Eccles, who adduces in support *Perseverance*'s 'mossel' for 'morsel' at 1171.

320 **superstitious charms** Mankind contrasts the righteous observations he has recorded with the type of diverting language he will shortly encounter.

321 'Remember, Man, that you are dust, and that you will return to dust' (Latin). A paraphrase of Job, 34.15 ('All fleshe shall come to naught at once, and all men shall turne againe vnto dust'), in language that has become familiar through funeral rituals: 'Ashes to ashes, and dust to dust'.

321 SD, 322 Mankind pins the paper with its motto on his chest. The word *arms* registers as heraldic, as in the phrase 'coat of arms', but it also possesses the sense of something used for defence or offence. Eccles compares *Mary Magdalene*, 57: 'Here xall enter the iij Mariis . . . wyth sygnis ofe the passyon pryntyd ypon ther brest' (line 992 SD). Mankind may wear this paper until 583.

315 SD] *Bevington*   317 SD] *Adams*   319 remorse] *Manly;* remos MS   321, 324, 325 *et*] (&)   321 SD] *this edn; He points to the cross depicted on his breast* | *Bevington; He makes the sign of the cross* | *Lester*   322 SD] *Manly subst.*

NEW-GUISE

> The weather is cold, God send us good fires!
> *'Cum sancto sanctus eris et cum perverso perverteris.*
> *Ecce quam bonum et quam jocundum'*, quod the devil to
>   the friars,   325
> *'Habitare fratres in unum.'*

MANKIND

> I hear a fellow speak; with him I will not mell.
> This earth with my spade I shall assay to delve.   [*Digs.*]
> To eschew idleness, I do it mine own self.
> I pray God send it his foison!   330

> [*Enter* NOWADAYS *and* NOUGHT,
> *making their way through the audience.*]

323 **weather is cold** New-Guise's complaint recalls those of shepherds and other figures from the lower orders in medieval drama, who often testify to their susceptibility to the elements. Cf. the first Shepherd in *Shearmen*, 8: 'I wasse so were of this cold weddur / Thatt nere past wasse my might' (ll. 232–3).

324 'With the holy you shall be holy, and with the perverse you shall be perverted' (Latin). New-Guise adapts Psalms, 18.25–6: 'With the holy thou wylt be holy: with a perfect man thou wylt be perfect. With the cleane thou wylt be cleane: and with the frowarde thou wylt be frowarde.' Dillon sees this as 'an ironical forecast of Mankind's instability' (Dillon, *'Mankind'*, 55).

325–6 *Ecce . . . unum* 'Behold how good and how pleasant . . . [it is] for the brothers to live as one' (Latin). Quoting the Vulgate's version of Psalms 132.1 (KJV 133.1), New-Guise tweaks religious authority in suggesting that the unity of the brothers (here = friars) pleases the devil; he implies that churchmen (including, perhaps, Mercy) live in sin. Such 'anti-monastic' satire was popular throughout

the Middle Ages and survived through the Reformation. See Szittya.

325 **quod** said

327 **mell** both 'have anything to do, meddle', and 'speak, converse'. Although the general sense seems the more likely, the force of *speak* in this line hints that Mankind is avoiding talking with the *fellow* he has heard. A common expression, especially in the negative, in the Corpus Christi cycle; witness Joseph to Mary in *Doctors*, 216: 'With men of myght can I not mell' (line 221).

328 **assay** attempt. Cf. Noah in *York Plays*: 'To wyrk this werke here in this feylde / Al be myselfe I will assaye' (Play 8, ll. 95–6).
    delve dig with a spade (in preparation for planting). On the religious and social overtones of Mankind's delving, see pp. 15–16.

329 **eschew** forgo, avoid. For the biblical associations of this verb, cf. 2 Timothy, 2.16: 'But eschewe thou vnhooli and veyn spechis, for whi tho profiten myche to vnfeithfulnesse' (Wycliffe).

330 **foison** blessing, bounty. 'God's foison' was proverbial; see Whiting, G228.

328 SD] *Adams subst. after 330*   330 SD] *Enter . . .* NOUGHT *Manly; making . . . audience*] *Bevington subst.*

NOWADAYS

> Make room, sirs, for we have be long!
> We will come give you a Christmas song.

NOUGHT

> Now I pray all the yeomanry that is here
> To sing with us with a merry cheer!

> [*Sings.*]
> It is written with a coal, it is written with a coal,   335

NEW-GUISE, NOWADAYS [*encouraging the audience to sing along*]

> It is written with a coal, it is written with a coal,

NOUGHT

> He that shitteth with his hole, he that shitteth with his
> hole,

331 **Make room** Nowadays orders the audience to move as he enters. Cf. similar orders by the Vices at 474, 612, 701. Heap reports that in the 1976 Medieval Players' production, such cries were 'frequently genuinely functional' – that is, they performed necessary work in moving audience members out of the actors' way (Heap, 101).
be long been delayed (i.e. we are late) (*MED* long *adj.*[1] 2.d)

332 **Christmas song** *Christmas* here is probably shorthand for any festive revelry occurring during the Christmas season, or similar to such a Christmas revel (see *MED* Criste-mas(se) *sb.* 2a). Like Mischief's mockery of Mercy at 45ff., the earthy vernacular of the song contrasts with the more formal Latin of the Church.

333 **pray** ask
yeomanry respectable commoners (especially those who cultivate their own land)

334 **cheer** spirit, mood (*MED* chere *sb.*[1] 5); and also: happy expression (*MED* *sb.*[1] 3). In the *York Plays*, Herod orders the court: 'Do rewle vs than in riche array, / And ilke man make tham mery chere' (Play 16, ll. 147–8).

335 **written . . . coal** i.e. in a low fashion, as though graffiti or other common writing. Once cool, coals were proverbially worthless; cf. Whiting, C331. See also Pecock, 166: 'he write sum seable cros or mark or carect with cole or chalk in the wal of his chaumbre or hal.'

337 **He . . . hole** i.e. everyone. Part of this line's humour comes from its obscenity, part from the hilariously unnecessary specification of *with his hole*. Early editors found this 'vulgar song' (Manly) 'unprintable' (Adams) and omitted it from their editions. Adams censored most of 346 as well.

335 SD] *Manly*   336–42] *om. Manly; Adams omits 337–42*   336 SD] *Adams subst.*   336 [2]with a coal] *Eccles;* cetera *MS*

NEW-GUISE, NOWADAYS

He that shitteth with his hole, he that shitteth with his
hole,

NOUGHT

But he wipe his arse clean, but he wipe his arse clean,

NEW-GUISE, NOWADAYS

But he wipe his arse clean, but he wipe his arse clean,   340

NOUGHT

On his breech it shall be seen, on his breech it shall be
seen!

NEW-GUISE, NOWADAYS

On his breech it shall be seen, on his breech it shall be
seen!

ALL *(Sing)* [*except Mankind.*]

Holyke, holyke, holyke! Holyke, holyke, holyke!

NEW-GUISE

Ay, Mankind, God speed you with your spade!
I shall tell you of a marriage: 345

339 **But** unless
  arse posterior (US ass). Cf. Cain in
  Killing of Abel, 13: 'Com kis myne ars!
  Me list not ban' (line 61).
341 **breech** underpants, drawers, or tights
  (*MED* brech *sb.* 1). Cf. *PP C-text*: 'Yut
  am y challenged in our chapitre-hous
  as y a childe were / And balayshed
  on the bare ers and no brech bytwene'
  (Passus 6, ll. 156–7).
343 SD Mankind almost certainly
  declines to sing here and earlier in the
  song; note his negative response to the
  Vices at 327, 348–9.
343 **Holyke . . . holyke** perhaps merely
  festive nonsense words, though Eccles
  saw this line as distorting 'holy' and
  suggesting 'hole-lick'. For the former,
  cf. Revelation, 4.8: *'sanctus, sanctus,
  sanctus'* ('holy, holy, holy'); for the latter,

cf. 145. The adverb 'wholly' could be
spelled 'hoolliche', 'holiche', 'holyke',
'holilich', 'hoolich' and 'holych' (*OED*
wholly I). When referring to a plural
or collective noun, this word could
mean 'all of them, all together, in a
body', a sense appropriate to the new
group identity forged by the song. The
audience has been tricked into loose
speech, and so has joined the sinful
fraternity of the Three Ns.
344 **God speed** a proverbial blessing,
  especially in the traditional phrase
  'God speed the plough!' (appropriate
  for Mankind's occupation as farmer)
345 **marriage** conjunction: see *junctly* at
  347; but also a word that, as New-
  Guise defines it in the following lines,
  continues the tension between holy and
  profane. See 347n., and *OED sb.* 5a.

338 ²he . . . hole] *Eccles;* cetera *MS*   339, 340 ²wipe . . . clean] *Eccles;* cetera *MS*   341 ²it . . . seen]
Eccles; cetera *MS*   342 ²breech . . . seen] *Eccles;* cetera *MS*   343 SP, SD] *(*Cantant omnes*)   except
Mankind*] *this edn*

I would your mouth and his arse, that this made,
    Were married junctly together.

MANKIND

Hie you hence, fellows, with braiding!
Leave your derision and your japing!
I must needs labour, it is my living.   350

NOWADAYS

What, sir? We came but late hither.

Shall all this corn grow here
That ye shall have the next year?
If it be so, corn had need be dear,
    Else ye shall have a poor life.   355

NOUGHT

Alas, good father, this labour fretteth you to the bone.
But for your crop I take great moan;
Ye shall never spend it alone!
    I shall assay to get you a wife.

How many acres suppose ye here, by estimation?   360

NEW-GUISE

Ay, how ye turn the earth up and down!
I have be in my days in many good town

346 **this** perhaps either the spade (which represents Mankind's occupation as well as labour in this world generally, and which New-Guise may snatch from him briefly), or the song (which Nought has led). New-Guise will be the first to be hit with the spade.

347 **married junctly** joined firmly. But *junctly* (jointly) also suggests the Latin *iunctus*, a common word for describing the joining of man and woman in marriage.

348 **braiding** reproach (i.e. Mankind's scolding). This usage predates the sole citation given by the *OED* (*vbl. sb.*[2]).

349 **japing** tricks, mockery

350 **must needs** have to

351 **but late** only recently

354 **dear** high-priced

355 **poor life** impoverished existence. Nowadays plays on both *dear* (354) and Mankind's *living* (350).

356 **fretteth** wears down

357 **crop** i.e. the yield of *corn* (354) when harvested
    take great moan make significant complaint

358 **spend it** i.e. spend the money which the *crop* (357) brings in

360 **here** are here

346 your . . . made] *om. Adams*   348 Hie] *(Hey)* braiding | *(bredynge)*

Yet saw I never such another tilling!

MANKIND

Why stand ye idle? It is pity that ye were born!

NOWADAYS

We shall bargain with you and neither mock nor scorn.   365

Take a good cart in harvest and load it with your corn,

And what shall we give you for the leaving?

NOUGHT

He is a good stark labourer, he would fain do well.

He hath met with the good man Mercy in a shrewd sell.

For all this, he may have many a hungry meal.   370

Yet, will ye see he is politic:

Here shall be good corn, he may not miss it.

If he will have rain, he may over-piss it;

And if he will have compost, he may over-bless it

A little with his arse, like –   [*Bends, as if to defecate.*]   375

---

364 **stand ye idle** Cf. Matthew, 20.6: 'And about the eleuenth houre, he went out, and founde other standyng idle, and saide vnto them: why stande ye here all the day idle?'
pity . . . born Cf. Matthew, 26.24: 'It had ben good for that man, yf he had not ben borne.'
367 **leaving** remnant, remainder
368 **stark** strong, sturdy
fain gladly, willingly
369 **shrewd sell** i.e. bad or unfortunate bargain (with *sell* taken as a verbal noun; cf. also *MED* shreued *adj.* 2b). Nought implies that Mankind's meeting with Mercy has been unfortunate (*shrewd*) for Nought, New-Guise and Nowadays, and for their plans. Cf. Chaucer's *Legend of Good Women*: 'Of these two here was a

shrewed lees' (1545).
370 **For all this** despite his labour and bargain
hungry meal meal which will leave him hungry
371 **politic** wise
373 **over-piss** urinate on (as irrigation). Cf. a similar (if more obvious) insult in *PP B-text*: 'A Bretoner, a braggere, he bosted Piers als / And bad hym go pissen with his plowgh, pyuysshe sherewe!' (Passus 6, ll. 154–5).
374 **over-bless** consecrate (ironic: he is to do so by defecating, 375). See *MED* overblissen *v.*, citing this passage alone. See also *MED* overblissing *ger.*, which cites *Speculum Sacerdotale* (*c.* 1425) on 'overblessing'.
375 SD Nought is connected with defecation in the play; cf. 783 and n.

374 compost] *(compasse)*   375 SD] *this edn; Makes a rude gesture* | *Lester*

MANKIND

Go and do your labour! God let you never thee!
Or with my spade I shall you ding, by the holy Trinity!
Have ye none other man to mock but ever me?
    Ye would have me of your set?
Hie you forth lively, for hence I will you drive.   380
    [*Hits them with the spade.*]

NEW-GUISE

Alas, my jewels! I shall be shent of my wife!

NOWADAYS

Alas! And I am like never for to thrive,
    I have such a buffet.

MANKIND

Hence I say, New-Guise, Nowadays and Nought!
It was said before, all the means shall be sought   385
To pervert my conditions and bring me to nought.
    Hence, thieves! Ye have made many a leasing.

NOUGHT

Married I was for cold, but now am I warm!
Ye are evil advised, sir, for ye have done harm.
By Cock's body sacred, I have such a pain in my arm   390

---

376 **thee** prosper. Mankind quotes Mercy
from 304 almost verbatim.
377 **ding** hammer, strike
379 **set** group; with implications of 'sect'
(to which this word is etymologically
related: cf. Latin *secta*)
380 **Hie** get, remove
lively quickly, vigorously
381 **jewels** i.e. testicles, 'family jewels'.
Heap notes that the 1976 Medieval
Players' production had its 'best
running gag' in relation to New-Guise's
concern for his *jewels*, alluded to again
at 429, 441 and 496 (Heap, 102).
shent of lost regarding, incapable with

(i.e. impotent)
383 **buffet** beating, series of blows
385 **before** i.e. by Mercy, at 296
387 **leasing** lie, falsehood (*OED sb.*).
Cf. Isaiah, 59.3: 'our lippes speake
leasinges, and your tongue setteth out
wickednesse.' Cf. 568 and n.
388 **now . . . warm** Nought continues
the chorus of responses to Mankind's
buffets: he is *warm* from the beating he
has been given. This contrasts with the
cold of 323.
390 **Cock's** God's. A euphemism (like
today's 'Gosh'). Cf. Ophelia in *Ham*
4.5.61: 'By Cock they are to blame.'

380 SD] *Manly subst.*   385 shall] *(xull); xulde Manly*

I may not change a man a farthing.

> [*New-Guise, Nought and Nowadays start to go.*]

MANKIND

Now I thank God, kneeling on my knee.   [*Kneels.*]

Blessed be his name! He is of high degree.

By the subsidy of his grace that he hath sent me,

> Three of mine enemies I have put to flight.   [*Rises.*]   395

> Yet this instrument, sovereigns, is not made to

> > defend.   [*Points to his spade.*]

David saith, '*Nec in hasta, nec in gladio, salvat Dominus.*'

NOUGHT

No, marry, I beshrew you, it is *in spadibus*!

Therefore Christ's curse come on your *headibus*,

> To send you less might!   400

> > *Exeunt* [*New-Guise, Nought and Nowadays*].

MANKIND

I promit you these fellows will no more come here,

For some of them, certainly, were somewhat too near.

---

391 **change** i.e. reach into my purse to make change for

394 **subsidy** help, assistance, granting. Most often possessing a specialized sense (referring to funds granted to the monarch by Parliament), this word was sometimes used metaphorically. *OED* cites Ryman's *Poems* of 1492: 'Petir and Paule and seintis alle . . . For subsidie to you we calle' (line 250).

396 **instrument** his spade

397 *Nec . . . Dominus* a Latin version of David's words to Goliath in 1 Samuel, 17.47, which reads in full: 'And all this assembly shall know that the LORD saveth not with sword and spear: for the battle is the LORD's, and he will give you into our hands'; Mankind's implication is that his *instrument* (396) is only temporarily sufficient for the 'battle' against evil.

398 *in spadibus* Nought's made-up Latin for 'with a spade'; it recalls Mischief's mockery of Mercy at 45ff., ineptly supplying a plural Latin ablative (*spadibus*) in contrast to the singular nouns of 396 (*instrument*) and 397 (*hasta, gladio*). The *–ibus* ending sounds uniquely Latinate, and amusing, in this play.

399 *headibus* i.e. head (continuing the mock Latin, with plural ablative in place of the singular)

400 **might** strength

401 **promit** promise (cf. *promition* at 316)

391 SD] *Adams subst.*   392 SD] *Adams*   394 the subsidy] *MS (*Þe subsyde*) as read by Bevington;* Þe sbsyde *MS as read by SG;* the fesyde *MS as reported by Manly;* this spade *Manly (Kittredge);* Þe side *Furnivall & Pollard;* the ayde *Adams*   395 SD] *this edn*   396 SD] *Adams subst.*   397 hasta] *Manly;* hastu *MS*

My father, Mercy, advised me to be of a good cheer
And again my enemies manly for to fight.

I shall convict them, I hope, every one.   405
Yet I say amiss, I do it not alone.
With the help of the grace of God I resist my fon
And their malicious heart.

With my spade I will depart, my worshipful sovereigns,
And live ever with labour to correct my insolence.   410
I shall go fetch corn for my land; I pray you of patience;
Right soon I shall revert.   [*Exit.*]

[*Enter* MISCHIEF.]

MISCHIEF

Alas, alas, that ever I was wrought!
Alas the while, I am worse than nought!
Sithen I was here, by him that me bought,   415
I am utterly undone!

403 **father** i.e. his spiritual father, religious instructor. Cf. 86n., 150n.
404 **again** against. This means position (*OED adv., prep., conj.*, B.6) rather than repetition (i.e. *again*): far from counselling another assault, Mercy in his lone conversation with Mankind has explicitly told him *not* to associate with them (cf. esp. 297–9).
manly . . . fight i.e. to fight as a man. Cf. the phrasing in Samuel's poetic abridgment of the book of Joshua: 'For to be strong the Lord him bad, / and manly for to fight' (Samuel, ll. 5–6).
405 **convict** overcome, vanquish – with a hint of the persuasion implied in 'convince', to which the word *convict* here is related (*OED* convince I.1). For biblical parallels, cf. Ephesians, 5.11.

410 **with** by means of
insolence prideful disobedience. Cf. *Devil Conjured*, where the bad are 'restrained by good, to correct their malice, and insolence' (E3ᵛ).
411 **corn** seed grain (for one of the cereal crops)
412 **revert** come back from, return (*OED* I.2a)
413 Meredith observes that this is the text's first 'absolute break'; Mischief reintroduces himself 'almost as though he is restarting the play' (Meredith, *Acting*, 28).
wrought made, created
414 **nought** nothing (with play on the character Nought)
415 **by . . . bought** Mischief invokes Mercy's favourite oath (see 9 and n.)

412 SD1, SD2] *Manly*   413] SCENE II *Eccles*   414 am] *Manly; not in MS*

125

I, Mischief, was here at the beginning of the game
And argued with Mercy, God give him shame!
He hath taught Mankind, while I have be wane,
　　To fight manly again his fon.　　　　　　　　　420

For with his spade, that was his weapon,
New-Guise, Nowadays, Nought he hath all to-beaten.
I have great pity to see them weepen.
　　Will ye list? I hear them cry.
　　　*They [New-Guise, Nowadays and Nought] cry
　　　[from offstage].*
Alas, alas! Come hither, I shall be your borrow.　　425

[Enter NEW-GUISE, NOWADAYS *and* NOUGHT.]

Alack, alack! *Vene, vene!* Come hither with sorrow!

417 **beginning . . . game** start of the 'play'. Mischief highlights the trouble he has started, and hints that he knows he is in a play. For the phrasing here, cf. *Alexander-Cassamus*: 'And at the begynnyng of this fresh[e] game / A corowne anon vp-on his hed set was' (st. 3, ll. 7–8). On metatheatre in the play, see 97 and n.
419 **wane** lacking, deficient (*OED a.* 1, citing this passage)
422 ***he hath** MS *hath*. For this construction, see 535.
all to-beaten beaten into pieces. Cf. 249n.
424 **list** listen
424 SD a common piece of stage business in medieval drama. Cf. the devils in *N-Town*: '*Omnes demones clamant*: Harrow and owt what xal we say harrow / we crye owt and alas' (ll. 410–11).
425–50 The stage business in these lines seems to include the following

actions: the Three Ns complain of their pains; Mischief expresses mock compassion in order to lure them closer; once they come near, Mischief batters Nowadays's head so that it disappears; Nought comically describes Nowadays's predicament while New-Guise protects himself; Mischief restores Nowadays's head; and the four troublemakers huddle to plan more mischief against Mankind.
425 **borrow** bail, deliverer from prison.
426 **Alack** an interjection, like *alas* (with which it often appears for variation), that advertises the pain of a situation
Vene Come! (Latin; an abbreviated form of the imperative *vene/venete*, from the verb *venire*)
with sorrow a phrase with two meanings here: both 'with your sorrows, troubles' and, as an exclamation, 'confound it!'. See *MED sorwe sb.* 5d.

419 wane] *(vane)*　422 he hath] *Lester (Brandl);* hath *MS;* hath he *Furnivall & Pollard*　424 SD *They . . . cry] (*Clamant*) from offstage] this edn*　425 SD] *Manly*　426, 433 *Vene, vene*] *(ven ven)*

Peace, fair babes, ye shall have an napple tomorrow!
Why greet ye so, why?

NEW-GUISE

Alas, master, alas, my privity!

MISCHIEF

Ah, where? Alack! Fair babe, ba me! 430

*[New-Guise starts to remove his breeches, but Mischief
stops him.]*

Abide! Too soon I shall it see.

NOWADAYS

Here, here, see my head, good master!

MISCHIEF

Lady, help! Seely darling, *vene, vene*!

I shall help thee of thy pain;

I shall smite off thy head and set it on again. 435

*[Mischief batters Nowadays's head, pulling his clothing
over it.]*

NOUGHT

By our Lady, sir, a fair plaster!

---

427 **fair babes** Mischief's passionate speech, beginning with his first *Alas* (413), has led into a mother-hen performance that will be curtailed comically by stage violence at 435ff. With this (mock) compassion, cf. Mercy's tenderness at 307.
an napple i.e. an apple; Mischief's informal baby talk (see also 75n.). Cf. 'A child's love, if lost with a pear, may be gained with an apple' (Whiting, 74).

429 **privity** private parts, genitals (his *jewels*, 381). Cf. Chaucer's 'The Monk's Tale': 'His Mantel over his hypes caste he / For no man sholde seen his privetee' (2714–15). Cf. 381n.

430 **ba me** Kiss me! Baby talk indicating intimacy. Cf. the Wife of Bath in her

Prologue: 'Com ner, my spouse, let me ba thy cheke' (433), and see 307n., 427n.

431 **Abide** Wait!
it i.e. the effect of Mankind's assault

432 **my head** the site of the *buffet* (383) Nowadays has suffered

433 **Lady, help** Mischief somewhat ironically calls for help from the Virgin Mary; cf. 106 and n.
Seely harmless, defenceless

434 **help thee of** alleviate

435 **smite . . . head** Mischief's comforting words clearly give way to humorous stage aggression.

436 **plaster** healing or soothing measure (*OED sb.* 1b) – ironic. Cf. New-Guise's use of this word at 247.

427 an napple] *(a* nappyll*)*; an apple *Lester* 430 SD] *Knittel & Fattic subst. after 429* 435 SD] *this edn*

Will ye off with his head! It is a shrewd charm!

As for me, I have none harm.

I were loath to forbear mine arm.

    Ye play *in nomine patris*, chop!   440

NEW-GUISE

Ye shall not chop my jewels, an I may.

NOWADAYS

Yea, Christ's cross, will ye smite my head away?

There! Where? On and on! Out! Ye shall not assay.

    I might well be called a fop.

MISCHIEF

I can chop it off and make it again.   445

    [*Reveals Nowadays's head.*]

NEW-GUISE

I had a shrewd *recumbentibus* but I feel no pain.

---

437 **shrewd charm** mischievous spell
439 **forbear** lose, surrender (*OED v.* 4b)
440 **play** do, act (like this). Nought presumably mimes the action he has just witnessed Mischief perform against Nowadays. He may even act it out against New-Guise, who protests in the following line.
  in nomine patris in the name of the Father (Latin); traditional beginning of a benediction, accompanied by the sign of the cross. Mischief may finish this gesture by boxing Nowadays's ears; see Nought's mention of a *shrewd charm* (437), and cf. Mercy's more serious use of this verse at 902.
441 New-Guise perhaps describes what Nought has just done; he may speak this from the ground or floor, and/or while covering his crotch: cf. 381n., 446n.
  an I may if I can prevent it
442 **Christ's cross** by Christ's cross (an oath)

443 **There . . . Out** Mischief continues to mistreat Nowadays, even pretending to strike off his head. Nowadays probably ducks his head inside his clothing and pretends, with this line, to grope for it. Smart notes the parallel, 'bringing to life' action in the mummers' plays (Smart, '*Mankind*', 22). See p. 12.
  On and on continuously, again
  assay try (my mettle) – with the implication of assaulting me further
444 **fop** fool (*OED* 1). Cf. Cayphas in *N-Town*, 276: 'spek man spek / spek thou fop hast thou scorn to speke to me?' (ll. 75–6).
445 **make it again** restore it. Cf. 443n.
446 *recumbentibus* a 'lie-down' blow. Humorously derived from the Latin *recumbere*, 'to lie down, recline'. For a similarly comic employment, see Heywood, *Proverbs*, 87: 'Had you some husband, and snapte at him thus, / Iwys he would geue you a recumbentibus' (ll. 231–2).

442 Yea] *(ye)*   Christ's] *Manly subst.;* crastys *MS as read by Furnivall & Pollard*   443 Where . . . on] *(were on & on);* wer on anon *Manly (Kittredge)*   445 SD] *this edn*

NOWADAYS

And my head is all safe and whole again.

Now touching the matter of Mankind,

Let us have an interlection, sithen ye be come hither.

It were good to have an end.　　　　　　　　450

[*They whisper with their heads together.*]

MISCHIEF

How, how? A minstrel? Know ye any aught?

NOUGHT

I can pipe in a Walsingham whistle, I, Nought, Nought.

MISCHIEF

Blow apace, and thou shall bring him in with a flute.

[*Nought plays.*]

TITIVILLUS [*from offstage*]

I come with my legs under me.

MISCHIEF

Ho, New-Guise, Nowadays, hark ere I go:　　　455

When our heads were together I spake of *si dedero*.

---

449 **interlection** formal conversation: a coinage based on Latin for 'a speech between (or among)'. Note that Mischief and the Vices continue to use Latin humorously (cf. 440, 446) even while out of Mercy's presence.
sithen seeing that
450 **have an end** be done with (this business), bring (it) to a conclusion
450 SD Cf. 451 and n., and 456 and n.
451 **How, how** Mischief most likely delivers this after their whispered conference.
aught at all
452 **Walsingham whistle** a souvenir whistle connected with the pilgrimage to the shrine of Our Lady of Walsingham in Norfolk (on which, see Smart, 'Concluded', 296). Bury St Edmunds, the area where *Mankind* probably originated, lay between Walsingham and London. It is ironic that Nought possesses (and has mastered the playing of) this whistle, a religious pilgrim's trinket – and, further, that such is the means to summon Titivillus.
453 **apace** immediately, quickly
454 **with . . . me** i.e. quickly, expeditiously
456 *si dedero* if I give (Latin). Mischief raises the issue of passing the hat or plate amongst the audience to pay for their performance – the first reference we have to money being paid by those attending a play in England. With this phrasing cf. Lydgate's *Isopes Fabules*, which indicts the corrupting power of money thus: 'Si dedero ys now so mery a song, / Hath founde a practyk by lawe to make a preef / To hang a trew man & saue an errant theef' (Lydgate, *Minor Poems*, ll. 327–9).

447 safe] *(saue)*　450 SD] *this edn*　451 aught] *(out)*　453 SD] *Bevington*　454 SD] *Manly subst.*

NEW-GUISE

> Yea, go thy way! We shall gather money unto, [*Exit Mischief.*]
> Else there shall no man him see.
>
> [*to the audience*] Now ghostly to our purpose,
>   worshipful sovereigns,
> We intend to gather money, if it please your negligence,   460
> For a man with a head that is of great omnipotence.

NOWADAYS

> Keep your tail, in goodness I pray you, good brother!
> He is a worshipful man, sirs, saving your reverence.
> He loveth no groats, nor pence of twopence;
> Give us red royals if ye will see his abominable
>   presence.   465

NEW-GUISE

> Not so! Ye that may not pay the tone, pay the tother.

458 **him** i.e. Titivillus

459 **ghostly . . . purpose** a conventional rhetorica l tag for introducing new topics in contemporary preaching. Cf. 'Goostli to oure purpos, Jerusalem is as mykil for to say as sight of pees, and it bitokeneth contemplacion in perfighte love of God' (*Scale*, 2.1129). See Fletcher, 'Meaning'.

460 **your negligence** (deliberate) error for *your reverence* (cf. 463)

461 **For** both 'as the agents of' and 'for the sight (of whom)'
head . . . omnipotence In addition to suggesting Titivillus's power (where *great omnipotence* modifies *man*), this line may imply that Titivillus wears an oversize mask, or large false head (i.e. with *great omnipotence* modifying *head*). The bustle of activity here and *Mankind*'s allegorical staging generally may enable both readings.

462 **tail** tally, reckoning (*OED sb.*[2] IV. 4a, b)
in goodness i.e. accurately

463 **He** Titivillus, the 'man with a head' (461)

464 **groats** a coin worth four or five pence (pennies); this varied depending on whether the coin was minted.
pence of twopence a silver coin worth two pennies

465 **red royals** gold coins. This type of coin had been recently introduced as English currency. At this time a gold *royal* would have been worth approximately twenty-four *groats* or sixty *twopence* (464). Nowadays escalates the value of coins in his list to suggest the great worth of seeing Titivillus.
abominable detestable, odious. MS spelling, *abhomynabull*, reflects a common (if erroneous) belief that the word derived from Latin *ab homine*, that is, 'away from man, inhuman, beastly' (see *OED* headnote).

466 **Not so** New-Guise responds to Nowadays's insistence on receiving only *red royals* (465) by telling the assembled audience that any coins will do.
tone . . . tother one . . . other

457 Yea] *Manly subst.;* yo *MS*   SD] *this edn*   459 SD] *Adams*   461 is] *Adams (Brandl); not in MS*   464 twopence] *(*to pens*)*   466 may] *(*mow*)*

[They collect money from the audience.]

At the goodman of this house first we will assay.

God bless you, master! Ye say us ill, yet ye will not say
nay.

Let us go by and by and do them pay.

Ye pay all alike; well mote ye fare!   470

NOUGHT

I say, New-Guise, Nowadays: '*Estis vos pecuniatus?*'

I have cried a fair while, I beshrew your *patus*!

NOWADAYS

Ita vere, magister. Come forth now your *gatus*!

He is a goodly man, sirs; make space and beware!

[Enter TITIVILLUS, *with a net in his hand.]*

---

467 **goodman . . . house** the master of
the place, which might have been,
variously, a private home (*OED* house
sb.[1] I.1), an inn or tavern (*OED* 2c), or
a religious house (*OED* 4a).

468 **Ye . . . nay** You speak ill of us,
but will not deny us our pay. New-
Guise comically suggests a way for
the leading figure of the place (the
goodman, 467) to reward the Vices
(with the audience's first contribution)
even while appearing to disapprove of
these same Vices.

469 **by and by** amongst the audience
do make (as at 82–3)

470 **all alike** equally
mote might

471 *Estis vos pecuniatus* 'Are you full of
money?' (Latin)

472 **cried** begged for money (amongst
the audience)
beshrew curse
patus mock Latin for 'pates', as in
collective 'heads'; cf. 'bald-pate' and

'clod-pate' in *OED*, where these are
metonyms for 'one who has a bald
head' and 'blockhead', respectively.

473 *Ita vere, magister* Thus indeed,
master (Latin). Nowadays invokes the
medieval schoolroom, Titivillus being
the schoolmaster. Cf. 478n.
your from your
gatus mock Latin for 'gates'; here the
implication is that Titivillus comes forth
from the gates of hell. Cf. Matthew,
16.18, and *Saddlers*, 372, which opens
'outside the gates of Hell'.

474 **goodly** perhaps both 'excellent,
good-looking' and 'large in size or
stature'. See *make space* in this line
and cf. 461.

474 SD On Titivillus's net, cf. 303 and
n. Meredith, *Acting*, suggests that
Titivillus could also be carrying a sack
with the board he will use at 533; this
sack would allow Titivillus to steal
away Mankind's discarded corn and
rosary beads.

SD] *Adams subst.* 468 us] *Bevington;* as *MS* 470 mote] *(mut)* 472, 473 *patus . . . gatus*]
pates . . . gates *Lester* 474 SD] *Manly subst.*

131

Mankind

TITIVILLUS

> *Ego sum dominantium dominus* and my name is Titivillus. 475
> Ye that have good horse, to you I say *caveatis*!
> Here is an able fellowship to trice them out at your
> > gates.

> *Ego probo sic:*   (*speaks to New-Guise*)
> > Sir New-Guise, lend me a penny.

NEW-GUISE

> I have a great purse, sir, but I have no money.
> By the mass, I fail two farthings of an ha'penny; 480
> > Yet had I ten pound this night that was.

TITIVILLUS (*speaks to Nowadays*)

> What is in thy purse? Thou art a stout fellow.

NOWADAYS

> The devil have the whit! I am a clean gentleman.

475 *Ego . . . dominus* I am the Lord of
Lords (Latin). A blasphemously ironic
quotation of Deuteronomy, 10.17: 'For
the Lorde your God, is God of Gods,
and Lorde of Lordes, a great God, a
mightie and a terrible, whiche regardeth
no mans person, nor taketh rewarde.'
Cf. *Processus Talentorum*, 309 (line 15),
where Pilate also utters a version of this
line with structural irony.

476 *caveatis* beware (Latin)

477 **able fellowship** i.e. the Three Ns
(who are called *fellows* throughout the
play)
trice carry (as plunder; *OED v.* 1)
***them** here modernized from MS
hym
your gates This echo of *your gatus*
(473) confirms the proximity of the
worldly space to the devil's domain; in
each case, the crossing of thresholds is
dangerous.

478 *Ego probo sic* I prove it thus (Latin).
A schoolroom phrase, introducing
a logical demonstration. Cf. *Pierce*

Penniless: 'it is no matter what Sic
probo and his pennilesse companions
prate' (B2). Cf. also Mercy's proof at
165ff. and see 473 and n.

480 **By the mass** a mild oath
fail come, fall short by

481 **ten pound** ten pounds. See *OED
sb.*[1] 2b: 'A large sum of money, freq.
contrasted with penny, shilling, or
mark' (chiefly plural).
this . . . was last night. The
implication is that New-Guise has
been a spendthrift.

482 **stout** upstanding, valiant. Like *Sir
New-Guise* (478), the compliment
helps deepen the humour of these
figures' pennilessness.

483 ***The . . . whit** May the devil have the
(small) amount I possess (ironic, given
Nowadays's fellow conversationalist).
See *MED* wight *sb.* 2 and *OED* whit
sb.[1] 1b, which cites *Robt. Devyll (c.*
1480): 'The devyll have the whyt that
he was soreye therfore.' MS reads
qwyll for *whit*.

477 them] *this edn;* hym *MS;* hem *Eccles*   478 SD] *(loquitur ad newgyse) opp. 477*   481 ten pound]
(x[ll]) 482 SD] *(loquitur ad nowadays) opp. 482*   483 the whit] *Eccles (Adams);* qwyll *MS*

I pray God I be never worse stored than I am.

It shall be otherwise, I hope, ere this night pass. 485

TITIVILLUS (*speaks to Nought*)

Hark now! I say thou hast many a penny.

NOUGHT

Non nobis, Domine, non nobis, by Saint Denny!

The devil may dance in my purse for any penny;

It is as clean as a bird's arse.

TITIVILLUS

Now I say yet again, *caveatis*! 490

Here is an able fellowship to trice them out of your

gates.

Now I say, New-Guise, Nowadays and Nought,

Go and search the country, anon it be sought,

Some here, some there; what if ye may catch aught?

If ye fail of horse, take what ye may else. 495

clean elegant or proper (*OED a.* 7, 9), with an ironic implication of one whose purse has been 'cleaned out'; cf. 487–9, where *clean* is repeated, and *OED a.* 14.

484 **worse stored** more poorly provided, in possession of less money

486 **Hark now** Nought is the only one of the Three Ns whom Titivillus does not try to flatter. On Nought's characterization, see List of Roles 4n.

487 *Non nobis . . . nobis* Not to us, O Lord, not to us (Latin). A quotation from Psalms, 115.1: 'Geue praise not vnto vs O God, not vnto vs, but vnto thy name.' **Saint Denny** St Denis, the patron saint of France. Used for its rhyme and also for a play on French *denier*: at this time, like the English *penny* (488), made of silver and of relatively small value. Cf. 75 and n.

488 proverbial: 'The Devil dances in an empty pocket' (*ODEP*, D233). The implication is that poverty is both the curse of and breeding ground for mischief.

489 **clean . . . arse** proverbial: 'As bare as a bird's ass' (cf. Dent, B391)

490–1 By repeating most of 476–7, Titivillus neatly closes a frame on the intervening stage business.

493 **anon . . . sought** immediately let it (the countryside) be searched. For this sense of *sought* cf. *OED* seek *v.* 10a: 'To search, explore (a place) in order to find something'. Modern ears perhaps expect, after *anon*, either *be it* or an auxiliary such as *let*. For another instance of Titivillus's syntactical inversion, see 522n.

494 **what . . . aught** You may chance upon some plunder.

486 SD] (loquitur ad nought*) opp. 486* 487 *Non*] Manly; No *MS* 490] *Repeated and cancelled in MS* 491 them] (hem*)* 493 it] (yt*);* that yt *Manly*

NEW-GUISE

Then speak to Mankind for the *recumbentibus* of my
jewels.

NOWADAYS

Remember my broken head in the worship of the five
vowels.

NOUGHT

Yea, good sir, and the sciatica in my arm.

TITIVILLUS

I know full well what Mankind did to you.

Mischief hath informed me of all the matter through.   500

I shall venge your quarrel, I make God avow.

Forth, and espy where ye may do harm.

Take William Fide, if ye will have any mo.

---

496 New-Guise earlier spoke of his *jewels*
(cf. 381 and n., 441) and *recumbentibus*
(446). Here the latter probably means
the 'blow', 'striking of'.

497 **my broken head** Nowadays has
complained of his head at 432; he was
probably injured by Mankind after
380.

five vowels a difficult passage: this is
probably an error (either Nowadays's or
a scribe's) for the 'five wells' of Christ's
(five) wounds on the Cross, conceived
as *wells* flowing with redemptive blood
(cf. 221 and n.). For this image, see Fig.
11 and cf. *MED* welle *sb.* 2a.c, citing,
inter alia, Lydgate's *The Testament*
(*c.* 1475): 'At welles five licour I shal
drawe / To wasshe the ruste of my
synnes blyve, . . . I mene the welles of
Crystes woundes five' (*Minor Poems*,
1.335, ll. 161–5,). Nowadays thus
asks Titivillus to revere his wounded
head as one would Christ's wounds,
mistakenly saying *vowels* for 'wells'.
There may also be a play on the *vowels*
representing demonstrative cries of
pain ('O', 'I', etc.), as they did in some
contemporary comic songs (Eccles,

citing R.L. Greene).

498 **sciatica . . . arm** Because sciatica is
typically felt in the hips, legs or back,
Nought's line has a humorous aspect
he does not intend.

500 **Mischief . . . informed** presumably
following his exit after 456 and before
Titivillus's entrance at 474

501 **venge** revenge
I make . . . avow I pledge before God
(an ironic oath, given the speaker)

502 **Forth** go forth
espy search for, discover

503 **William Fide** the first of a cluster of
ten personal references, most of which
can be connected with individuals living in and around Cambridgeshire and
Norfolk during the period *Mankind*
was composed (see Fig. 7, p. 26).
Many of these men were sturdy land-
owners connected in some way with
the administration of justice. We can
imagine them to be of the class of *sovereigns that sit* (29). One of the figures
is described as a potential accomplice
(503), six as targets (505–7, 509–10,
513), and three as men to be avoided
(511, 514–15).

---

500 hath] *Manly;* hat *MS*   me] *Furnivall & Pollard (Brandl);* not in *MS*   503 William] *Furnivall
& Pollard;* w *MS;* with you *Manly*

I say, New-Guise, whither art thou advised to go?

NEW-GUISE

First I shall begin at Master Huntington of Sawston,   505
From thence I shall go to William Thurlay of Hauxton,
And so forth to Pichard of Trumpington.
    I will keep me to these three.

NOWADAYS

I shall go to William Baker of Walton,
To Richard Bollman of Gayton;   510
I shall spare Master Wood of Fulbourn,
    He is a *noli me tangere.*

NOUGHT

I shall go to William Patrick of Massingham,
I shall spare Master Allington of Bottisham
And Hammond of Swaffham,   515
    For dread of '*in manus tuas*' queck.

505–7 *Sawston . . . Hauxton . . . Trump-ington* formed a trio of villages just south of Cambridge (making New-Guise's expedition an efficient one; see Fig. 7). Smart traces a Huntingdon family in Sawston in 1428, a John Thyrlowe to 'Hawkeston' (spelled, also, 'Hauston') in 1450, and a John and William Pychard to Trumpington between 1450 and 1489 (Smart, 'Continued', 52).

509–12 (East) *Walton* and *Gayton* are in Norfolk, to the east of King's Lynn; *Fulbourn* is to the east of Cambridge. Smart has identified a William Baker in East Walton (d. 1491) (Smart, 'Continued', 52–3) and an Alexander Wood at Fulbourn (d. 1479) (49–50); Wood was Justice of the Peace in 1471, giving Nowadays good reason to *spare* him.

512 *noli me tangere* do not touch me (Latin): Christ's injunction to Mary

Magdalene after the Resurrection (cf. John, 20.17); hence, someone to be avoided (see 509–12n.)

513–15 *Massingham* and *Swaffham* (one of two villages so named) are in Norfolk; like Walton and Gayton (509–10), they are east of King's Lynn. *Allington* is almost certainly William Allington of Bottisham, Justice of the Peace from 1457, later speaker of the Commons (1472), and knight (1478). He was exiled with Edward IV in September 1470, serving as the king's standard-bearer in April 1471. See Wedgwood, 1.9.

516 *in manus tuas* 'into your hands' (Latin). Christ's final words upon the Cross; cf. Luke, 23.46: 'And when Iesus had cryed with a loude voyce, he sayde: Father into thy handes I commende my spirite. And when he thus had sayde, he gaue vp the ghost.' A conventional prayer for the dying – though with

505 Master] *(M)*   516] *Brandl (Manly); after 517 MS*

Fellows, come forth, and go we hence together.

NEW-GUISE

Sith we shall go, let us be well ware and whither.

If we may be take, we come no more hither.

Let us con well our neck-verse, that we have not

a check.   520

TITIVILLUS

Go your way, a devil way, go your way all!

I bless you with my left hand: foul you befall!

Come again, I warn, as soon as I you call,

A' bring your advantage into this place.

[Exeunt all but Titivillus.]

To speak with Mankind I will tarry here this tide   525

And assay his good purpose for to set aside.

The good man Mercy shall no longer be his guide.

512, this is the second in a pair of brazen misappropriations of Christ's speech. The potential blasphemy of the line – a criminal quoting, at the moment of his execution, Christ's passion – extends that of Titivillus at 475. Contrast with *Everyman*, 881, 887–8.

queck Nought mimics the choking sound one would make when hanged (i.e. for committing a crime against *Master Allington of Bottisham* or *Hammond of Swaffham*, 514–15). Cf. *OED* queck *sb.*, *v.*¹, *v.*². Cf. 808.

518 **well . . . whither** aware of where, to what place; with a possible pun on the more familiar pairing 'where' and 'whither'. Cf. Katherina in *TS* 4.5.37: 'Whither away, or where is thy abode?'

519 **take** taken, arrested (for our crimes)

520 **con** learn, memorize

neck-verse a biblical verse that, when read in Latin, could redeem a criminal from hanging (on the assumption that the ability to read

Latin proved the man was of a religious order, and thus outside the jurisdiction of secular authority). Often the initial verses of Psalm 50 (KJV 51) were so used. Mercy will quote the beginning of this psalm at 830. Cf. Pilia-Borza in *Jew of Malta*, who speaks of seeing a Friar 'within 40 foot of the gallows, conning his neck-verse' (4.2.16–17).

check impediment, stumbling block

522 **left hand** The left hand was conventionally seen as unlucky, ominous, and even of the devil; cf. 'sinister'. See *2 Honest Whore*: 'I am the most wretched fellow: sure some left-handed Priest christned me, I am so vnlucky' (F1ᵛ).

foul you befall i.e. may you have misfortune (a curse). For his *left hand* blessing, Titivillus inverts his syntax. Cf. 493n.

524 **advantage** profit, gain

525 **tide** time, hour

526 **assay . . . aside** try to divert him from his proper course

520 con] *Manly;* com *MS*   524 SD] *Adams subst.*

I shall make him to dance another trace.

Ever I go invisible, it is my jet,
And before his eye thus I will hang my net   530
To blench his sight. I hope to have his foot-met.
    To irk him of his labour I shall make a frame:
This board shall be hid under the earth privily;
    [*Hides a board.*]
His spade shall enter, I hope, unreadily;
By then he hath assayed, he shall be very angry   535
    And lose his patience, pain of shame.
I shall ming his corn with drawk and with darnel;
It shall not be like to sow nor to sell.
Yonder he cometh; I pray of counsel.
He shall ween grace were wane.   540

528 **trace** step. Cf. 93n., 95–6.
529 **Ever** always
    jet fashion, habit (cf. 103n.)
530 **net** Satan was traditionally portrayed as trying to entrap mankind with a net (cf. 303 and n.).
531 **blench** turn aside, divert (*OED v.*[1] 4)
    foot-met foot measured; cf. 'belly-met' at 143 and n. Titivillus relates that he hopes to take the 'measure' of Mankind. Cf. *OED* met *a.* 1, defining as 'measured' and citing *First Shepherds'*, 125: 'This botell . . . It holdys a mett potell' (ll. 694–8). See also Matthew, 7.2: 'For with what iudgement ye iudge, ye shalbe iudged: And with what measure ye meate, it shalbe measured to you agayne.'
532 **irk** (make) weary, tired (*OED v.*[1] 3)
    frame snare (*OED sb.* 7b). This use predates the *OED* quotation, Barclay's *Shyp of Folys* (1509): 'The deuyll . . . labours to get vs in his frame' (1.164)
534 **enter** i.e. into the ground

unreadily uneasily, with difficulty; this use predates the *OED* entry's citation.
535 **By then** when, once, after
536 **pain of shame** upon pain of shame (a mild oath). This phrase is used twice in *Nature* (ll. 450, 977).
537 **ming** intermix, mingle (*MED* mengen *v.*). Cf. Leviticus, 19.19: 'Thou shalt not . . . sow thy fielde with mingled seede.'
    drawk . . . darnel weeds common to grainfields. Cf. *OED* drawk, which defines this plant as *Bromus secalinus*, and *MED* darnel *sb.*, which identifies darnel as *Solium temulentum*. A farmer like Mankind would hate to have these weeds amongst his corn. Cf. also the episode of the tares in Matthew, 13.37.
538 **like** likely. Mankind's *corn* (537) will be too impure to sow or sell.
539 **I . . . counsel** I beg you to keep our secret.
540 **ween** think, surmise
    wane lacking, absent (*OED a.* 1).

533 hid] (hyde)   SD] *Adams subst. after 536*   534 unreadily] (on redyly)

[*Enter* MANKIND, *carrying a bag of corn.*]

MANKIND

Now God of his mercy send us of his sand!

I have brought seed here to sow with my land.

While I over-delve it, here it shall stand.

[*Puts the corn down and Titivillus goes out with it.*]

In nomine Patris et Filii et Spiritus Sancti, now I will
           begin. [*His spade hits the board.*]

This land is so hard it maketh unlusty and irk.   545

I shall sow my corn at venture and let God work!

[*Looks for his bag.*]

Alas, my corn is lost! Here is a foul work!

I see well by tilling little shall I win.

Here I give up my spade for now and for ever.

[*Throws down his spade.*]

Here Titivillus goeth out with the spade.

Titivillus means to lead Mankind into the (prideful) sin of despair by making him believe that grace (arguably available to all Christians owing to Christ's sacrifice) is not available to him. Cf. John, 1.17: 'For the lawe was geuen by Moyses: but grace and trueth came by Iesus Christe.'

541 **of his sand** as a message, present (*OED sb.*¹). Cf. Caiaphas in *Tapiteres*, 282: 'Some feende of his sand has he sente' (line 31).

542 **with my land** my land with

543 **over-delve** dig up, turn over (the earth)
it . . . it the land . . . the (bag of) seed

544 *In . . . Sancti* In the name of the Father, and the Son, and the Holy Ghost (Latin). Mankind righteously recites the well-known benediction that originates in Matthew, 28.19: 'Go ye therfore, & teache all nations, baptizing

them in the name of the father, and of the sonne, and of the holye ghost.'

545 **hard** i.e. hard to dig (because of Titivillus's *board*, 533)
unlusty indisposed to activity or exertion
irk weary, tired. Mankind repeats Titivillus's word from 532.

546 **at venture* by chance, haphazardly (i.e. sowing it without properly preparing the ground). MS reads *at wynter*; here emended for sense: Mankind seems to refer to a slothful mode of planting. For the phrase 'beware of that adventure', see 847.

548 **by . . . win** I shall gain little by farming.

549 SD1 Heap reports that the 1976 Medieval Players' production had Mankind do a double-take when he did not hear his discarded spade hit the

To occupy my body I will not put me in dever.   550
I will hear my evensong here ere I dissever.
   This place I assign as for my kirk.
Here in my kirk I kneel on my knees.
[Kneels and prays with his rosary.]
Pater noster, qui es in caelis . . .

[Enter TITIVILLUS.]

TITIVILLUS *[aside to the audience]*
   I promise you I have no lead on my heels.   555
   I am here again to make this fellow irk.

Whist! Peace! I shall go to his ear and tittle therein.
[to Mankind] 'A short prayer thirleth heaven'; of thy
                     prayer blin.
Thou art holier than ever was any of thy kin.

ground: 'because Titivillus . . . caught it' (Heap, 99).

550 **I . . . dever** I will not endeavour (cf. *OED* devoir *sb.* 2)

551 **hear . . . here** MS reads *here . . . here*, making it impossible to say which word is the verb and which the adverb. This verbal play, called *paranomasia* and, more specifically in medieval rhetoric, *annominatio*, is very common in Latin poetry and in the works of Langland. See Schmidt, 59–60. For a second instance, see 836 and n.

evensong the church service celebrated shortly before sunset (also called *vespers*)

dissever depart

552 **assign as for** (will) appoint (*OED* assign *v.* 3)

kirk church

554 *Pater . . . caelis* Our Father, who art in heaven . . . (Latin). Mankind begins the Lord's Prayer or 'Paternoster', found in Matthew, 6.9 and Luke, 11.2.

The actor would most likely lower his voice as Titivillus begins to speak.

555 SP A second hand in the MS has written 'new g' below the original speech prefix for Titivillus; this also occurs at 565 and 589. Similar assignment of Mischief's speech to Nowadays occurs at 642 and 664. See pp. 36–38 for discussion.

555 **lead . . . heels** i.e. I am not slow; proverbial (Dent, L136), continuing the theme of speed and mobility he has announced at 454.

557 **Whist** hush
tittle whisper

558 **A . . . heaven** proverbial (Tilley, P555). Titivillus speaks ironically, as he means his whispered words to divert Mankind from righteousness. Cf. Ecclesiasticus/Sirach, 35.17: 'The prayer of the humble pierceth the clouds' (KJV).
thirleth pierces, penetrates
blin cease, leave off

553 SD] *Adams subst.*   554 SD] *Manly*   555 SP, 565 SP, 589 SP] new g *added in a second hand after SPs MS*   555 SD] *Lester subst.*   558 SD] *Manly subst.*

Arise and avent thee! Nature compels.   560

MANKIND [*to the audience, as he rises*]

I will into thy yard, sovereigns, and come again soon.

For dread of the colic and eek of the stone

I will go do that needs must be done.

[*Puts down his rosary.*]

My beads shall be here for whosomever will else.   *Exit.*

TITIVILLUS

Mankind was busy in his prayer, yet I did him arise.   565

He is conveyed, by Christ, from his divine service.

Whither is he, trow ye? Iwis I am wonder wise;

I have sent him forth to shit leasings.

If ye have any silver, in hap pure brass,

Take a little powder of Paris and cast over his face,   570

And even in the owl-flight let him pass.

560 **avent** escape (i.e. from confinement, into the open air) (*OED v.* 2)
Nature compels i.e. you must relieve yourself. Titivillus has made Mankind feel the need to urinate and defecate.
562 **colic . . . stone** two ailments that Mankind fears could result from not immediately relieving himself. The *colic* refers to 'severe paroxysmal griping pains in the belly' (*OED sb.* 1); *the stone* refers to 'A hard morbid concretion in the body, esp. in the kidney or urinary bladder, or in the gallbladder' (*OED sb.* 10a).
564 **beads** rosary beads. Medieval Christians (like many modern-day Roman Catholics) often prayed with the help of a string of beads divided into units of eleven: one large, and ten small. The small beads represent prayers called Aves, the large ones Paternosters (cf. 554 and n.) and Glorias. Leaving his rosary beads 'for whomsomever will else' would seem a careless act signifying Mankind's lapse into sin.
565 SP See 555 SPn.

567 **trow** know
Iwis indeed
wonder wondrously
568 **shit leasings** pass lies. Titivillus implies that he has gained control of, and corrupted, Mankind's body. Mankind's absence from the performance space for 12 lines makes his decline more believable. He charged the Vices with making *many a leasing* at 387 (cf. n.).
569 Titivillus begins an *ad hoc* speech to the audience, demonstrating his virtuoso skill with a petty deception.
in hap perchance; i.e. not actually silver, but *brass*
570 **powder of Paris** a white compound, perhaps made of arsenic, used in magic and alchemy (*OED* powder *sb.*[1] 5d)
his face i.e. the surface of the coin
571 **even . . . pass** at dusk pass the coin off as legitimate. The person receiving the coin would be tricked in poor light. For *owl-flight* as dusk (i.e. the time owls would begin flying), see *OED* owl *sb.* compounds C2b.

561 SD] *Adams subst.*   563 SD] *Bevington subst.*   564] *First copied and cancelled at 562*   else] *(ellys)*
in cancelled version of the line at 562; cumme *MS version of the line at 564*

Titivillus can learn you many pretty things.

I trow Mankind will come again soon,
Or else I fear me evensong will be done.
His beads shall be triced aside, and that anon.   575
   Ye shall a good sport if ye will abide.
Mankind cometh again, well fare he!
I shall answer him *ad omnia quare*.
There shall be set abroach a clerical matter.
   I hope of his purpose to set him aside.   580

[*Enter* MANKIND.]

MANKIND

Evensong hath be in the saying, I trow, a fair while.
I am irk of it; it is too long by one mile!
Do way! I will no more so oft over the church-stile.
[*Discards paper badge.*]
   Be as be may, I shall do another.
Of labour and prayer, I am near irk of both;   585
I will no more of it, though Mercy be wroth.

---

572 **pretty** clever, ingenious
574 ironic: Titivillus of course wants Mankind to miss his prayers.
575 **triced** carried off (cf. Titivillus at 477)
576 **shall** i.e. shall have
578 *ad omnia quare* to his every question (Latin)
579 I will set in motion a plan worthy of a cleric (i.e. an ingenious device); cf. *2H4* 4.2.14: 'Alack, what mischiefs might he set abroach.'
580 **of** from
581 **be** been
  in the saying i.e. underway, in the process of being said
582 **it . . . mile** i.e. the service is longer

than I am willing to endure.
583 **Do way** put away, have done with. Having discarded his spade (549) and beads (564), Mankind similarly abandons the paper he wrote (and probably affixed to his gown) at 321–2. Cf. New-Guise's use of *Do way* when he discards his halter at 623.
  will i.e. will go
  stile an arrangement of steps over a fence, here marking the boundary of the churchyard
584 **Be . . . may** be as it may, however it may be
  another otherwise; i.e. he will not go to church.
586 **wroth** angry

576 a] se a *Manly*   580 SD] *Manly*   583 SD] *this edn*   584–6] *Added at foot of page with cross as location mark opp. 584 MS*

My head is very heavy, I tell you forsooth.
I shall sleep full my belly an he were my brother.
[*Sleeps and snores.*]

TITIVILLUS [*to the audience*]
An ever ye did, for me keep now your silence.
Not a word, I charge you, pain of forty pence.   590
A pretty game shall be showed you ere ye go hence.
Ye may hear him snore; he is sad asleep.
Whist! Peace! The devil is dead! I shall go round in
                                    his ear.
[*Whispers in Mankind's ear.*] Alas, Mankind, alas!
                    Mercy hath stolen a mare!
He is run away from his master, there wot no man
                                    where;   595

587 **My . . . heavy** Heap relates that in the 1976 Medieval Players' production, 'Titivillus was putting pressure with his hands on the top of Mankind's head' while the latter spoke this line (Heap, 99).
forsooth in truth
588 I am going to get my bellyful of sleep, even if Mercy were my own brother. Mercy has twice said to Mankind 'Do truly your labour' (300, 308), and has cautioned him to 'keep your holy day' (300); with this line Mankind confirms his disregard of these warnings.
589 SP See 555 SPn.
589 If you have ever kept quiet, please do so now for me. Titivillus continues to address the audience directly, gaining their complicity in his *good sport* (576) in the same way the Three Ns have solicited the audience's help. Cf. 333–43, 457–74. Brannen calls this 'The height of the audience involvement with evil' in the play (Brannen, 17).
590 **pain of** at the penalty of (i.e. should you wake Mankind)

591 **pretty game** Titivillus repeats his *pretty* from 572 and combines it with Mischief's keyword, *game* (69, 417).
592 **sad** sound, deep (*OED a.* and *adv.*)
593 **The devil is dead** proverbial, implying that a task is nearly finished (Dent, D244). Titivillus chooses an ironic saying, as at 558 (see n.).
round At 303, Mercy predicted to Mankind that Titivillus 'will round in your ear', where 'round' = whisper, speak privately to. Cf. the Bastard in *KJ*, who indicts France for having 'rounded in the ear / With that same purpose–changer, that sly divel, / That broker, that still breaks the pate of faith' (2.1.566–8).
594 **stolen a mare** the same crime (horse theft) that Titivillus has mentioned three times previously: 476–7, 490–1, 494–5. For possible wordplay on *mare* see 600n.
595 **He** Mercy (who, extending the image of the *stolen . . . mare*, is likened to a horse who has run away from his *master*)
there . . . where no man knows (*wot*) where

588 SD, 589 SD] *Adams subst.*   594 SD] *Adams*   hath] *this edn; not in MS;* has *Lester (Brandl)* stolen] (stown)

Moreover, he stole both a horse and a neat.

But yet I heard say he brake his neck as he rode in
France;
But I think he rideth on the gallows, to learn for to
dance,
Because of his theft, that is his governance.
Trust no more on him, he is a married man.　　　　600
Mickle sorrow with thy spade before thou hast wrought.
Arise, and ask mercy of New-Guise, Nowadays and
Nought.
They can advise thee for the best; let their good will be
sought,
And thy own wife brothel, and take thee a leman.

596 **neat** a bovine animal: ox, bullock, cow or heifer (*OED sb.*[1])
597 **heard say** i.e. heard tell, heard it reported
  brake broke
598 **rideth . . . gallows** is being hanged on the gallows
  to . . . dance i.e. learning how to *dance* while being hanged. The grim joke concerns the resemblance between the convulsions of a hanged body and a *dance*. Cf. *OED* dance 3b, and *Honest Lawyer*: 'Well, if there be no remedie, I hope, / I shall not dance alone vpon the rope' (K1ᵛ).
599 **governance** mode of living
600 **married man** Following *mare* (594), MS *marryde* here seems to pun on both *married* and *marred*. Spellings recorded in the *MED* suggest the words may have been pronounced similarly; cf. marien *v.* and merren *v.* The *married* reading would play on the inappropriateness of a priest's having a wife (see Coogan, 4: 'Unless Mercy is indeed a priest, and therefore bound to celibacy, the words of Titivillus are

meaningless'). The *marred* reading would signify a troubled person, with an implication of 'ruined', 'finished': *OED* marred *a.* 1, 2a. This was a conventional alliterative phrase; cf. Stanzaic *Morte*, 99–100: 'The king gan loude cry and call, / As marred man of wit unsaught' (ll. 3188–9).
601 i.e. you have created much sorrow *before* this with your spade (as at 398ff.). The use of *wrought* here may ironically echo God's creating power in the Bible; cf. Isaiah, 26.12: 'Lorde vnto vs thou shalt prouide peace: for thou also hast wrought all our workes in vs.'
602 **ask mercy of** seek forgiveness from (with an ironic play on the figure Mercy, whose *good will* (603) these figures clearly lack)
604 *****brothel** i.e. let go into ruin (MS *brethel*). Here the modern variant of *brethel* (which appears in the plural form at 707); each referred to a worthless person, with the implication of sexual looseness. See *OED* brothel *sb.*
  leman girlfriend, mistress

597 as] *Manly, MS as read by Furnivall & Pollard;* ab *MS*　603 can] *(*cun*)*　604 brothel *(*brethell*)*

143

[*to the audience*] Farewell, every one, for I have done
                            my game,   605
For I have brought Mankind to mischief and to shame.
                                                            [*Exit.*]

MANKIND [*Wakes.*]

Whoop! Ho! Mercy hath broken his neckercher, avows,
Or he hangeth by the neck, high up on the gallows.
Adieu, fair masters! I will haste me to the ale-house
    And speak with New-Guise, Nowadays and Nought   610
A' get me a leman with a smattering face.

[*Enter* NEW-GUISE, *making his way through the audience,
                    with a noose around his neck.*]

NEW-GUISE

Make space, for Cock's body sacred, make space!
Ah ha! Well overrun! God give him evil grace!
    We were near Saint Patrick's way, by him that me
                            bought.

607 **Whoop! Ho** Mankind presumably awakes dramatically, as if from a nightmare.
neckercher neckerchief, here humorous slang for *neck*
avows assuredly, certainly (see *OED* vous *int.*); perhaps a colloquial reduction of the phrase heard at 624: *I make avow!*
611 **smattering** 'Ready for smacking or kissing' (i.e. because attractive) (*OED ppl. a.* 1, glossing this usage)
SD Here and elsewhere the Vices use the proximity of the audience to their advantage; cf. SDs at 330, 336, 459, 466, 555, 605, 696 and 701. On staging *Mankind*, see Heap and Meredith, *Acting*.
612 **Make space** New-Guise ostentatiously calls attention to himself.

613 **overrun** out-run. New-Guise may cast a glance over his shoulder to indicate that he has escaped the law.
him i.e. the officer of the law he has *overrun*
614 **Saint Patrick's way** St Patrick's Purgatory, long the site of pilgrimages by European Christians in the Middle Ages. Located at Lough Derg, County Donegal, in Northern Ireland, this site consisted of a cave into which pilgrims would descend (sometimes sleeping there overnight) in hopes of seeing the entrance to Purgatory. New-Guise may mention this site to exaggerate the distance he has travelled, as well as to suggest how close he has come to dying (i.e. *Saint Patrick's way* as a colourful way of saying 'death').

605 SD] *Adams*   Farewell] (*Harwell*)   606 SD] *Manly*   607 SD] *Adams subst.*   611 SD *Enter* NEW-GUISE] *Manly*   making . . . audience] *Lester subst.*   with . . . neck] *Adams subst.*

I was twitched by the neck; the game was begun.   615
A grace was, the halter burst asunder: *ecce signum*!
[*Holds up the broken rope.*]
The half is about my neck; we had a near run!
'Beware', quod the goodwife, when she smote off her
husband's head, 'beware!'
Mischief is a convict, for he could his neck-verse.
My body gave a swing when I hung upon the case.   620
Alas, he will hang such a likely man, and a fierce,
For stealing of an horse, I pray God give him care!

Do way this halter! What devil doth Mankind here,
with sorrow?
Alas, how my neck is sore, I make avow!

by . . . bought New-Guise uses Mercy's favourite oath; cf. 9 and n., 415 and n.

615 **twitched** pulled up, jerked; cf. *dance* (598).

616 **A grace was** it was a grace that
halter noose
asunder apart, in two
ecce signum Behold the proof (Latin). New-Guise evidently displays the broken noose mentioned in 617.

617 **near** closely contested

618 The line describes a woman beheading her husband even while warning him to be careful. Rather than recalling a lost folktale or jest, it probably constitutes an early 'Wellerism'; cf. 126 and n.
quod said

619 Mischief has been pronounced guilty (*is a convict*) as we see from (*for*) the fact that he knew (*could*) his neck verse (see 520n.). New-Guise has just witnessed Mischief trying to escape punishment.

620 **case** a type of legal action, here comically identified as an instrument of execution. For *case*, see *OED sb.*[1] 6c, which cites Lambarde from

1591: 'Suits at the Common Law, for remedie in Cases, where no proper helpe was formerly knowne . . . called the Action or Writ upon the Case'. See also *OED* 6d.

621 **he** i.e. the executioner
likely . . . fierce i.e. such a handsome (*likely*) and brave (*fierce*) man (as me). For *likely*, see *OED* 5, which cites Malory: 'The damoysel beheld the poure knyght, and sawe he was a lykely man' (2.2.77).

622 **I . . . care** New-Guise curses the executioner (*him*) for nearly killing him. Cf. the First Pharasie in *Chester* (*Christ at the House of Simon the Leper*), 265: 'God give him care, / that was so great of price!' (ll. 363–4).

623 **Do way** New-Guise presumably removes the rope from his neck with a show of contempt. Cf. 583 and n.
What devil i.e. what the devil (a mild oath)
with sorrow confound it! (an exclamation). Cf. Mischief at 426 and n.

624 New-Guise begins a theatrical lament to gain Mankind's attention.

616 burst] (brast) SD] *Adams*   620 upon] (vpp on)   621 likely] (lyghly); lightly *MS as reported by Manly*   624 avow] (a vowe)

MANKIND

    Ye be welcome, New-Guise! Sir, what cheer with you?   625

NEW-GUISE

    Well sir, I have no cause to mourn.

MANKIND

    What was that about your neck, so God you amend?

NEW-GUISE

    In faith, Saint Audrey's holy band.

    I have a little disease, as it please God to send,

    With a running ringworm.   630

[Enter NOWADAYS, *with stolen items from a church.]*

NOWADAYS

    Stand a-room, I pray thee, brother mine!

    I have laboured all this night; when shall we go dine?

    A church here beside shall pay for ale, bread and wine.

    Lo, here is stuff will serve.

625 **what . . . you** i.e. how are you doing?

627 **so . . . amend** i.e. may God reform you. Cf. Jeremiah, 26.13.

628 **Saint . . . band** St Audrey was reported to have died from a neck tumour, which she saw as punishment for the vanity of her younger years (when she wore necklaces and other ornaments). Thus neck-bands called 'tawdry-lace', from a corruption of Sain*t-A*udrey, came to be sold at fairs and were hallowed at her shrine in Ely Cathedral (Eccles). See *OED* tawdry lace, cf. *Walsingham whistle* (452), and see p. 25.

630 **running ringworm** literally, a fungus (*tinea sycosis* or *tinea circinata*) that spreads over the skin. See *OED* ringworm as well as *OED* running *ppl. a.* 6b, which cites this passage and also Higins from 1585: '*Herpes*, Some call it

the shingles, some ye running worme, some wild fire' (441). New-Guise also puns on the *running* he has had to do to escape from the law (cf. 613, 617) and the way a rope 'rings' his neck.

631 **a-room** aside; cf. *Hickscorner*: 'Aware, fellows, and stand a-room' (1.154). Like New-Guise at 612, Nowadays calls attention to his entrance by demanding space.

632 **laboured . . . night** Nowadays boasts of his industry – ironic, given his real activity. Cf. Luke, 5.5: 'And Simon aunswered, and sayde vnto hym: Maister, we haue laboured all nyght, and haue taken nothyng.'

634 **here is stuff** Nowadays evidently displays properties representing pilfered church goods such as plate and/or candlesticks (cf. 633). With such theft cf. Spenser's Kirkrapine in *FQ*, esp. 1.3.17–18.

629 disease] *(dyshes)*   630 SD] *Adams subst.*

NEW-GUISE

Now by the holy Mary, thou art better merchant than I!   635

[*Enter* NOUGHT.]

NOUGHT

Avaunt, knaves, let me go by!
I cannot get and I should starve.

[*Enter* MISCHIEF, *wrapped in broken chains.*]

MISCHIEF

Here cometh a man of arms! Why stand ye so still?
Of murder and manslaughter I have my belly-fill.

NOWADAYS

What, Mischief, have ye been in prison? An it be
                                        your will,   640
Meseemeth ye have scoured a pair of fetters.

MISCHIEF

I was chained by the arms: lo, I have them here.

---

636 Nought enters boisterously ordering the audience to give him room.

637 I can't succeed at stealing anything, even if I starved.

638 **man of arms** Mischief presumably enters bearing chains and/or shackles and may wear, on his legs, a *pair of fetters* that Nowadays soon notices (see 641); he thus puns on *man of arms* as meaning (1) soldier, knight or other armed man; and (2) someone whose arms have recently been restrained.

639 **murder and manslaughter** While both terms indicate the killing of another person, *manslaughter* is a slightly lower offence in English law; it occurs when a person causes 'the death of another unintentionally by culpable negligence or as a consequence of some

unlawful act, or does so intentionally but under provocation, while suffering from diminished responsibility' (*OED* manslaughter *sb.* 2).

belly-fill belly-full. Cf. *belly-met* at 143, and *full my belly* at 588.

640 **An** if

641 **Meseemeth** it seems to me
scoured . . . fetters worn smooth (by long wearing) a pair of restraints (*fetters*) on the lower legs. Lester compares Heywood, *Pardoner*: 'thou shalt not escape me, / Till thou hast scouryd a pare of stokys' (ll. 614–15).

642 SP In MS a later hand has added 'novad' (i.e. Nowadays) next to the prefix for Mischief; this occurs also at 664. Cf. 555 SPn. and pp. 36–8.

642 **them** i.e. the *chains* (643)

635 SD] *Manly subst.*   637 SD *Enter* MISCHIEF] *Manly   wrapped in broken chains*] *Adams subst.*
641 scoured] *(scoryde)*   642 SP, 664 SP, 670 SP] 'novad' *or* 'nowad' *added in a second hand after SPs*

The chains I burst asunder and killed the jailer,
Yea, and his fair wife halsed in a corner;
   Ah, how sweetly I kissed the sweet mouth of hers!   645

When I had do, I was mine own butler;
I brought away with me both dish and doubler.
Here is enough for me; be of good cheer!
   Yet well fare the new chesouns!

MANKIND

I ask mercy of New-Guise, Nowadays and Nought.   650
   [*Kneels.*]
Once with my spade I remember that I fought.
I will make you amends if I hurt you aught
   Or did any grievance.

NEW-GUISE

What a devil liketh thee to be of this disposition?

MANKIND

I dreamt Mercy was hanged, this was my vision,   655
And that to you three I should have recourse and
               remotion.

644 **halsed** embraced; *OED* halse *v.*², citing *Sir Generides* (*c.* 1430): 'There thei halsed and thei kist' (line 9614). Walker suggests this episode 'sounds very like the rape of the jailer's wife' (Walker, 259).
646 **do** done
  mine own butler I served myself, as though I were in charge of the place's wine and plate.
647 **dish and doubler** dishes and platters. The alliteration recalls that at 639.
649 **new chesouns** new condition (i.e. the situation we find ourselves in owing to my crimes); *chesoun* is an aphetic form of the Old French

achesoun (occasion, cause, motive); cf. *OED* chesoun *sb.*
651 i.e. at 380–7
654 What brought you to this frame of mind? Mankind's change of heart towards them is puzzling until Nowadays realizes that Titivillus has been involved: see 659–60. The oath *what a devil* is thus ironic.
655 **vision** scene revealed to me (in my dream)
656 **I . . . remotion** I should come to you for help. In indicating directions to follow to obtain aid, the alliterative pair *recourse and remotion* is essentially redundant.

643 burst] (brast) 648 enough] (a now) 650 SD] *Bevington* 655 hanged] (hange)

Now, I pray you heartily of your good will.

I cry you mercy of all that I did amiss.

NOWADAYS [*aside*]

I say, New-Guise, Nought: Titivillus made all this;

As sicker as God is in heaven, so it is. 660

NOUGHT [*to Mankind*]

Stand up on your feet! Why stand ye so still?

[*Mankind rises, trembling.*]

NEW-GUISE

Master Mischief, we will you exhort

Mankind's name in your book for to report.

MISCHIEF

I will not so; I will set a court.

Nowadays, make proclamation, 665

A' do it *sub forma juris*, dastard!

NOWADAYS

Oyez! Oyez! Oyez! All manner of men and common

women

657–8 I beg you on the basis of your good will to forgive me for everything I have done wrong. Mankind evidently kneels here (see 661), as he has earlier done with Mercy at 212ff. The phrase 'I pray you heartily' repeats Nowadays from 129.

660 **sicker** certainly

as . . . heaven an ironic oath, in the context of the preceding line

661 **Why . . . still** Nought's question seems to indicate that Mankind shakes with fear.

663 The allusion seems to be to an official or quasi-official record (*your book*) in which Mankind's name is to be entered.

report give an account of, describe

664 SP See 642 SPn.

set a court call a court into session

666 *sub forma juris* legally, under the

form of law (Latin)

dastard fool (see *OED* dasart and *OED* dastard, which suggest this word derived from *daze* + *ard* in a manner similar to the formation of *dullard* and *drunkard*)

667 Nowadays begins parodying the role of a beadle or usher in a manor court, where the lord of a manor had jurisdiction over his tenants in civil and minor criminal matters.

Oyez! Oyez! Oyez! The customary call for respectful silence in a court. Cf. *Country Justice*, 46: 'He may cause three *Oyes* for silence, to be made.'

All . . . women perhaps elegant variation of 'common men and women', though *common women* offers a sexual joke. On 'common woman' as 'harlot', see *OED* common A.I.6a.

659 SD] *Manly* 661 SD1] *Bevington* SD2] *this edn* 665] *Eccles; opp. 665 MS; printed as SD* | *Manly* 667] *Eccles; MS lines* Oyet / women /

To the court of Mischief either come or send!

Mankind shall return; he is one of our men.

MISCHIEF

    Nought, come forth, thou shall be steward.   670

NEW-GUISE

    Master Mischief, his side-gown may be sold.

    He may have a jacket thereof, and money told.

    Nought writes.

MANKIND

    I will do for the best, so I have no cold.

    Hold, I pray you, and take it with you.

    [*Takes off his gown and hands it to New-Guise.*]

    And let me have it again in any wise.   675

NEW-GUISE

    I promit you a fresh jacket after the new guise.

668 **either ... send** either appear in person or send a representative. Eccles points out that tenants had to either attend the manor court or send excuses (called 'essoins').

669 **return** make official reply (to our demands); for this legal sense, see *OED v.*[1] 16a.

he ... men The implication is that Mankind has become one of the ill-doers; perhaps also, that he is bound to answer (*return*) Mischief's questions the same way a tenant would be obligated to obey the lord of a manor. Cf. 668n.

670 **steward** The *steward* of the manor transacted his lord's legal and financial affairs, presided over the manor court in his absence, and kept its records.

671 **his side-gown** Mankind's long cloak. See *OED* side *a.* 3: 'Reaching or hanging far down on the person; long'.

672 He could have a (shorter) jacket made from this, and we could count the money (gained from selling the extra cloth); cf. *OED* tell *v.* 22b. Smart cites statutes of 1463 and 1482 that forbid short gowns (Smart, 'Concluded', 304).

672 SD Nought has been charged to act as *steward* at 670 and will ineptly record the events of the trial.

673 **do ... best** act for the best result. Cf. Chaucer, 'Melibee': 'I speke for youre beste' (line 271).

so ... cold as long as I don't get cold; a comic set-up to the subsequent, drastic shortening of his protective outer garment

675 **in any wise** by all means. Mankind means that he wants the gown back regardless, but his words ironically anticipate the radical alterations that we soon see.

676 **fresh** new (with resonances, perhaps, of 'bright' and 'fine')

after ... guise in the new fashion (with obvious play on the speaker's name)

668 either] *(othere)* 671 sold] *Manly;* tolde *MS* 672 SD] *(Nought scrib) opp.* 674 674 SD] *Adams subst. after 673*

MANKIND

Go and do that 'longeth to your office,

A' spare that ye may!   [*Exit New-Guise with the gown.*]

NOUGHT

Hold, Master Mischief, and read this.   [*Gives a paper.*]

MISCHIEF

Here is [*reading*] '*Blottibus in blottis,*   680

Blottorum blottibus istis.'   [*Strikes Nought.*]

I beshrew your ears, a fair hand!

NOWADAYS

Yea, it is a good running fist.

Such an hand may not be missed.

NOUGHT

I should have done better, had I wist.   685

MISCHIEF

Take heed, sirs, it stands you on hand.

[*Reads.*] '*Curia tenta generalis,*

677 '**longeth** belongs
678 **spare . . . may** Leave in place as
much (material) as you're able.
680–1 ***Blottibus . . . istis*** parody Latin,
with words in various cases playing on
the sense of *blot* as 'to cover (paper)
with worthless writing' (*OED* blot *v.*[1]
2). Not quite nonsense, the sentence
might have registered upon the ears of
those familiar with Latin as playfully
approximating 'You (pl.) have blotted
blots in your blotting.'
682 **beshrew** curse
fair hand legible handwriting.
Mischief's irony here may be
accompanied by some slapstick stage
violence; cf. the repeated references to
hand (682, 684, 686) and *fist* (683), the
latter of which 'may not be missed'
(684).

683 **good running fist** fluid (cursive)
handwriting (*MED* fist *sb.*[1] 4, citing
this passage); ironic, with pun on
fleeing Mischief's blows
685 **wist** known. Nought presumably
means he would have produced better
writing (*done better*) had he known he
would be struck for his poor effort.
686 Be careful, gentlemen, for this
concerns you. In his threat Mischief
continues the play on *hand* from the
preceding lines.
***stands** emended by Lester (MS
stoude). Cf. *The pedlers prophecie*
(1595): 'looke to this geare, it stands
you in hand' (*Pedlers*, E2ʳ).
687–93 Seeming to continue to read
Nought's record, Mischief utters a
parody of the proceedings in a manorial
court. The Latin and English here add

678 may] mow *Manly*   SD *Exit New-Guise*] *Manly* *with the gown*] *Adams subst.*   679 SD] *Adams subst.*   680 SP] 'novght' *added in a second hand after SP MS*   680 SD] *Bevington subst.*   681 SD] *this edn*   686 stands] *Lester (Brandl);* stoude *MS*   687 SD] *Adams Curia*] *Furnivall & Pollard;* Carici *MS*

In a place there good ale is,
Anno regni regitalis
   Edwardi nullateni   690
On yesterday in February –'. The year passeth fully,
As Nought hath written; here is our Tully!
'*Anno regni regis nulli!*'

NOWADAYS

What ho, New–Guise! Thou makest much tarrying.
That jacket shall not be worth a farthing.   695

[*Enter* NEW-GUISE, *through the audience.*]

NEW-GUISE

Out of my way, sirs, for dread of fighting!
  Lo, here is a feat tail, light to leap about!
    [*Shows Mankind's gown now cut down to a jacket.*]

NOUGHT

It is not shapen worth a morsel of bread;
There is too much cloth, it weighs as any lead.
I shall go and mend it, else I will lose my head.   700

up to: 'A general court having been held in a place where there is good ale, in the regnal year of Edward the Nought, on yesterday in February, the year ends, as Nought has written – here is our Tully – in the regnal year of no king.' *Tully* (692) refers to Marcus Tullius Cicero, the Roman orator known for his impeccable style; Mischief's compliment to Nought is quite ironic. Because at this date the year officially ended in March, Mischief may be accurate in suggesting that 'The year passeth fully' (i.e. completely) in February. On the implications of this passage for dating the play, see pp. 28–9.

696 **for . . . fighting** lest we fight
697 **feat** elegant, well-fitting. Cf. *OED a.* and *adv.* 3.
  tail the hanging rear portion of a coat
  light . . . about light enough to leap about in
698 **shapen** shaped, cut. Cf. Malory, 243: 'but in mockage ye shall be called La Cote Male Tayle, that is as moche to saye, the euyle shapen cote' (9.6–7).
699 **as** as much as
  lead an object made of lead, such as a cauldron or large pot; or, perhaps, the weight, called a 'lead', used to measure the depth of water
700 **lose my head** continuing the play on beheading seen at 435–7

694 tarrying] *Manly; not in MS;* troublynge *Brandl* 695 SD *Enter* NEW-GUISE] *Manly* through the audience] *Bevington subst.* 697 SD] *Lester subst.*

[*to the audience*] Make space, sirs, let me go out.

[*Exit, with the jacket.*]

MISCHIEF

Mankind, come hither! God send you the gout!

Ye shall go to all the good fellows in the country about;

Unto the goodwife when the goodman is out.

'I will', say ye.

MANKIND   I will, sir.   705

NEW-GUISE

There are but six deadly sins, lechery is none,

As it may be verified by us brethels every one.

Ye shall go rob, steal and kill as fast as ye may gone.

'I will', say ye.

MANKIND   I will, sir.

NOWADAYS

On Sundays on the morrow early betime   710

Ye shall with us to the ale-house early to go dine

A' forbear mass and matins, hours and prime.

---

701 **Make space** This exit fits the pattern of the aggressive entrances established at 612, 631 and 696.

702 **God . . . gout** an ironic blessing: the *gout* is a painful inflammation of the smaller joints (especially of the big toe).

703 **Ye shall go** Mischief gives a mock 'charge' to Mankind; by responding in the affirmative, Mankind may confirm he is 'one of our men' (669), i.e. 'one of us'.

706 **but** only
six deadly sins Following his injunction for Mankind to visit the *goodwife* (704), Mischief omits lust from the list of deadly sins (pride, covetousness, lust, anger, gluttony, envy and sloth), thus reducing these seven to *six*.

707 **brethels** worthless fellows (see *OED*, and 604 and n.)

708 **gone** go

710 **Sundays** the day of the Sabbath in the Christian tradition, given over to worship and rest. Mercy has earlier commanded Mankind to observe the Sabbath (see 300 and n.).
on the morrow in the morning
early betime early in the day. Cf. Ophelia's song: 'Tomorrow is Saint Valentine's Day, / All in the morning betime' (*Ham* 4.5.48–9).

712 **forbear** abstain from
mass . . . prime Nowadays describes the 'offices' of the medieval church, which began at daybreak (or earlier) with *matins* (from the Latin for 'belonging to the early morning'), proceeded to the *mass* (the celebration

701 SD1] *this edn*   SD2] *Adams subst.*   706 are] *(*arn*)*

'I will', say ye.

MANKIND   I will, sir.

MISCHIEF

Ye must have by your side a long *da pacem*,

As true men ride by the way for to unbrace them,   715

Take their money, cut their throats, thus over-face them.

'I will', say ye.

MANKIND   I will, sir.

[*Enter* NOUGHT, *with the jacket cut down even more.*]

NOUGHT

Here is a jolly jacket! How say ye?

NEW-GUISE

It is a good jake-of-fence for a man's body.

[*Puts it on Mankind and they chase him.*]

Hey, dog, hey! Whoop whoo! Go your way lightly!   720

---

of the Eucharist, where consecrated bread representing Christ's body is served in imitation of the Last Supper), and included set *hours* for prayer and devotion (see *OED* canonical *a.* (and *sb.*) 1b), one of which was *prime*, the first such 'hour' in the day – usually observed at 6 a.m. or sunrise. Nowadays's point is that their visit to the *ale-house* (711) will replace these unpleasant, early activities.

714 *da pacem* peace-maker (literally, 'give-peace' in Latin): a sword or dagger. Mischief's ironic euphemism borrows the beginning of a popular prayer; cf. '*Da pacem domine*' ('Give us peace, O Lord'), found in both *Primer*'s '*Officium beate marie. Per aduentum*' (1531, f. clii) and in Sternhold, *Psalms*, 266–71.

715 **true men** faithful, upright citizens. See *OED* trueman, and cf. *1H4* 2.2.90: 'The thieves have bound the true men.'

for to in order to

unbrace undress (i.e. so as to reveal any hidden *money*, 716)

716 **over-face** overwhelm, intimidate through brazenness (*OED v.* 1a, citing this instance as its first usage)

718 **jolly** splendid, good-looking (here ironic); cf. *R3* 4.3.43: 'To her go I, a jolly thriving wooer.' Meredith suggests that the 'shortening of the gown parallels Mankind's acceptance of evil', moving him 'visually from respectability to high fashion, and from decency to vulgarity' (Meredith, *Acting*, 35).

719 **jake-of-fence** protective jacket; *jake* is short for 'jacket' here and *fence* is a shortened form of 'defence' (see *MED* fens *sb.* 2b).

720 **Hey, dog, hey** New-Guise teases Mankind as though he were a dog (see 721n.), perhaps quoting a popular song; cf. *Pammelia*: 'My Dame has in her hutch at home, a little dog, hey dog hey, with a clog' (C1ʳ).

717 SD] *Adams subst.*   719 SD] *Lester subst.*

Ye are well made for to run.

MISCHIEF

Tidings, tidings! I have espied one!

Hence with your stuff, fast we were gone!

I beshrew the last shall come to his home.

ALL

Amen! 725

[Enter MERCY.*]*

MERCY

What ho, Mankind! Flee that fellowship, I you pray!

MANKIND

I shall speak with thee another time, tomorn, or the
next day.

We shall go forth together to keep my father's year–day.

A tapster, a tapster! Stow, stot, stow!

Whoop whoo Cf. Mankind's similar interjections upon waking at 607.
lightly quickly
721 New–Guise comments sarcastically as Mankind is chased about the stage. Bevington suggests the shortened *jacket* (718) may resemble that of a racing dog – hence New–Guise's remark at 719.
722 **Tidings, tidings** i.e. there is news.
espied spotted, found out
one someone (Mischief sees Mercy approaching)
723 **stuff** i.e. the properties which the Vices have brought with them: New–Guise's *noose* (611 SD), Nowadays's 'items from a church' (630 SD), and Mischief's own *broken chains* (637 SD).
we were let us be
724 I curse the last one still here.
725 **Amen** This assent is in keeping with the Vices' confederation, but there is a chance that the entire Latin phrase in the MS, '*amen dicant omnes*', may also be spoken aloud by Mischief in parody

of a priest. Metre and rhyme suggest this phrase is pronounced in full at the close of the anti–monastic ballad 'Friars, ministri malorum', which, alternating English and Latin lines, ends: 'fader ffyrst in trinite, / *ffilius atque fflamen*. / *Omnes dicant Amen*' (*Historical Poems*, 164–5).
727 **tomorn** tomorrow
728 **to . . . year–day** to observe the anniversary of my father's death (*OED* year–day 2). In contrast to what Mankind suggests in the next line, such services were typically solemn.
729 Mankind calls for one who will serve beer or ale (see 'common tapster of Bury' at 274 and n.), analogizing this request to the cry of a falconer summoning his bird; cf. *Magnificence*, Neuss, 125: 'Stow, bird, stow, stow! / It is best I feed my hawk now' (ll. 966–7). He imagines this bird as a woman, for which the word *stot* is a disparaging term, akin to 'slut'. See *MED* stot *sb*. 2a.

721 run] *(ren)* 725] *(amen dicant omnes)* 725 SD] *Manly* 727 thee] *Manly; not in MS* 729 stot] *(statt)*

MISCHIEF

Ah, mischief go with thee! Here I have a foul fall.   730

Hence, away from me, or I shall beshit you all.

NEW-GUISE

What ho, ostler, ostler! Lend us a football!

Whoop how! Anow, anow, anow, anow!

[Exeunt all but Mercy.]

MERCY

My mind is dispersed, my body trembleth as the aspen

leaf.

The tears should trickle down by my cheeks, were

not your reverence.   735

It were to me solace, the cruel visitation of death.

Without rude behaviour I cannot express this

inconvenience.

730 Mischief is apparently tripped by his companions as they attempt to exit; he curses them, ironically using his own name.

731 **beshit** shit upon

732 **ostler** innkeeper. See *OED* 1b, from *hosteler*, one who keeps an *hostel*.
    football Perhaps responding to Mischief's *fall* (730), New-Guise calls for a football to initiate a formal version of this boisterous game in which tripping often occurs. In *KL*, Kent will paint football as socially low: 'Nor tripped neither, you base football player' (1.4.84–5). Because it sometimes included entire villages, and quickly got out of hand, football was also seen as a dangerous game, and thus in some localities restricted by law to particular seasons.

733 New-Guise probably performs some aggressive activity (perhaps directed at Mercy) as he speaks this line.
    Anow now (*MED* anou *adv.*)

734 **dispersed** scattered, distracted. See

MED dispersen *v.* 1c, citing as its sole instance this line. This verb is almost always used with demonstrably plural subjects, such as sheep, cows, crowds of people, letters, money, etc.
    trembleth . . . leaf a conventional simile, reflecting the European aspen's botanical name, *populus tremula*. Cf. Golding: 'I trembling like an aspen leaf stood sad and bloodlesse quyght' (14.245).

735 **were . . . reverence** except that I have respect for you

736 Even death would be a comfort (*solace*) to me now.

737 ***cannot** emended by Manly from MS *kan* for sense: Mercy is explaining the awkwardness of his situation.
    inconvenience offence, moral impropriety. From late Latin *inconvenientia*, 'inconsistency'. For its moral reference, see *OED sb.* 2, citing *The Play of the Sacrament*: 'Agaynst god yf ye haue wroght eny Inconuenyence' (line 897).

730 Ah] *(A)* thee] *Lester; not in MS*   733 SD] *Adams subst.*   734] SCENE III *Eccles*   737 cannot] *Manly;* kan *MS*

Weeping, sighing and sobbing were my sufficience.
All natural nutriment to me as carrion is odible.
My inward affliction yieldeth me tedious unto your
                      presence.   740
I cannot bear it evenly that Mankind is so flexible.

Man unkind, wherever thou be! For all this world was
                  not apprehensible
To discharge thine original offence, thraldom and
                       captivity,
Till God's own well-beloved son was obedient and
                       passible.

738 **sufficience** sustenance, what will sustain (me) (*OED* 3, citing this passage). See also 2 Corinthians, 9.8: 'alle thingis euermore hauynge al sufficience' (Wycliffe).

739 All ordinary nourishment is now as hateful (*odible*) to me as rotten flesh (*carrion*). For *odible*, see Lydgate's *Fall of Princes*: 'His olde hatreed was so venymous / And so odible to destroie me' (ll. 4014–15). For *carrion*, commonly associated with flies, vultures and stench, see *OED sb.* (and *a.*) 2a.

740 What I feel inside makes me a wearying spectacle for you.

741 **evenly** with evenness of mind
flexible pliant (hence easily misled, ready and able to change). See *OED* flexible, *a.* (*sb.*) 3b, and cf. *3H6* 1.4.141: 'Women are soft, mild, pitiful, and flexible.'

742 **Man unkind** a pun (with *Mankind* from 741), and common phrase. Cf. the Digby *Christ's Resurrection*: 'O, most vnkind man! / What creatur may or can / The from sclaunder kepe?' (*Religious Plays*, 180, ll. 380–2); and the two fifteenth-century ballads, 'Unkind Man, Take Heed of Me', and 'Why Art Thou, Man, Unkind?'

in *Religious Lyrics*, 158–62. Cf. 280 and n.
apprehensible capable of attaining (*MED*, citing this passage as sole instance). Mercy's point is that, until Christ's sacrifice, humanity (*all this world*) was not aware enough to atone for original sin.

743 **original offence** humanity's first disobedience in the Garden of Eden
thraldom bondage, servitude. Cf. *Monologue*, 113: 'The children of Israel – to thraldom Institute / In the land of Egipte without refute'.
captivity The Latin form of this word (*captivitas*), like its English equivalent, is used in the Bible to describe the bondage of the Israelites. Here the idea is metaphorical, alluding to the captivity of sin.

744 **obedient** Cf. Philippians, 2.8: 'He humbled hym selfe, made obedient vnto death, euen the death of the crosse.'
passible capable of suffering or feeling. See *OED a.* 1a, and cf. Lydgate's 'The Fifteen Ooes of Christ': 'Wich thow sufferedist, to saue man fro myschaunce, / And for our love were pacyently passyble' (Lydgate, *Minor Poems*, 1.242, ll. 127–8).

739 carrion] *(caren)*

Every drop of his blood was shed to purge thine
iniquity.   745
I discommend and disallow thine often mutability.
To every creature thou art dispectuous and odible.
Why art thou so uncourteous, so inconsiderate? Alas,
woe is me!
As the vane that turneth with the wind, so thou art
convertible.

In trust is treason; thy promise is not credible;   750
Thy perversious ingratitude I cannot rehearse.
To God and to all the holy court of heaven thou art
despectible,

746 **discommend** find fault with, disapprove of. Cf. Kent to Oswald in *KL* 2.2.107–8: 'To go out of my dialect, which you discommend so much'.
often frequent (an adjective; cf. *OED adv.* and *a.* B).
mutability changefulness. Cf. *flexible* at 741.

747 **dispectuous** contemptible (*MED* despectuous *adj.*). Cf. *Legendys*, 281: 'If ony lyf of more despecteuousnesse / She coude han fondyn in ony thyng' (ll. 10358–9). See also *despectible* at 752.

748 ***uncourteous** rude, ignoble (*MED* uncourteis *adj.*). Repeated at 768, *uncourteous*, with its root word *court*, helps frame a string of judicial references that effectively counterpoint the mock trial conducted by Mischief (664–725). Bevington reads MS as offering '*ouer curtess*', i.e. 'over-courteous', though Manly and others read *on*, i.e. 'un-'.

749 **As . . . wind** proverbial: 'as wavering (variable) as the weathercock' (Tilley, W223)
convertible changeable, able to be converted or turned towards something.

Cf. Chaucer, 'The Cook's Tale': 'Al have he no part of the minstralcye; / For thefte and riot, they ben convertible' (4394–5).

750–1 *MS reads *þis promes* and *Thys peruersyose*; we follow Manly in emending to extend the personal application of Mercy's apostrophe. Cf. *thine* (743, 745, 746) and *their* (762).

750 **In . . . treason** proverbial, suggesting that trust is in this case delusive; cf. *ODEP*, 842.

751 **perversious** wicked (*MED* and *OED*, citing only this instance)
rehearse give an account of, narrate

752 ***God and MS** *go on*. Eccles's emendation provides a convincing object to Mercy's statement; Mercy uses the phrase 'to God' at 20 and 280, as does Mankind at 223.
court of heaven with play on *uncourteous* (see 748 and n.). Cf. Constance on her dead son in *KJ* 3.4.87: 'I shall meet him in the court of heaven.'
despectible contemptible, unworthy (*MED*, citing, as with 747's *dispectuous*, only this instance).

746 thine] *MS* (*Þin*) *as read by Eccles;* Þis *MS as reported by Manly*   mutability] *Manly;* imutabylyte *MS*   748 uncourteous] *Manly subst.;* ouer curtess *MS as read by Bevington;* on curtess *MS as reported by Manly*   749 vane] *(*fane*)*   750 thy] *Manly;* Þis *MS*   751 Thy] *Manly;* Thys *MS*   752 God and] *Eccles;* go on *MS*

As a noble versifier maketh mention in this verse:
'Lex et natura, Cristus et omnia jura
Damnant ingratum, lugent eum fore natum.'   755

O good Lady and mother of mercy, have pity and
                              compassion
Of the wretchedness of Mankind, that is so wanton
                              and so frail!
Let mercy exceed justice, dear mother, admit this
                              supplication,
Equity to be laid on party and mercy to prevail.

Too sensual living is reprovable, that is nowadays,   760
    As by the comprehense of this matter it may be
                              specified.
New-Guise, Nowadays, Nought with their allectuous
                              ways

753 **noble versifier** No other trace of these (simple) verses survives; here the phrase seems a way of dignifying the Latin.

754–5 'Law and Nature, Christ and all Justice condemn the ungrateful one, and lament his very birth' (Latin). Puttenham cites similar rhyming Latin in his indictment of the practice of 'monastical men' and 'every scholar and secular clerk' who, when they 'wrote any short poem or matter of good lesson, put it in rhyme, whereby it came to pass that all your old proverbs and common sayings, which they would have plausible to the reader and easy to remember and bear away, were of that sort as these' (Puttenham, 103–4).

756 **good Lady** i.e. Mary

758 **Let . . . justice** Punning on his own name, Mercy asks that forgiveness triumph over punishment. Cf. Portia

in *MV* 4.1.192–3: 'earthly power doth then show likest God's / When mercy seasons justice.'

759 **Equity . . . party** Mercy's *supplication* (758) or plea is that fairness (*Equity*) be given to one side in this trial of Mankind; see *OED* party *sb.* 3a, which sees the phrase *on a party* as referring to one side (as in a legal disputation). For *Equity* see *OED* 1, 2, and, for its legal sense, cf. Lear to the Fool: 'thou, his yoke-fellow of equity, / Bench by his side' (*KL* 3.6.37–8).

760 The current habit of living too sensually is reprehensible (*reprovable*); with pun on Nowadays's name.

761 **comprehense** observation, understanding (*MED*, citing this instance alone)
    specified made plain

762 **allectuous** alluring, seductive (*MED*, citing this instance alone; from Latin *allectare*, 'entice')

754 ²*et*] *Manly;* sit *MS*

They have perverted Mankind, my sweet son,
            I have well espied.

Ah, with these cursed caitiffs, an I may, he shall not
                  long endure.
I, Mercy, his father ghostly, will proceed forth and
                  do my property.   765
Lady, help! This manner of living is a detestable pleasure.
Vanitas vanitatum, all is but a vanity.

Mercy shall never be convict of his uncourteous condition.
With weeping tears by night and by day I will go
                  and never cease.
Shall I not find him? Yes, I hope. Now God be my
                  protection!   770
[*Calls.*] My predilect son, where be ye? Mankind,
                  ubi es?   [*Exit.*]

---

764 **caitiffs** wretches, villains. With *cursed*, a conventional alliterative phrase; cf. the Second Pharisee in *The Glovers Playe* (in *Chester*, 238): 'O cursed caytyffe, yll moote thow thee!' (st. 28, line 205).
an I may if I have my way
765 **do my property** exercise my distinctive quality or attribute (i.e. providing mercy). See *OED* property *sb.* 5a, b, and cf. Haphazard, the Vice, in *Apius*, 2.118: 'By the gods, I know not how best to devise, / My name or my property well to disguise.'
767 *Vanitas vanitatum* vanity of vanities (Latin). See Ecclesiastes, 1.2: '*vanitas vanitatum dixit Ecclesiastes vanitas vanitatum omnia vanitas*'; 'Vanitie of vanities, sayth the Preacher: vanitie of vanities, all is vanitie' (Geneva). This well-known biblical passage introduces an indictment of the worldly *pleasure*

(766) that Mercy detests. Cf. 909.
768 **convict . . . condition** overcome by his (Mankind's) ignoble state. For *convict* as 'overcome', see 405n.; for *uncourteous*, see 748n.
771 **predilect** chosen or favoured in preference to others. *OED*, like *MED*, cites this and 872 as the first examples of this word in English. From post-classical Latin *praedilectus*, 'well-beloved, preferred'.
where be ye a familiar plaintive tag, Latinized later in the line (see following note)
ubi es? Where are you? (Latin). Perhaps a version of Genesis, 3.9, where God searches for Adam (arguably wayward, like Mankind): 'And the Lorde called Adam, & sayde vnto hym: where art thou?' (Vulgate: *vocavitque Dominus Deus Adam et dixit ei ubi es*). See also 775–6 and n.

771 SD1] *Adams*   SD2] *Lester*

[*Enter* MISCHIEF *and* NEW-GUISE.]

MISCHIEF [*to the exiting Mercy*]

My prepotent father, when ye sup, sup out your mess.
Ye are all to-gloried in your terms; ye make many a lease. –
Will ye hear? He crieth ever, 'Mankind, *ubi es?*'

NEW-GUISE

Hic hic, hic hic, hic hic, hic hic! 775
That is to say, here, here, here! Nigh dead in the creek.
If ye will have him, go and seek, seek, seek!
Seek not overlong, for losing of your mind!

[*Enter* NOWADAYS.]

NOWADAYS

If ye will have Mankind, ho, *Domine, Domine, Dominus!*

---

772 **prepotent** greatly powerful or authoritative (*OED*), from classical Latin *praepotent–*, *praepotens*, 'superior to others in power, outstandingly powerful'
father ironically reversing Mercy's *son* (771)
sup . . . mess Swallow up your meal. Like his earlier *ba me* (cf. 430 and n.), Mischief's playful injunction mimics a parent speaking to a child – here, a directive during a meal. See *OED* sup *v.*[1] and *OED* mess *sb.*[1] 2a: 'A portion or serving of liquid or pulpy food such as milk, broth, porridge, boiled vegetables, etc'. An ironic reversal of *prepotent father*.
773 **to-gloried** overly proud, exultant
terms style of speaking (*OED* term *sb.* 14a)
774 Mischief shifts address as he calls attention to Mercy's behaviour.
775–6 New-Guise's *hic*/here pairing continues the 'where be ye'/'*ubi es*'

conjunction of 771 – *hic* means 'here' in Latin – but, as Marshall (112) points out, it also exactly replicates phrasing in *Edmund* (81). In this narrative of the Bury monastery's patron saint, Edmund's severed head, responding to a search party's clamour of '*Ubi es?*', cries out 'her, her, her' (i.e. 'here'), which is immediately glossed in Latin as 'Hic, hic, hic' (ll. 32–4).
776 **Nigh** nearly
778 **for losing** for fear of losing
779 *Domine . . . Dominus* Lord, Lord our Lord (Latin). Cf. Psalms, 8.2: '*Domine Dominus noster quam admirabile est nomen tuum in universa terra quoniam elevata est magnificentia tua super caelos*', translated in the Bishops' Bible as 'O God our Lorde, howe excellent is thy name in all the earth? for that thou hast set thy glory aboue the heauens' (8.1). Nowadays perhaps accompanies this Latin with a parodic liturgical gesture.

772 SD] *Lester subst.* 776 Nigh] *Manly subst.;* my *MS* dead] *(dede)* 778 SD] *this edn;* Enter NOWADAYS *and* NOUGHT, *who urinate with their backs to the audience.* | *Lester*

Ye must speak to the shrieve for a *cape corpus*,   780
Else ye must be fain to return with *non est inventus.*
[*to Nought*] How say ye, sir? My bolt is shot.
NOUGHT [*from offstage*]
I am doing of my needings – beware how ye shoot!

[*Enter* NOUGHT, *with his foot befouled.*]

Fie, fie, fie! I have foul arrayed my foot.
Be wise for shooting with your tackles, for God wot   785
My foot is foully overshot.

---

780 **shrieve** sheriff. Cf. *OED* sheriff, which relates this word etymologically to 'shire-reeve'.

cape corpus take the body (Latin). An arrest warrant, the phrase coming from Latin *capias*, 'thou mayest take' and *corpus*, 'body' (*OED*); cf. the erotic parody in *FQ*, where Cupid, angry with Mirabella, 'In great displeasure, wild a *Capias* / Should issue forth, t'attach that scornefull lasse. / The warrant straight was made' (6.7.35).

781 **fain** content, glad under the circumstances (*OED a.* and *adv.* 2)

non est inventus The person is not to be found (Latin): 'a phrase used by a sheriff in returning a writ, as a statement that the defendant is not to be found in the sheriff's jurisdiction' (*OED*)

782 **My . . . shot** i.e. I'm done speaking (with implication of having run out of things to say); cf. the proverb 'A fool's bolt is soon shot' (*ODEP*, 276). Nought, just out of sight (see 783 and n.), will understand this to mean that Nowadays is doing the same thing he is.

783 **doing . . . needings** satisfying my bodily needs (here, most likely defecating). With whatever realism,

and whether visible, Nought has clearly begun to relieve himself while Nowadays speaks (779–82). Nought's phrase and action contrast markedly with Mercy's *do my property* (765), which implies a vocational or allegorical function rather than bodily necessity. Cf. 375 SD.

shoot aim, with play on 'shit', of which *schott* (MS) is an alternate spelling. Nought offers generally applicable advice on the need for care when eliminating. His *beware* is sometimes taken to indicate that Nowadays joins him in this loose stage business, although Nought in the next line blames only himself for this faulty aim.

784 **arrayed** befouled, defiled; see *OED* array *v.* 10c., and cf. *Johan Johan*: 'And bycause it is arayed at the skyrt / Whyle ye do nothyng skrape of the dyrt' (ll. 256–7).

785 **wise for** careful when

shooting discharging (here, urine or faeces) from your body

tackles gear, tools; cf. *MED* takel *sb.* 3, with quotation from 1425 referring to the male sexual organ.

wot knows

786 **foully overshot** i.e. befouled (with faeces or urine)

---

780 shrieve] (schryue)   782 SD] *Lester*   shot] *Manly subst.;* schett *MS*   783 SD1] *this edn*   783 SD2] *this edn*

MISCHIEF

> A parliament, a parliament! Come forth, Nought,
> > behind.
>
> A counsel! Believe, I am afeard Mercy will him find.
>
> How say ye, and what say ye? How shall we do with
> > Mankind?

NEW-GUISE

> Tish, a fly's wing! Will ye do well?   790
>
> He weeneth Mercy were hung for stealing of a mare.
>
> Mischief, go say to him that Mercy seeketh everywhere.
>
> He will hang himself, I undertake, for fear.

MISCHIEF

> I assent thereto; it is wittily said and well.

NOWADAYS

> Whip it in thy coat; anon it were done.   795
>
> Now Saint Gabriel's mother save the clouts of thy shoon!
>
> All the books in the world, if they had be undone,

---

787 **parliament** i.e. 'Let's assemble!' (see *MED* parlemente *sb.* 2a)
Nought, behind Mischief may ask Nought to stand *behind* the rest owing to the stench of his *foully overshot* foot (786).

788 **counsel** conversational gathering
Believe i.e. believe me
afeard afraid

789 ²**How** what. Cf. York in *R2* 2.2.104: 'How shall we do for money for these wars?'

790 **Tish** an exclamation of impatience or contempt (see *OED* tush *int. sb.*³)
fly's wing i.e. a worthless thing (see *OED* wing *sb.* I.1e, citing this passage)
Will . . . well Do you wish to succeed?

791 **weeneth** believes

792 **seeketh** i.e. for Mankind (hence the following line)

793 **hang himself** New-Guise may

brandish the very noose that he has earlier worn (cf. 611 SD, 616 and n., 617).

795 **Whip it** conceal it quickly (see *OED* whip *v.* 2a, citing this passage). Nowadays may address Mischief, who will presently brag that he has the noose (801). The word *Whip* here ironically anticipates Mercy's *baleys* (807).

796 **Saint . . . shoon** May St Gabriel's mother save your shoes (*shoon*)! A mock blessing, given the inappropriateness of the intercessor (as an archangel, *Gabriel* would have no *mother*) and the object to be saved: *clouts* usually referred to patches, as when a cobbler repaired shoes. It also described the heavy plates or nails that some country folk attached to the bottom of their shoes to increase their wear. See *OED* clout-shoe 1, 2.

797 **undone** opened

---

795 Whip] (qwyppe); I whip *Manly*   796 clouts] *Manly;* clothes *MS*

Could not ha' counselled us bet.
Here Mischief exits [and returns immediately with MANKIND].

MISCHIEF

Ho, Mankind! Come and speak with Mercy, he is here
        fast by.

MANKIND

A rope, a rope, a rope! I am not worthy.   800

MISCHIEF

Anon, anon, anon! I have it here ready,
    With a tree also that I have get.
    [They bring in a gallows.]

Hold the tree, Nowadays! Nought, take heed and
        be wise!

NEW-GUISE

Lo, Mankind, do as I do: *[Puts his own head in the noose.]*
        this is thy new guise.
Give the rope just to thy neck; this is mine advice.   805

        [Enter MERCY, *with a rod.]*

MISCHIEF

Help thyself, Nought! Lo, Mercy is here!

798 **bet** better
799 **fast** close. Cf. Warwick in *2H6*
3.2.189: 'And sees fast by a butcher
with an axe'.
800 **rope** i.e. with which he might hang
himself
802 **tree** gallows. Mischief presumably
refers to a makeshift wooden stand that
will represent a formal structure for
hanging. For the 'dry tree' as gallows,
see *OED sb.* 4a, citing *Perseverance*, 10:
'Pyncecras parys & longe pygmayne /
& euery toun in trage euyn to the dreye
tre' (ll. 176–7).
get got

803 **Hold . . . Nowadays** The *tree* seems
to be of manageable enough size for
Nowadays to hold it upright without
the help of Mischief (who gives the
orders here), Nought (who is told
to stand by and observe) or New-
Guise (who mimes choking while
demonstrating the noose).
804 **new guise** punning, once again, on
his own name
805 **Give . . . neck** Put the noose just like
this around your neck. See *OED* give
v. 41, which discusses this obsolete
sense 'where *put* or *set* would now be
used'.

798 ha'] *(a)* SD *Here Mischief exits*] *(*hic exit myscheff*) and . . .* MANKIND] *Manly* 802 SD,
804 SD] *Adams subst.* 805 thy] *Manly subst.;* pye *MS* SD] *Lester subst.*

He scareth us with a baleys; we may no longer tarry.
[*They run about. New-Guise strangles on the rope.*]

NEW-GUISE

Queck, queck, queck! Alas, my throat! I beshrew you,
marry!
Ah, Mercy, Christ's copped curse go with you, and
Saint Davy!
Alas, my weasand! Ye were somewhat too near.   810
Exeunt [*all but Mercy and Mankind*].

MERCY

Arise, my precious redempt son! Ye be to me full dear.
[*aside*] He is so timorous, meseemeth his vital spirit
doth expire.

MANKIND

Alas, I have be so bestially disposed, I dare not appear.
To see your solacious face I am not worthy to desire.

807 Mercy's wielding of the *baleys* neatly reverses the situation from earlier in the play, when the Vices had held it (see 73 and n., 76 and n.).

808 As his companions scurry about in fear of Mercy's rod, New-Guise makes the sound of being strangled by the noose he has so cavalierly been demonstrating to Mankind. Cf. 516 and n.

809 **copped** saucy, crabbed (*OED ppl. a.* 4b)
Saint Davy i.e. St David, patron saint of Wales

810 **weasand** wind-pipe, or throat generally

811 **redempt** redeemed. See *OED* redempt *pa. pple.* and *ppl. a.*, citing this and *Everyman* (Q3, Q4) as its only instances; cf. 'I cum with Knowlege for my redemcyon / Redempt with herte and full of contrycyon' (*Everyman*, 548–9).

812 **timorous** fearful

vital spirit living force (located, according to medieval physiology, in the heart). Cf. Stanyhurst, 54: 'When fro Neoptolemus thee vital spirit abated' (3.346).

813 **bestially disposed** oriented to living as a beast does. Cf. the words of Wrath to the Pilgrim in ther degre. Lydgate's translation of Guillaume de Deguileville's *The Pilgrimage of the Life of Man*: 'I cause hem that they may nat se / But bestyally in ther degre. / I trouble hem (in especyal) / That they be verray bestyal' (Lydgate, *Minor Poems*, 420, ll. 15625–8).
I . . . appear Here Mankind reveals the very *fear* that New-Guise has predicted at 793.

814 **solacious** that which gives solace (*OED*). Cf. Skelton, Henderson, 75, on Chaucer in 'Phyllyp Sparowe': 'His mater is delectable, / Solacious, and commendable' (ll. 790–1).

807 SD] *Bevington subst.*   810 SD *all . . . Mankind*] *Adams subst.*   812 SD] *Lester*   is] ys ys *MS*

MERCY

Your criminous complaint woundeth my heart as
a lance.   815
Dispose yourself meekly to ask mercy, and I will
assent.
Yield me neither gold nor treasure, but your humble
obeisance,
The voluntary subjection of your heart, and I am
content.

MANKIND

What, ask mercy yet once again? Alas, it were a vile
petition.
Ever to offend and ever to ask mercy, it is a puerility.   820
It is so abominable to rehearse my iterate transgression,
I am not worthy to have mercy, by no possibility.

MERCY

O Mankind, my singular solace, this is a lamentable
excuse.
The dolorous tears of my heart, how they begin to
amount!
O pierced Jesu, help thou this sinful sinner to reduce!   825

815 **criminous** guilty; cf. the anonymous
fifteenth-century poem *Knyghthode*,
46: 'But vse not the medycyne extreme
/ Save in thin vtterest necessitee, /
That is, the crymynous to deth to
deme' (st. 39, ll. 1244–6).
816 **Dispose** prepare, make ready; cf.
bestially disposed at 813.
ask mercy i.e. ask *for* mercy, though
the speaker's name here makes for
a situational pun. Mercy counsels
Mankind to *ask mercy anon* at 305;
Mankind complies at 541 and, with
unintentional irony, says at 650: 'I ask
mercy of New-Guise, Nowadays and

Nought.' Cf. also 819, 820, 859, 863.
817 **obeisance** obedience, submission.
Cf. Nature in *Nature* (93), who urges
Man 'To honour your maker wyth
humble obeysance' (line 72).
819 **it . . . petition** i.e. it would be a
loathsome request
820 **puerility** childishness
821 **iterate** repeated, iterated
824 **dolorous** grievous, distressful (*OED*
2); cf. *AC* 4.2.39: 'You take me in too
dolorous a sense.'
amount increase, rise (*OED v.* 4a)
825 **pierced** i.e. because nailed to the cross
and poked with a spear (see John, 19.34)

825 pierced] (piessie)

Nam haec est mutatio dexterae Excelsi; vertit impios
et non sunt.

Arise and ask mercy, Mankind, and be associate to me.

Thy death shall be my heaviness; alas, 'tis pity it
should be thus.

Thy obstinacy will exclude thee from the glorious
perpetuity.

Yet for my love ope thy lips and say '*Miserere mei,*
Deus!'   830

MANKIND

The egal justice of God will not permit such a sinful
wretch

To be revived and restored again; it were impossible.

---

reduce recover from error. See *OED v.*
8a: 'To lead or bring back from error
in action, conduct, or belief, *esp.* in
matters of morality or religion', citing
the *Digby Mysteries* (*c.* 1485): 'Whan I
erryd, thu reducyd me, Iesus' (5.313).
This renders literally the Latin roots:
re-ducere, to lead back.

826 For this is the effect of the right
hand of God; he overturns the
impious, and they are no more
(Latin). A combination of lines from
two places in the Bible. Cf. Psalms,
76.11 (77.10 KJV), *et dixi nunc*
coepi haec mutatio dexterae Excelsi,
translated as: 'And I sayde, this is
my death: but the ryght hande of the
most hyghest [may graunt] me yeres';
and Proverbs, 12.7: '*verte impios*
et non erunt domus autem iustorum
permanebit', 'God ouerturneth the
[estate of the] wicked, and they
stande not: but the house of the
ryghteous shall stande.'

827 **associate** joined in companionship
(*OED ppl. a.* 1); cf. *Enough*: 'to be
associate with the righteous' (G1').

828 **shall be** would be (i.e. were it to
occur with you in this unrepentant
state)

829 **perpetuity** i.e. afterlife. On the
perpetual duration of the Christian
afterlife, see John, 3.16: 'For God so
loued the worlde, that he gaue his
only begotten sonne, that whosoeuer
beleueth in hym, shoulde not
perishe, but haue euerlastyng lyfe.'
This term also had a specific sense
in the law and institutional practice
which implied 'endless or indefinite
duration or existence' (*OED sb.* 1b,
citing a 1455 reference to 'eny benefice,
college, chauntre, or other Office of
perpetuete').

830 **for my love** for love of me. Cf. *Son*
40.5: 'Then if for my love thou my
love receivest'.
Miserere mei, Deus 'Have mercy upon
me, God' (Latin). A common biblical
phrase, found (in various forms) in
Job, 19.21; Matthew, 15.22; and Mark,
10.48. It begins Psalms 50, 55, 56 (KJV
51, 56, 57), and appears in ten others.
See 520n. on *neck-verse*.

831 **egal** impartial, equal; see *OED* egall
a., and cf. *MV* 3.4.13: 'Whose souls do
bear an egall yoke of love'.

832 Contrast Mercy's *impossible* action
with Mischief's claim to have restored
Nowadays's head at 435 and 445.

---

826 *haec . . . dexterae*] *Bevington;* hic . . . dextre *MS*   829 thee] *Manly; not in MS*

MERCY

    The justice of God will as I will, as himself doth preach:
    Nolo mortem peccatoris, inquit, if he will be reducible.

MANKIND

    Then mercy, good Mercy! What is a man without
                mercy?   835
    Little is our part of paradise where mercy ne were.
    Good Mercy, excuse the inevitable objection of my
                ghostly enemy.
    The proverb saith, 'The truth trieth the self.' Alas,
                I have much care.

MERCY

    God will not make you privy unto his last judgement.
    Justice and Equity shall be fortified, I will not deny.   840
    Truth may not so cruelly proceed in his strait argument

833 **will . . . will** is disposed as I am disposed (i.e. by virtue of my *property*, 765); see *OED* will *v.*[1] 10a; cf. Romans, 9.15 (of God): 'For he sayth to Moyses: I wyll shewe mercy to whom I shewe mercy: And wyll haue compassion, on whom I haue compassion.'

834 *Nolo . . . inquit* 'He said: "I do not want the death of a sinner"' (Latin). A paraphrase of Ezekiel, 33.11: '*dic ad eos vivo ego dicit Dominus Deus nolo mortem impii*', 'Tell them, as truely as I liue saith the Lorde God, I haue no pleasure in the death of the wicked.' **he** i.e. the sinner (from *peccatoris* in the Latin phrase) **reducible** reclaimable, brought back to right conduct (*OED a.* 1a, citing this passage alone); cf. *reduce* (825).

836 **where . . . were** where mercy does not exist. The implication (perhaps continuing the legal analogy invoked by *perpetuity* at 829 and continued at

839) is that humans will have no access to paradise without the intercession of mercy. The MS reading, *were mercy ne were*, repeats the figure of *paranomasia* or *annominatio* seen in 551 (see n.).

837 **inevitable objection** unavoidable attack. See *OED* objection *sb.* 2, citing this instance and *Arcadia*, 1590: 'The partes either not armed, or weakly armed . . . should haue bene sharpely visited, but that the aunswere was as quicke as the obiection' (27ᵛ).

838 **The truth . . . self** i.e. truth is its own test (and, hence, best witness). See Whiting, T514. Lester cites a fifteenth-century lyric: 'The trewth In dede hyt-selff well preffe' (*Religious Lyrics*, 267).

840–1 Mercy's mention of *Justice, Equity* and *Truth* in these lines invokes (along with his ever-present identity) the 'four daughters of God' (Mercy, Truth, Righteousness and Peace). This group

833 preach] *Manly;* precyse *MS*   834 be reducible] *MS* (be redusyble*) as read by Eccles* ('reducylle' *changed to* 'be redusyble' *by a later hand);* reducylle *MS as read by Bevington*

But that Mercy shall rule the matter without
controversy.

Arise now and go with me in this deambulatory.
Incline your capacity; my doctrine is convenient.
Sin not in hope of mercy; that is a crime notary. 845
To trust overmuch in a prince it is not expedient.

In hope when ye sin ye think to have mercy, beware of
that adventure.
The good Lord said to the lecherous woman of
Canaan —

was generated, during the Middle Ages, from an imaginative interpretation of Psalms, 85.10: 'Mercy and trueth are met together: righteousnes and peace haue kissed [eche other]' (Bishops'; 84.11, Vulgate). They appear as characters in *N-Town* (*Mary Play*) (ll. 1137–1248) and *Perseverance* (ll. 3129–3560), where they discuss the means by which the soul may be saved.

841 **strait** strict, allowing no evasion (i.e. because it represents the unavoidable facts of Mankind's sin). See *OED a.* 8a, where the sense pertains to 'a commandment, law, penalty, vow'.

843 **Arise now** This is the third time (cf. 811, 827) that Mercy has asked Mankind to stand up.
deambulatory place to walk (often covered). See *OED sb.* B, quoting Lydgate's *Chronicle of Troy* (*c.* 1430): 'Fresche alures..That called were deambulatoryes, / Men to walke to geder twayne & twayne, / To kepe them drye when it dyde rayne'.

844 **Incline** turn, orient. Cf. Psalms, 17.6: 'I call vpon thee O God, for thou wilt heare me: incline thine eare to me, hearken vnto my wordes.'
capacity attention, mental ability (*OED* 4, 5); cf. *LLL* 5.2.376–8: 'Your capacity / Is of that nature that to

your huge store / Wise things seem foolish.'
doctrine teaching, instruction
convenient morally proper; cf. *OED a.* 5, citing *Coventry Mysteries* (*c.* 1400): 'It is not convenient a man to be / Ther women gon in travalynge' (149).

845 **notary** well-known, notorious (*OED a.* 1, citing this passage); extending the legal tropes of the previous lines, this word also invokes that sense of *notary* which refers to an individual responsible for recording official information. The pun may intentionally redound upon one who relies, almost legalistically, on the forgiveness technically available from the Church.

846 Do not count on a prince being willing to forgive you (i.e. after the fact); cf. 854.

847 i.e. be careful not to sin thinking that you will be granted mercy. Lester compares Ecclesiasticus/Sirach, 5.4: 'Say not, I have sinned, and what harm hath happened unto me?' (KJV).

848–53 To support his *doctrine* (844) of 'Sin not in hope of mercy' (845), Mercy provides a compressed sermon; he cites scripture, quoting its words, and applies its truths to Mankind's current situation. Here

844] *Manly subst.;* My doctrine ys conuenient Inclyne yowyr capacite *MS*

169

The holy gospel is the authority, as we read in
                                    scripture –
'*Vade et iam amplius noli peccare.*'   850

Christ preserved this sinful woman taken in adultery;
    He said to her these words, 'Go and sin no more.'
So to you, go and sin no more. Beware of vain
                                    confidence of mercy;
Offend not a prince on trust of his favour, as I said
                                    before.

If ye feel yourself trapped in the snare of your ghostly
                                    enemy,   855
    Ask mercy anon; beware of the continuance.
While a wound is fresh it is proved curable by surgery,
    That if it proceed overlong, it is cause of great
                                    grievance.

Mercy recounts the 'woman taken in adultery' incident wherein 'the scribes and pharisees brought vnto hym [i.e. Jesus] a woman taken in adulterie.' Dispersing the accusers by asking that only those without sin remain, 'When Iesus had lyft vp hym selfe, & sawe no man but the woman, he sayde vnto her: Woman where are those thine accusers? Hath no man condempned thee? She sayde, No man Lorde. And Iesus sayde, Neither do I condempne thee: Go, and sinne no more' (John, 8.3–11).

850–3 In the space of four lines, Mercy repeats Christ's words of absolution three times (first in Latin). He thus signals the absolution that, in representing a priest, he has granted Mankind. See 848–53n. and 850n.

850 'Go, and sin no more' (Latin); the Vulgate's version of John, 8.11,

translated by Mercy at 852.
851 **preserved** kept safe from harm, saved the life of
853 **confidence of** trust in
854 *I MS *he*. We follow Manly's emendation for sense. Cf. Mercy's *I said before* (880).
855 For the conventional imagery of Satan's *snare* or net, cf. 303n.
856 **continuance** going on (i.e. in such a state of sin) (*OED* 3a); see *Confessio Amantis*, 377: 'And thus cam into remembrance / Of Senne the continuance' (7.5109–10). Perhaps also with the legal valence of an adjournment of a suit or trial until a future date (*OED* 2).
857–8 Cf. the proverb 'A green wound is soon healed' (Tilley, W927), and *2H6* 3.1.284–6: 'stop the rage betime, / Before the wound do grow uncurable; / For, being green, there is great hope of help.'

851 adultery] *(a wowtry)*   854 I] *Manly;* he *MS*

MANKIND

> To ask mercy and to have, this is a liberal possession.
> Shall this expeditious petition ever be allowed,
> as ye have insight?   860

MERCY

> In this present life mercy is plenty, till death maketh
> his division;
> But when ye be go, *usque ad minimum quadrantem* ye
> shall reckon your right.

> Ask mercy and have, while the body with the soul hath
> his annexion;
> If ye tarry till your decease, ye may hap of your
> desire to miss.
> Be repentant here, trust not the hour of death; think
> on this lesson: 865
> *'Ecce nunc tempus acceptabile, ecce nunc dies salutis.'*

859 **To . . . have** i.e. to ask for mercy and to be granted it
liberal possession ample thing (i.e. to have). Here *liberal* suggests both 'abundant' (*OED a*. 2b) and 'free from restraint' (*OED* 3a) – the latter deriving from the line's first half, where mercy seems available for the asking.

860 **expeditious** quickly made (*OED a*. 1, first citation from 1610)
ever be allowed always be granted

861 **present life** i.e. life on earth. A concept found frequently in the New Testament, where it is contrasted with the afterlife. Cf. 1 Timothy, 4.8: 'godlinesse is profitable vnto all things, which hath the promes of the life present, and of that that is to come' (Geneva).
division separation (i.e. between the living and the dead)

862 **go** gone (i.e. dead)
usque . . . quadrantem all the way to the last farthing (Latin). A paraphrase, with variation, of Matthew, 5.26: 'Uerely I say vnto thee, thou shalt not come out thence, tyll thou hast payde the vtmost farthyng.'

863 **his annexion** union (of body and soul); *MED* annexion (a) (citing this passage). This term must have had a technical meaning relating to the legal institution of the Church, for it appears in a satirical list of over fifty items of 'Romishe marchaundise' in *Freewyl* (27), a list that includes not only 'pardons, graces, priuileges' but also: 'offices and benefices, administrations, commaundries, prebendes, pensions, resignations, vnions, incorporations, annexions, reseruals, regresses, renuntials, resignals, vacations, exchanges'.

864 **may . . . miss** may not attain what you want. Cf. *OED* hap *v*.[1] 1a.

865 **here** i.e. on earth, in *this present life* (861)

866 'Behold, now is the accepted time; behold, now is the day of salvation' (Latin); from 2 Corinthians, 6.2. Cf. also Isaiah, 49.8, of which this is a paraphrase.

862 shall] *Manly;* scha *MS*   863 soul] *Manly;* sowe *MS*   his] *MS as reported by Manly (* hys*); yys MS*

171

All the virtue in the world if ye might comprehend
Your merits were not premiable to the bliss above,
Not to the least joy of heaven, of your proper effort to
ascend.
With mercy ye may; I tell you no fable, scripture
doth prove.   870

MANKIND

O Mercy, my suavious solace and singular recreatory,
My predilect special, ye are worthy to have my love;
For without desert and means supplicatory
Ye be compatient to my inexcusable reprove.

Ah, it sweameth my heart to think how unwisely I have
wrought.   875

---

867 (even) if you happened to possess all the virtue in the world
868 **merits** good works viewed as entitling a person to reward from God (*OED sb.* II.4a *Theol.* In *pl.*)
premiable deserving of reward (*OED*) **to** both 'so as to qualify you for' and 'in the eyes of'
869 **proper** own
870 **no fable** i.e. the truth; cf. Chaucer's 'Physician's Tale': 'this is no fable, / But knowen for historial thyng notable' (155–6).
871 **suavious** pleasing, agreeable (*OED*, sole entry from 1669; ultimately deriving from Latin *suavis*, 'sweet, agreeable')
singular special, private
recreatory a source of comfort or recreation (*OED*, citing only this passage; the coinage derives from Medieval Latin *recretorium*, 'place to be refreshed')
872 **predilect** a specially favoured one (see 771n.)
873 **desert** merit, worth
means supplicatory ways of making supplication (i.e. a petition or

other entreaty); see *OED* supplicatory *a.*, citing this passage as its first instance.
874 **compatient** sympathetic, compassionate; *OED*, citing 1 Peter, 3.8: 'In preyer be ye compacient' (Wycliffe).
to in the face of, with
reprove Mankind may mean a generalized shame; but this word also had a related sense involving insult or other open scorn – which could refer to his dismissive lines towards Mercy at 727–9. For *reprove* as shame see *OED* reproof 1 (of which *reprove* is a variant spelling), and cf. 1 Timothy, 3.7: 'For it bihoueth hym to haue also good witnessing of hem that ben with outforth, that he falle not in to repreef, and in to the snare of the deuel' (Wycliffe). For *reprove* as insult, scorn, see *OED* reproof 2.
875 **sweameth** grieves
wrought done (*OED* work *v.* past tense, B.I.1). If *reprove* in 874 is taken as utterance, the (now obsolete) sense of *wrought* meaning 'To utter, speak, say' (*OED* 4b) may apply.

---

867 world] *Manly;* word *MS*   868 premiable] (premyabyll)

172

Titivillus, that goeth invisible, hung his net before
my eye
And by his fantastical visions seditiously sought,
To New-Guise, Nowadays, Nought caused me to
obey.

MERCY

Mankind, ye were oblivious of my doctrine monitory.
I said before, Titivillus would assay you a brunt.   880
Beware from henceforth of his fables delusory.
The proverb saith, '*Jacula praestita minus laedunt.*'

Ye have three adversaries and he is master of them all:
That is to say, the Devil, the World, the Flesh and
the Fell.

876 Cf. 530n.
877 **fantastical visions** imaginary
scenes (*OED* fantastic 1a), i.e. unreal
images that Titivillus has succeeded
in conjuring up: see 594–9, and
cf. *Gwydonius*: 'knowing that these
fantastical visions and presupposed
passions, would in time (if he tooke
not heed) proue but too true' (fol. 26,
sig. Iii).
seditiously sought pursued rebel-
liously (see *OED* seditiously *adv.* and
sedition *sb.* 1, 2). Cf. Golding (116),
of the gods: 'And through this partiall
loue of theirs seditiously increast / A
hurlyburly' (9.509–10).
878 After planting *fantastical visions*
(877) in Mankind's mind (cf. 594–9),
Titivillus instructed him to seek the
good will (603) of the Three Ns.
879–98 Heap notes that Mercy's speech
provides a 'good opportunity for a
tableau' (i.e. a group appearance of
almost all the play's characters) with
its naming of Titivillus and the Three
Ns (Heap, 103).
879 *doctrine** **monitory** warning,

cautionary command (see *OED*
monitory *sb.* and *a.*, B.1, citing this
passage as its first instance). The *MED*
identifies MS *manyterge* as an error;
see monitorie *sb.* and *adj.*
880 **I said before** i.e. at 301–4, where
Mercy has mentioned Titivillus's
invisibility and net, and predicted to
Mankind that this devil 'will round in
your ear' (303).
assay . . . brunt attack, try your
mettle by means of a blow or other
assault (see *OED* assay *v.* 14a; and
brunt *sb.*¹ 1, 2).
881 **delusory** false, deceitful (*MED*,
citing this as its only instance; *OED*
first entry is 1588).
882 *Jacula . . . laedunt* 'Foreseen darts
hurt less' (Latin). Cf. Salisbury, 44:
'Iacula quoque minus laedunt quae
praeuidentur' (27.14).
884 The World, the Flesh, and the
Devil formed a conventional trio of
temptations, an anti-trinity dangerous
to humankind. See Wenzel, 'Enemies'.
Flesh . . . Fell i.e. 'flesh'; see *OED*
flesh *sb.*¹ I.1a: '*flesh and fell*: the whole

879 monitory] *Eccles (Brandl)*; manyterge *MS*   883, 885 them] *Manly*; hem *MS*

The New-Guise, Nowadays, Nought, 'the World'
                    we may them call;   885
    And properly Titivillus signifieth the fiend of hell;

The Flesh, that is the unclean concupiscence of your
                    body.
    These be your three ghostly enemies, in whom ye
                    have put your confidence.
They brought you to Mischief to conclude your
                    temporal glory,
    As it hath be showed before this worshipful audience. 890

Remember how ready I was to help you; from such I
                    was not dangerous;
    Wherefore, good son, abstain from sin evermore
                    after this.
Ye may both save and spill your soul that is so precious.
    Libere velle, libere nolle God may not deny, iwis.

Beware of Titivillus with his net and of all envious will, 895

substance of the body'. For this phrase in conjunction with *World*, cf. Churchyard, 116, 'The Honor of a Soldier': 'World scrats and scrapes, pluckes flesh and fell from bone.'

889 **conclude** restrain, shut up from a course of action (*OED v.* 3a.)

893–4 Mercy argues that Mankind has freedom to determine what happens to his soul. For a strong and controversial statement as to humanity's free will, see the apocryphal book of Ecclesiasticus/Sirach, 15.14–17: 'Hee himselfe made man from the beginning, and left him in the hand of his counsell, If thou wilt, to keepe the Commandements, and to performe acceptable faithfulnesse. He hath set

fire and water before thee: stretch forth thy hand vnto whether thou wilt. Before man is life and death, and whether him liketh shalbe giuen him' (KJV).

893 **save and spill** rescue and (or) destroy. Cf. *Perseverance*: 'god hathe govym man fre arbritracion / whethyr he wyl hym self saue or hys soule spyll' (ll. 24–5).

894 *Libere ... nolle* Free to will, free not to (will) (Latin). Cf. *Freewyl*, 132–3: 'My God created me from the beginning, and left me into the handes of myne owne counsel, and settyng before me lyfe and death, good and yll, gaue me free power to choose whiche I woulde, as Ecclesiasticus doth testifie.' Cf. 893–4n.

894 *velle*] *Manley;* welle *MS*   895 envious] *Furnivall & Pollard (Manly);* enmys *MS*

Of your sinful delectation that grieveth your ghostly
substance.
Your body is your enemy; let him not have his will.
Take your leave when ye will. God send you good
perseverance!

MANKIND

Sith I shall depart, bless me, father, here; then I go.
[*Kneels.*]
God send us all plenty of his great mercy!　　　　900
MERCY

Dominus custodit te ab omni malo
In nomine Patris et Filii et Spiritus Sancti. Amen!
[*Mankind rises.*]　　　　　　　　　*Here exits Mankind.*

Worshipful sovereigns, I have do my property:

896 **sinful delectation** enjoyment of sin; also: enjoyment that is sinful
897 **body . . . enemy** a central moral of the play, for which Mercy draws upon, among other sources, Matthew, 26.41. See 195n.
him . . . his i.e. it . . . its
898 **perseverance** In addition to a general sense of 'persevering' (*OED* 1a), this word had, according to *OED*, a distinct theological valence: 'the action or fact of continuing or remaining in a state of grace, virtue, or religious fidelity; (*Theol.*) continuance in a state of grace until death. In early use freq. in blessings'. See also the term and concept's role in *Perseverance*.
899 **bless . . . here** Mankind most likely kneels to receive Mercy's blessing. If he does so, it would be the fifth time he has kneeled (see 212 SD, 392 SD, 553 SD, 650 SD). At 553 he also uses a locative *here*: 'Here in my kirk I kneel

on my knees.'
900 **God send** subjunctive: 'may God –'
mercy Mankind appropriately ends his dialogue by invoking his dramatic saviour.
901 'God wyll preserue thee from all euill' (Latin); from Psalms, 121.7 (120.7, Bishops').
902 *In . . . Sancti* 'in the name of the father, and of the sonne, and of the holye ghost' (Latin); from Matthew, 28.19. Mercy presumably concludes his formal blessing of Mankind with the sign of the cross. Cf. 440 and n.
903 **Worshipful sovereigns** Upon Mankind's exit, Mercy returns to direct address of the audience, using the term (*sovereigns*) he deployed three times at the play's beginning (13, 25, 29). See also 561.
property Cf. 765 and n.: Mercy repeats that line's promise to *do my property* but here uses the past tense.

899 SD] *this edn*　902 SD1] *this edn*　SD2] (hic exit mankend)

Mankind is delivered by my favoural patrociny.
God preserve him from all wicked captivity   905
And send him grace his sensual conditions to mortify!

Now for his love that for us received his humanity,
Search your conditions with due examination.
Think and remember the world is but a vanity,
As it is proved daily by diverse transmutation.   910

Mankind is wretched, he hath sufficient proof.
Therefore God grant you all *per suam misericordiam*
That ye may be playferes with the angels above
And have to your portion *vitam aeternam.* Amen!   [*Exit.*]

FINIS

904 **favoural patrociny** favouring (i.e. partisan) defence or protection. See *patrocinie* in *MED*, citing this passage alone.

905–6 **preserve . . . send** subjunctive: 'may God –'

906 **sensual conditions** orientations towards bodily pleasure. Cf. Jude, 1.19: 'These be they who separate themselves, sensual, having not the Spirit' (KJV).
mortify See 191 and n.

907 **for his . . . humanity** out of love for him (i.e. Christ) who became human for us. Cf. 830 and n.

908 **Search** examine, consider

909 **world . . . vanity** See 767 and n.

910 **diverse transmutation** various changes

911 **wretched** See Romans, 7.24: 'O wretched man that I am: Who shall deliuer me from the body of this death?'

912 ***grant** not in MS. Clearly a word has been omitted; we follow Eccles's suggestion. For a similar construction, see 144.
per suam misericordiam through his mercy (Latin). The last two words make up a popular biblical phrase; cf. 1 Peter, 1.3: 'Blessed be God the father of our Lorde Iesus Christe, which accordyng to his aboundaunt mercie begat vs agayne vnto a lyuely hope.'

913 **playferes** playfellows, companions; *OED* 1, citing the *Vernon Homilies* (*c.* 1390): 'Crist pleyed with hym as pley fere' (57/276).

914 ***vitam aeternam*** eternal life (Latin). Cf. John, 3.15: 'That whosoeuer beleueth in hym, perishe not, but haue eternall lyfe.'

908 Search] (Serge) 912 grant] Eccles; not in MS; kepe Manly; give Brandl 913 angels] Manly; angell MS 914 SD] this edn

176

THE
SUMMONING
OF
EVERYMAN

LIST OF ROLES

MESSENGER
GOD
DEATH
EVERYMAN
FELLOWSHIP   5
KINDRED
COUSIN
GOODS
GOOD DEEDS
KNOWLEDGE   10
CONFESSION
BEAUTY
STRENGTH
DISCRETION
FIVE WITS   15
ANGEL
DOCTOR

LIST OF ROLES This list is based on the figures' order of appearance. For discussion of casting possibilities, see Appendix 3.

1 MESSENGER a prologue figure, not in the Dutch source play, *Elckerlijc*. See pp. 61–7. Because prologues typically deliver information, dramatists since the classical period have often used messengers in this function. Death is also called a 'messenger' at 63, 114, 266 and 329.

2 GOD the Christian deity, sometimes (as at 29–34) understood to encompass Jesus Christ, his son (see Fig. 11). Productions often place this figure on a raised throne or other structure, and sometimes have God observe the entire play; see pp. 68–9. Referred to as 'Adonai' (cf. 245) in early twentieth-century theatre programmes to avoid offending religious sensibilities

3 DEATH God's servant; a messenger and summoner (i.e. one who officially summons another before justice) who represents the inevitability of mortality. See Figs 12 and 15 for early illustrations.

4 EVERYMAN the representative human figure. See pp. 53–4, 58 and Fig. 15 for an early illustration.

5 FELLOWSHIP good companionship, friends

6 KINDRED those related by blood or descent

7 COUSIN a relative more distant than sisters and brothers (i.e. than 'Kindred' – see List of Roles 6n.)

8 GOODS worldly possessions. Some productions have surrounded Goods with moneybags from the beginning of the performance. See pp. 50–1 and Fig. 13.

9 GOOD DEEDS the first female figure so identified in the play, representing virtuous acts, particularly those sanctioned by religion, such as giving alms and charity. *Elck* has '*Duecht*', which may be translated as 'Virtue'. See pp. 55–6 for the doctrinal significance of good deeds. Some productions have Good Deeds lying onstage from the

beginning of the performance. See Appendix 3.

10 KNOWLEDGE Everyman's *guide* (522) to religious salvation, Knowledge stands separately from Everyman, representing external truth and instruction rather than wisdom that Everyman might possess. See p. 56 and Figs 17 and 18. Like Good Deeds, a female figure

11 CONFESSION A *holy man* who dwells in the *house of salvation* (539–40), Confession stands for one of the holy sacraments and functions as a priest figure in the play (cf. 543–72). In *Elck*, Confession is female.

12 BEAUTY physical attractiveness; portrayed as female in a woodcut on the verso of the title-page in Q4 (see Fig. 16)

13 STRENGTH physical power. Portrayed as male in the woodcut of Q4 (see Fig. 16), Strength is nevertheless identified as 'She' at 829. See 829n. and p. 61.

14 DISCRETION practical judgement. Conley argues that 'prudence' is implied by this term, as in *Elck*'s '*Vroetscap*' (Conley, 'Identity'). For this sense see *1H4* 5.4.118–19: 'The better part of valour is discretion.'

15 FIVE WITS the five senses: hearing, seeing, tasting, touching, smelling

16 ANGEL a holy servant

17 DOCTOR a teacher rather than a physician. *OED sb.* 1a cites three sixteenth-century instances of 'doctor' as holy teacher (one description of Paul, two of Christ), including Matthew, 23.10: 'Be not called doctors: for one is your doctor, euen Christ' (Geneva). Like prologues, theatrical epilogues were sometimes delivered by figures clothed authoritatively, often wearing robes, caps, laurel crowns, and bearing other symbols of authority such as scrolls, books and staffs. Cawley, pointing out precedents for this figure in Expositor who speaks at the end of the *Sacrifice of Isaac* (in *Chester*), the Doctor ending the *Brome Play*, and 'Machabre the Doctoure' closing *Dance of Death* (Lydgate, *Dance*), suggests we may hear in these figures 'the voice of the medieval preacher'.

LIST OF ROLES] *Hawkins subst.* 1–304] *Q3, Q4; not in Q1, Q2; Q3 serves as control text*

179

THE SUMMONING OF EVERYMAN

Here beginneth a treatise how the High Father of heaven sendeth Death to summon every creature to come and give account of their lives in this world, and is in manner of a moral play.

[*Enter* MESSENGER, *for the prologue.*]

MESSENGER
    I pray you all give your audience

0.1 **Here beginneth** an *incipit* (Latin 'It begins'), conventionally used by medieval scribes to mark the start of a new work. This verb's –eth ending, the dominant (Southern) form, is used consistently in the play to mark the third-person singular indicative. By Shakespeare's time, the (Northern) ending –(e)s is replacing –(e)th, as in *CE* 5.1.346: 'here begins his morning story right.'
    treatise 'A book or writing which treats of some particular subject . . . containing a formal or methodical discussion or exposition of the principles of the subject' (*OED* 1a). Contrast the formality here with *Elck*'s opening: 'Here begins a nice little book.'
    High Father i.e. God. Cf. Maria in the *Mercers' Play* (in *Chester*): 'the high Father of heavon I praye / to yeeld you your good deede todaye, / for his micle might' (ll. 181–3).
0.2 **summon** require a person's attendance. For death as summoner, see *Knack to Know*: 'Ah see my sonnes, where death, pall Death appeares, / To summon me before a fearfull Iudge' (B3ʳ). See Fig. 15.
    creature created thing; cf. 1 Timothy, 4.4: 'For euery creature of God [is] good.'

give account explain, make representation of (*OED* account *sb.* 9a, b). The first invocation of the play's central economic metaphor. See pp. 50–3, and cf. Romans, 9.14: 'So shal euery one of vs geue accompt of hym selfe to God.'
0.3 **in manner of** in the form or style of (*OED* manner *sb.* 10b)
    moral i.e. 'dealing with the rightness and wrongness of conduct; intended to teach morality or convey a moral; (hence also) having a beneficial moral effect, edifying' (*OED a*). Cf. the Introduction to Chaucer's 'Pardoner's Tale': 'Telle us som moral thyng' (325). In early usage, especially in relation to literary or pictorial representations, this term could signify the allegorical or emblematical, as with the Painter in *Tim* 1.1.92–4: 'A thousand moral paintings I can show / That shall demonstrate these quick blows of Fortune's / More pregnantly than words.'
1–21 This prologue, not in *Elck*, summarizes the play's message (10–11) and decorously introduces God, who otherwise (as in *Elck*) would have the burden of identifying himself.
1 **pray you** request, ask you (a polite phrase)

0 SD] *Adams subst.*

181

And hear this matter with reverence,
By figure, a moral play:
The Summoning of Everyman called it is,
That of our lives and ending shows   5
How transitory we be all day.
This matter is wondrous precious,
But the intent of it is more gracious
And sweet to bear away.
The story saith: Man, in the beginning   10
Look well and take good heed to the ending,

give your audience listen, attend
to. Cf. Brutus in *JC* 3.2.2: 'Then
follow me, and give me audience,
friends.' The play's epilogue likewise
characterizes *hearers* (904).
2 **matter** perhaps 'substance' of the
play (3), i.e. its facts or significance, as
distinct from its style (*OED sb.*[1] II.9a),
but an older sense of 'narrative' or
'tale' (*OED* II.8) may also apply. For
the former, cf. *RJ* 3.2.83–4: 'Was ever
book containing such vile matter /
So fairly bound?'; for the latter, cf.
Chaucer's 'Physician's Tale': 'For I
moot turne again to my matere' (104).
reverence (due) respect
3 **By figure** in its shape, form. But
perhaps also conveying the sense of
an emblem or type. See as well *OED*
figure *v.* 9b: 'To express by a metaphor
or image'.
moral instructive (as to rightness and
wrongness of conduct); cf. *OED a.* 2a.
4 *The Summoning of Everyman* the
full title of this play. The final word
here has sometimes been represented
as *Every Man*.
5 **ending** death
6 **transitory** fleeting, brief (i.e. not fixed
or permanent)
all day continually, always; cf. *OED*
alday *advb. phr.*, citing John Trevisa's
translation of the *Polychronicon*: 'We
dye alday but none overcome[th].'

7–9 The meaning of the matter is even
more gracious and sweet to learn
than the matter is precious itself.
The comparison here escalates the
prologue's praise.
8 **intent** object, purpose
more even more
gracious pleasing, attractive; cf. *Ham*
5.2.71: 'Thy state is the more gracious.'
The religious context also lends this
word the sense of divine 'grace'.
9 **bear** carry away (in the mind)
10–11 These lines invoke a proverb also in
Mundus et Infans: 'In what occupation
that ever ye be, / Always, ere ye begin,
think on the ending' (ll. 483–4; cf.
Dent, E128). With the admonition
of these line, cf. Ecclesiastes, 11.9:
'Be glad then (O thou young man) in
thy youth, and let thy heart be merie
in thy young dayes, folowe the wayes
of thyne owne heart, and the lust of
thyne eyes, but be thou sure that God
shall bryng thee into iudgement for
all these thinges.' They also suggest
the play's grounding in the popular
genre of *ars moriendi* or 'Art of Dying'
manuals. See pp. 45–6.
10 **saith** declares, states. Cf. Gower as
Chorus in *Per* 5.0.1–2: 'Marina thus
the brothel scapes, and chances / Into
an honest house, our story says.'
Man humanity, mankind (= the universal sense) (*OED* man *sb.*[1] 2)

7 wondrous] *Q4 (*wonderous*); wonders *Q3*   10 The] *Q3; *This *Q4*

Be you never so gay!
Ye think sin in the beginning full sweet,
Which in the end causeth the soul to weep,
When the body lieth in clay. 15
Here shall you see how fellowship and jollity,
Both strength, pleasure and beauty
Will fade from thee as flower in May;
For ye shall hear how our heaven king
Calleth Everyman to a general reckoning. 20
Give audience and hear what he doth say! [*Exit.*]

[*Enter* GOD.]

GOD

I perceive, here in my majesty,
How that all creatures be to me unkind,
Living without dread in worldly prosperity.

12 **gay** mirthful, light-hearted (*OED a.*
1a)
13 **full** entirely
15 **in clay** i.e. buried after death. Cf. 'An
Epitaph of Maister Edwards': 'in clay
his Carcas lyes' (*Epitaphes*, 142).
16–17 Jollity and Pleasure are not figures
in this play. But at 408, Everyman says
to Goods 'And all my life I have had joy
and pleasure in thee', and at 427–8 he
goes on to say 'Alas, I have thee loved,
and had great pleasure / All my life
days on good and treasure.'
17 **Both** and also
18 The fading flower was proverbial; cf.
Dent, F386.
20 **general reckoning** With *give account*
in the preface (see 0.2n.), this phrase
solidifies the actuarial nature of the
play's central moral (900–2): after our
deaths, God will measure our *Good
Deeds* (908) to determine whether our
account[s] are *whole and sound* (917). For
the economic metaphor, see pp. 52–3,
and cf. Job, 13.9: 'Shall that helpe you
when he calleth you to reckoning?' Cf.
885–6n. and *Mankind* 862.
21 SD2 Some productions have God
present for the entire performance,
seated on or slightly apart from the
stage before the Messenger enters.
He can watch the action from a raised
position (such as a throne).
22 **in my majesty** from the perspective
of my divinity; cf. *Elck*: 'from my
throne above' (1).
23 **How that** that
unkind playing on (1) out of their *kind*
or nature; (2) harsh, unpleasant. Cf.
Mankind 280n.
24 **dread** awe, reverence; cf. Psalms, 96.9:
'Worshyp you God in the maiestie of
holynesse: be you in dread of his face
all [that be in] the earth.'
worldly prosperity The theme of
wealth diverting humankind from its
social and spiritual obligations is central
to *Everyman*; see Harper & Mize.

14 ²the] *Q3;* thy *Q4* 21 doth] *Q3;* wyll *Q4* 21 SD1] *Adams* SD2] *this edn; God speketh* [*from
above*] | *Adams* 22 SP] *Q3* (God speketh)

Of ghostly sight, the people be so blind;   25
Drowned in sin, they know me not for their God.
In worldly riches is all their mind;
They fear not my righteousness, the sharp rod.
My law, that I showed when I for them died,
They forget clean, and shedding of my blood red.   30
I hanged between two, it cannot be denied;
To get them life, I suffered to be dead.
I healed their feet; with thorns hurt was my head.
I could do no more than I did, truly;
And now I see the people do clean forsake me.   35
They use the seven deadly sins damnable,

25 People lack spiritual vision. For *ghostly* as 'spiritual', see *Mankind* 27n.

26 **Drowned in sin** Cf. *Whipping*: 'drown'd with sinfulnes' (F8ʳ).

27 All their attention is on money (i.e. *worldly* rather than spiritual *riches*).

28 **sharp rod** i.e. severe instrument of punishment or correction; cf. Job, 21.9: 'the rod of God is not vpon them', and see *Enough*, 142: 'A straunge matter, when men have given over God: / They may be sure to be scourged with His sharp rod' (ll. 1416–17). The word 'sharp' here refers, by transference, to the sharp pain such an instrument would cause (rather than any pointed surface).

29 **law** emended to 'love' by Holthausen. Cawley defends *law* as 'the law of the New Covenant communicated by Christ through the Sacraments' (Cawley, 43).
showed exhibited, revealed; perhaps also with a sense of 'communicated'
when . . . died when, in the person of Christ, I died for their sins. This and the following four lines allude to the crucifixion (cf. Matthew, 27).

30 **clean** entirely, wholly

and . . . red i.e. and they (also) forget the shedding of my blood (on the cross).

31 Cf. Matthew, 27.38: 'Then were there two thieues crucified with hym: one on the ryght hande, and another on the left.'

32 **them** i.e. *the people* (25), rather than the *two* thieves (31). In Luke, 23.42–3, Christ assures only one of the thieves that he (the thief) shall be saved.

33 **healed their feet** Cf. John, 13.5–12, for the story of Jesus washing the disciples' feet. See *OED* heal $v.^1$ 3, for a figurative sense encompassing 'purify' and 'cleanse'. For the conjunction of *healed* and *feet*, see Hebrews, 12.13: 'And make straight paths for your feet, lest that which is lame be turned out of the way; but let it rather be healed.'
with . . . head Cf. Matthew, 27.29: 'And when they had platted a crown of thorns, they put it upon his head.'

36 **use** practise
seven deadly sins traditionally: pride, covetousness, lust, anger, gluttony, envy and sloth. Cf. *Mankind* 706n.
damnable liable to being condemned, damned (by God)

28 the] *Q3*; that *Q4* rod] *Q4*; rood *Q3* 29 law] *Q3*; love *Bevington* 30 forget] *Q3*; forgot *Q4* blood red] *Q3*; blod so redde *Q4* 31 two] *Q3*; two theues *Q4*

As pride, covetise, wrath and lechery
Now in the world be made commendable,
And thus they leave of angels the heavenly company.
Every man liveth so after his own pleasure,   40
And yet of their life they be nothing sure.
I see the more that I them forbear
The worse they be from year to year.
All that liveth appaireth fast.
Therefore I will, in all the haste,   45
Have a reckoning of every man's person.
For an I leave the people thus alone
In their life and wicked tempests,
Verily they will become much worse than beasts,
For now one would by envy another up eat: 50
Charity they do all clean forget.
I hoped well that every man
In my glory should make his mansion,
And thereto I had them all elect;

37 Conley ('Garbling') points out that while *Elck* follows traditional doctrine in citing 'Pride, Avarice, and Envy' as 'powerful among the Seven Deadly Sins' (11–12), *Everyman* modifies this list. *Everyman* retains 'Pride' and translates 'Avarice' (*'ghiericheit'*) as *covetise*, but adds *wrath* and *lechery*, and reinserts *envy* (*'nijt'*) at 50.

38 **Now . . . be** which now . . . are

40 **Every man** each person; though *man* is singular, the words *their* and *them* in the following lines indicate that the reference is still general. Cf. 66n.

41 **nothing sure** not at all certain

42 **forbear** endure, put up with; cf. Psalms, 99.8: 'O Lorde thou didst forbeare them.'

44 **appaireth** decays, falls off

45 **in . . . haste** as quickly as possible. Cf. *Jacob and Esau* (1568): 'But dressed it must be at once in all the haste' (5.1).

46 **person** the self, being, or individual personality of a man or woman (*OED sb.* 3a); here, the implication may be 'each person, individually'.

47–50 With this bleak vision cf. Galatians, 5.15: 'Yf ye byte and deuoure one another, take heede lest ye be consumed one of another'; and Albany in *KL* 4.2.49–50: 'Humanity must perforce prey on itself, / Like monsters of the deep.'

47 **an** if

48 **tempests** commotions, troubles; cf. *Elck*, *'tempeesten'* (27).

53 **mansion** dwelling place; cf. 2 Corinthians, 5.2: 'And herefore sigh we desyringe to be clothed wt oure mansion which is from heven' (Tyndale).

54 **elect** chosen for salvation or eternal life

41 nothing] *Q3;* not *Q4*   43 be] *Q3;* are *Q4*   47 an] *Q3* (and) *throughout for* an = if   51 do all] *Q3;* all do *Q4*

But now I see, like traitors deject,   55
They thank me not for the pleasure that I to them meant,
Nor yet for their being that I them have lent.
I proffered the people great multitude of mercy,
And few there be that asketh it heartily.
They be so cumbered with worldly riches   60
That needs on them I must do justice,
On every man living without fear. –
Where art thou, Death, thou mighty messenger?

[*Enter*] DEATH.

DEATH

Almighty God, I am here at your will,
Your commandment to fulfil.   65

GOD

Go thou to Everyman
And show him, in my name,
A pilgrimage he must on him take,

55 **deject** cast down from one's position, lowered in fortunes; lowered in character, abject, abased (*OED ppl. a.*, citing this passage)
57 **lent** given (temporarily; through the act of creation; cf. *creatures* at 23). See *Wisdom of Solomon*, 15.8: 'when his life which was lent him shall be demanded' (KJV), and cf. Goods: 'for a while I was lent thee' (440). See also 161–7, and pp. 50–1.
58 **great multitude** a large amount (*OED* 2c, in singular with mass noun)
59 **asketh** seek, ask for. For the availability of God's mercy, see Luke, 11.9: 'So I say to you, ask, and it will be given to you; seek, and you will find; knock, and it will be opened to you.'
60 **cumbered** encumbered, weighed down
61 **needs ... must** it is necessary
62 **living without fear** without (proper) humility or awe; cf. 2 Corinthians,

5.11: 'Therefore, knowing the fear of the Lord, we persuade men.' This rephrases *without dread* (24).
63 **mighty messenger** Death describes himself as 'Godys masangere' (line 177) in the *Death of Herod* (*N-Town*, 193).
65 **commandment** command
66 **Everyman** here, the single representative individual on which the play focuses. Cawley remarks upon the drama's habit of preparing us for specific personifications by introducing us first to the indefinite and abstract – as it has done at 40 with 'Every man' (Cawley, 30, 66n.). This recurs with Good Deeds (see 78, 481) and the Five Wits (see 168, 686).
67 **show** tell, communicate (the fact of)
68 **pilgrimage** journey; cf. the proverb 'Life is a pilgrimage' (Dent, L249), and *AYL* 3.2.129–30: 'how brief the life of man / Runs his erring pilgrimage.'

55 see] *Q3;* se that *Q4*   59 heartily] *Q3* (hertly)   63 SD *Enter*] *Adams*   64 SP] *Q3; om. Q4*

Which he in no wise may escape,
And that he bring with him a sure reckoning   70
Without delay or any tarrying.

DEATH

Lord, I will in the world go run over all
And truly outsearch both great and small.
Every man will I beset that liveth beastly,
Out of God's laws, and dreadeth not folly.   75
He that loveth richesse I will strike with my dart,
His sight to blind, and from heaven to depart –
Except that alms be his good friend –
In hell for to dwell, world without end.   *[Exit God.]*
Lo, yonder I see Everyman walking.   80
Full little he thinketh on my coming.

69 **in no wise** in no way, not at all
70 **he bring** i.e. he must bring
sure trustworthy, reliable
72 **run** almost certainly a mistranslation, based on aural error, of *Elck*'s *regneren* ('reign'). Cf. 'I shall go forth to reign in the world' (*Elck*, 58). On similar aural errors in the translation process, see Conley, 'Aural'.
74 **Every man** Here Death deploys the distributive ('all those who'), although in performance the distinction between *Every man* and *Everyman* might not be heard.
beset set upon
76 **richesse** wealth, opulence
dart Death was conventionally portrayed as holding a spear, arrow or javelin, called a *dart*, the touch of which brought death. The phrase 'death's dart' was conventional, as in *Cornelia*: 'What boote your teares, or what auailes your sorrow / Against th'ineuitable dart of Death?' (C2ʳ).
77 **from . . . depart** separate (him) from heaven
78 **alms** 'A meritorious action, a good

deed, a service to God, a charity. Often *ironically*' (*OED* 2). Because *alms* could convey a monetary sense, Death's conditional will indeed seem ironic until later in the play, when Good Deeds (i.e. *alms*) will call Everyman 'my special friend' (629).
79 **world without end** ironic use of a familiar phrase; cf. Paul in Ephesians, 3.21: 'Be prayse in the Churche by Christe Iesus, throughout all ages, worlde without ende. Amen.'
80 **walking** Along with frequent use of the verb *go*, and the *pilgrimage* metaphor (cf. 68 and n.), this suggests the play's devotion to the life-as-journey trope. See pp. 46–50.
81 Death's observation would have invoked biblical warnings about the suddenness of death and other ills; cf. 1 Thessalonians, 5.2–3: 'For yourselves know perfectly that the day of the Lord so cometh as a thief in the night. For when they shall say, Peace and safety; then sudden destruction cometh upon them, as travail upon a woman with child; and they shall not escape.'

72 run] *Q3 (*renne*)   73 truly] *Q4;* cruelly *Q3   74 will I] *Q3;* I wyll *Q4   76 richesse] *Q3 (*rychesse*);* ryches *Q4   77 to depart] *Q3;* depart *Q4   78 alms] *Q3;* almes dedes *Q4   79 SD] *Lester subst.*

187

His mind is on fleshly lusts and his treasure,
And great pain it shall cause him to endure
Before the Lord heaven king. –
Everyman, stand still! Whither art thou going   85
Thus gaily? Hast thou thy maker forget?

[*Enter*] EVERYMAN.

EVERYMAN
Why askest thou?
Wouldst thou wit?
DEATH
Yea, sir, I will show you.
In great haste I am sent to thee   90
From God, out of his majesty.
EVERYMAN
What? Sent to me?
DEATH
Yea, certainly.
Though thou have forget Him here,
He thinketh on thee in the heavenly sphere,   95
As, ere we depart, thou shalt know.
EVERYMAN
What desireth God of me?

82 *Elck* is less specific: 'Oh, Everyman, you will soon lose / what you think you hold firmly' (66–7).
83 **endure** last; stand
86 **gaily** perhaps, regarding Everyman's manner, 'airily, jauntily' (*OED* 2), with the possibility of 'brightly, showily, smartly, splendidly' dressed (*OED* 1) in reference to his clothing. At 12 and 466 *gay* refers to manners; at 614 it refers to dress.
Hast . . . forget? The first of many

such injunctions in the Bible is Deuteronomy, 6.12: 'Then beware lest thou forget ye Lorde.' 'Forgot' had not yet become the dominant past-tense form of 'forget'.
88 **Wouldst thou wit** Would you know the answer? (*OED* weet *v.* a)
89 **show** repeating the command God has given at 67
91 **out of** as an expression of
96 Cawley points out that this line lacks a companion rhyme (Cawley, 31).

86 SD *Enter*] *Adams subst.*   87 SP] *Q3*; om. *Q4*   88, 112, 143 wit] *Q3* (wete)   90 sent] *Q3* (sende)   96 ere] *Q3* (or) *throughout*   shalt] *Q3*; shall *Q4*

DEATH

> That shall I show thee:
> A reckoning he will needs have,
> Without any longer respite.   100

EVERYMAN

> To give a reckoning longer leisure I crave;
> This blind matter troubleth my wit.

DEATH

> On thee thou must take a long journey.
> Therefore thy book of count with thee thou bring,
> For turn again thou cannot by no way.   105
> And look thou be sure of thy reckoning,
> For before God thou shalt answer and show
> Thy many bad deeds and good but a few,
> How thou hast spent thy life and in what wise,
> Before the chief Lord of paradise.   110
> Have ado that we were in that way,
> For, wit thou well, thou shalt make none attorney.

EVERYMAN

> Full unready I am such reckoning to give.

100 **respite** delay
102 **blind** dark, obscure
   wit mind, intelligence
104 **book of count** account book (*count*
   is the aphetic form of 'account'); cf.
   Volpone: 'Get thee a cap, a count-
   booke, pen and inke, / Papers afore
   thee' (5.2.81–2). This literalizes the
   'reckoning' metaphor.
105 **turn again** return (here), go back; *OED*
   turn *v*. 66b cites Ruth, 1.11: 'But Naemi
   sayde: Turne agayne my doughters, why
   wolde ye go with me?' (Coverdale).
   by no way by no means
106 **sure** repeating God's word from 70
109 **wise** way
111 **Have ado** Bestir yourself; cf. *OED*
   ado, citing the *Paston Letters* (*c*. 1466):

'Fur I woll nowt have ado ther with'
(*Lett.* 566, 2.295).
we Some editors emend to *thou*,
reasoning that the pilgrimage
is Everyman's alone. But Death
accompanies Everyman for over
70 more lines (exiting after 183), and
the intimate nature of their dialogue
suggests a joint journey. Cf. 130 and n.
we . . . way i.e. that we be moving
along
112 **make none attorney** appoint no
deputy or agent
113 Kölbing, noting this line does not
rhyme with 114, suggests 'give now'
– a reading supported by *Elck*'s 'I
am hardly prepared just now to give
reckoning just for God alone' (96–7).

100 any longer] *Q3* (ony lenger*); lenger *Q4*   104 with] *Q3* (ẅ)   107 thou shalt] *Q3;* shalte thou
Q4   109 spent] *Q3;* spede *Q4*   111 ado that we] *Q4* (a do that we*); I do we *Q3;* ado that thou
Coldewey

I know thee not. What messenger art thou?

DEATH

    I am Death, that no man dreadeth,   115

    For every man I 'rest, and no man spareth,

    For it is God's commandment

    That all to me should be obedient.

EVERYMAN

    O Death, thou comest when I had thee least in mind!

    In thy power it lieth me to save;   120

    Yet of my good will I give thee if thou will be kind –

    Yea, a thousand pound shalt thou have –

    And defer this matter till another day.

DEATH

    Everyman, it may not be, by no way.

    I set not by gold, silver nor richesse,   125

    Ne by pope, emperor, king, duke ne princes;

---

115 **no man dreadeth** fears no man (i.e. rather than 'whom no man fears')

116 **'rest** arrest (*OED v.*³ 2, citing *CE* 4.4.3: 'To warrant thee as I am 'rested for'). Perhaps this hints also at the intransitive form, Death bringing all to what Jeremiah, 17.12 calls 'the place of our holy rest'.
no man spareth spare no man

117 **commandment** command (as at 65), without the formal sense of the 'ten commandments'; cf. Deuteronomy, 10.

119 Everyman repeatedly complains of being *unready*; see 81 and n., and cf. 113, 134, 187.

120 **In . . . save** It is in your power to save me.

121 **of . . . give** either (1) out of my good will I will give; or (2) of my goods I will give. See 389 and n. for similar ambiguity related to *good*.

122 **thousand pound** an extravagant sum, meant to suggest Everyman's possession of *worldly riches* (27); cf. *Elck*'s '*Duysant pont*', 'a thousand pounds' (103). In other works this will represent an undeniably attractive sum, as with Mistress Ford in *MW* 3.3.13–14: 'I had rather than a thousand pound he were out of the house.'

124–30 Cf. the proverb 'Death takes no bribe' (Dent, D149).

125 **set not by** do not regard, value

126 Cawley suggests that this list's descending order of rank may draw on the Dance of Death in Lydgate's treatment, where Death visits these figures in turn. See Lydgate, *Dance*, 2–23. *Elck* reads 'Pope, duke, king, nor count' (109).
Ne . . . ne neither . . . nor
princes Spelled *prynces* in Q3, this could also be represented (and/or heard) as 'princess'.

116 'rest] *Q3 (reste)*   no man] *Q3;* none *Q4*   121 thou] *Q3;* ye *Q4*   123 defer] *Q3;* [thou] differe *Bevington*   125 richesse] *Q3;* riches *Cawley*

For, an I would receive gifts great,
All the world I might get,
But my custom is clean contrary:
I give thee no respite. Come hence and not tarry.   130

EVERYMAN

Alas! Shall I have no longer respite?
I may say Death giveth no warning!
To think on thee it maketh my heart sick,
For all unready is my book of reckoning.
But twelve year and I might have abiding,   135
My counting book I would make so clear
That my reckoning I should not need to fear.
Wherefore Death, I pray thee, for God's mercy,
Spare me till I be provided of remedy.

DEATH

Thee availeth not to cry, weep and pray,   140
But haste thee lightly that thou were gone that journey,
And prove thy friends if thou can;
For, wit thou well, the tide abideth no man,

---

128 **get** possess, have at my control
129 **custom** habit, usage; perhaps also playing on the toll or duty levied on travellers: Death's *custom* is lives rather than money; cf. *OED sb.*[1] 4a.
130 **Come hence** come along, go there. Cf. *MED* comen *v.* 2: 'proceed, go' (esp. with *adv.* or *adv. clause* such as 'ther', 'thider', etc.). For a similar use of *come* where we would expect 'go', see 262. On *come* and *go* as keywords in *Everyman*, see pp. 47–9.
     not tarry do not tarry; we would expect 'tarry not'.
134 **all unready** entirely unprepared
135 yet if I might have a continuance of twelve years (cf. *OED* abiding *vbl. n.* 4). There may be a sense too of *But* as 'only, merely'.
136 **clear** to the good, positive; cf. *OED a., adv.,* and *sb.* 16a: 'Free from

any encumbrance, liability'. *OED* maintains that the financial sense of the verb *clear* (as in 'to clear an account or debt') came into use only in the 1590s.
138 **Wherefore** for which reason
139 **provided of** in possession of; cf. *MV* 2.4.23: 'I am provided of a torch-bearer.'
     remedy relief
140 **Thee availeth** it avails you
141 **lightly** quickly, at once (*OED adv.* 5)
     gone that journey on your way
142 **prove** test, determine the qualities of; also with the sense of 'to find by experience (a person or thing) to be (something)' (*OED* B.I.3, referencing approve *v.*[1] 9. *arch.*)
143 **tide . . . man** proverbial: 'The tide must be taken when it comes' (Dent, T323). Cf. *Tide.*

129 But] *Q3;* All *Q4*   141 ²that] *Q3* (yᵗ); yᵉ *Q4*   142 prove] *Q3* (preue)   143 thou] *Q3;* you *Q4*

And in the world each living creature
For Adam's sin must die of nature.   145

EVERYMAN

Death, if I should this pilgrimage take
And my reckoning surely make,
Show me, for saint charity,
Should I not come again shortly?

DEATH

No, Everyman: an thou be once there,   150
Thou mayst never more come here,
Trust me verily.

EVERYMAN

O gracious God in the high seat celestial,
Have mercy on me in this most need!
Shall I have no company from this vale terrestrial   155
Of mine acquaintance that way me to lead?

DEATH

Yea, if any be so hardy
That would go with thee and bear thee company.
Hie thee that thou were gone to God's magnificence,

144–5 recounting the Fall of Man (*Adam's sin*), which brought death to humanity; cf. the stakes of violating God's prohibition in Genesis, 2.17: 'But as touching the tree of knowlege of good and euyll thou shalt not eate of it: For in what daye so euer thou eatest therof, thou shalt dye the death.'
145 **of nature** by virtue of its essence
148 **for saint charity** for charity's sake, out of charitable compassion – from French *seint*, 'holy'. Cf. *Mankind* 212n. On charity in *Everyman*, see 344, 482n., 922.
149 **come again** return
152 **verily** in truth, truly
153 **in . . . celestial** enthroned high in heaven
154 **this most need** i.e. this, my greatest

hour of need; cf. *Ham* 1.5.178: 'So grace and mercy at your most need help you.'
155 **company** companionship, fellowship
vale terrestrial earthly plane. Cf. 'this earthly vale' (*Flower*, 36). This phrase, unusually poetic for Everyman at this point in the play, seems deployed here to balance and rhyme with *celestial* (153). Cf. the Host in *MW* 3.1.95–6, as he reconciles Doctor and Parson: 'Give me thy hand, terrestrial; so. Give me thy hand, celestial; so.'
157 **hardy** bold, daring; cf. *TNK* 1.1.204–5: 'nor be so hardy / Ever to take a husband.'
158 **bear** keep
159 Death repeats his order and construction from 141.
Hie hasten

151 mayst] *Q3;* must *Q4*   153 O] *Q3; om. Q4*   the] *Q3; om. Q4*   156 acquaintance] *Q4;* acqueynce *Q3*

Thy reckoning to give before his presence.   160

What, weenest thou thy life is given thee,

And thy worldly goods also?

DEATH

Nay, nay, it was but lent thee;

For as soon as thou art go,   165

Another a while shall have it and then go therefro,

Even as thou hast done.

Everyman, thou art mad. Thou hast thy wits five

And here on earth will not amend thy life;

For suddenly I do come.   170

EVERYMAN

O wretched caitiff, whither shall I flee,

That I might scape this endless sorrow?

Now, gentle Death, spare me till tomorrow,

That I may amend me

---

magnificence glorious presence, state of being; cf. More, 'The twelue propertees': 'So euery relique, ymage, or picture, / That doth pertaine to goddes magnificence' ('The vii. propertee', ll. 8–9). See also *OED sb.* 3 for use with possessive adjective ('your magnificence') as a title of respect or honour.

160 **give** present (for inspection)

161–7 repetition of a central point, concerning the temporary, borrowed nature of life. Cf. 57n., 440n.

161 **weenest** think, believe

165 **go** gone

166 **it** i.e. life, in the same way that others will possess one's *worldly goods* (162)

therefro away from there (*OED* therefrom *adv.*). The use of 'there' where we might expect 'here' may be owing to the futurity of the situation described.

167 **thou hast done** i.e. have lived your life

168 **wits five** the five bodily senses; *OED* wit *sb.* 3b, citing the *Interlude of the Four Elements* (*c.* 1515): 'I comforte the wyttes fyve, / The tastyng, smellyng, and herynge; / I refresh the syght and felynge / To all creaturs alyve' (*Interlude*, 19). A personification of the Five Wits will enter as one of Everyman's companions at 669.

171 **O wretched caitiff** Everyman reproves himself, perhaps speaking this and the following line as an aside.

172 **scape** escape

173 **gentle Death** flattery or wishful thinking on Everyman's part. Just as Everyman speaks of 'God' without qualification until 153 (*O gracious God*), so has he referred simply to *Death* until this moment. Death's self-description at 176ff. makes the modifier *gentle* humorously inapt.

161, 169 life] *Q3* (lyue)   168 mad] *Q4;* made *Q3*

With good advisement.   175

DEATH

Nay, thereto I will not consent,

Nor no man will I respite;

But to the heart suddenly I shall smite

Without any advisement.

And now out of thy sight I will me hie.   180

See thou make thee ready shortly,

For thou mayst say this is the day

That no man living may scape away.   [*Exit.*]

EVERYMAN

Alas, I may well weep with sighs deep!

Now have I no manner of company   185

To help me in my journey, and me to keep;

And also my writing is full unready.

How shall I do now for to excuse me?

I would to God I had never be get!

To my soul a full great profit it had be,   190

For now I fear pains huge and great.

The time passeth. Lord, help, that all wrought!

---

175 **good advisement** due deliberation (*OED sb.* 2a); perhaps with a sense of 'advice, counsel' (*OED* 5). For the conjunction of *advisement*(s) with *amend* (174), cf. Jeremiah, 26.13: 'Therfore amende your wayes, and your aduisementes, and be obedient vnto the voyce of the Lorde your God.'

178 **to ... smite** Cawley compares Chaucer's 'Pardoner's Tale': 'There cam a privee theef men clepeth Deeth / That in this contree all the peple sleeth, / And with his spere he smoot his herte atwo' (675–7).

179 **Without any advisement** Death sardonically repeats Everyman's word from 175: he needs no deliberation or counsel to take Everyman's life.

182–3 You should understand this as the one day no one may avoid. Just as Death has quoted Everyman's *advisement* (see 179 and n.), with *thou mayst say* he repeats the latter's pique from 132: 'I may say Death giveth no warning!'

186 **keep** guard, protect

187 **my writing** his *counting book* (136)

188 **How** what; cf. *R2* 2.2.104: 'How shall we do for money for these wars?'; and see *Mankind* 789n.

     for to in order to, so as to

189 **be get** been born, begotten

190 **it** i.e. not having been born (189)

192 **time passeth** Cf. *Elck*: 'Time is passing quickly, it is after noon' (173). This observation – Everyman painfully feeling time slipping through his fingers

180 thy sight] *Q3;* syght *Q4*   183 SD] *Adams*   190 full] *Q3;* om. *Q4*

For though I mourn, it availeth nought.
The day passeth and is almost ago;
I wot not well what for to do.   195
To whom were I best my complaint to make?
What an I to Fellowship thereof spake
And showed him of this sudden chance?
For in him is all mine affiance.
We have in the world so many a day   200
Be good friends in sport and play.
I see him yonder, certainly.

[*Enter* FELLOWSHIP.]

I trust that he will bear me company;
Therefore to him will I speak to ease my sorrow. –
Well met, good Fellowship, and good morrow.   205
FELLOWSHIP
Everyman, good morrow, by this day.
Sir, why lookest thou so piteously?
If anything be amiss, I pray thee me say,
That I may help to remedy.
EVERYMAN
Yea, good Fellowship, yea: 210

– forms the basis of Faustus's great closing soliloquy in *Faustus*.
wrought made, created; cf. Isaiah, 26.12: 'Lorde vnto vs thou shalt prouide peace: for thou also hast wrought all our workes in vs.'
193 **mourn** feel grief, regret
   availeth helps
194 **ago** gone
195 **wot** know
196 **complaint** utterance of grief
197 **Fellowship** Everyman turns first to a figure of friendship and sociability.
   spake spoke
198 **chance** accident, turn of events

199 **affiance** trust, confidence, faith; cf. *H5* 2.2.126–7: 'O how hast thou with jealousy infected / The sweetness of affiance!'
203 **bear me company** Cf. 158.
205 **good morrow** good morning. Cf. *Elck*: 'Good day, Fellowship!' (184).
206 **by this day** a mild oath; cf. Benedick: 'By this day, she's a fair lady!' (*MA* 2.3.236). Fellowship will use it again at 236; the phrase is his alone in *Everyman*.
207 **piteously** wretchedly
208 **me say** tell me
209 **remedy** make right

195 for] *Q3; om. Q4*   202 SD] *Bevington subst.*   206 SP] *Q3* (Felawshyp speketh)

I am in great jeopardy!

FELLOWSHIP

My true friend, show to me your mind.
I will not forsake thee to my life's end
In the way of good company.

EVERYMAN

That was well spoken, and lovingly.   215

FELLOWSHIP

Sir, I must needs know your heaviness;
I have pity to see you in any distress.
If any have you wronged, ye shall revenged be,
Though I on the ground be slain for thee,
Though that I know before that I should die.   220

EVERYMAN

Verily, Fellowship, gramercy.

FELLOWSHIP

Tush, by thy thanks I set not a straw.
Show me your grief and say no more.

EVERYMAN

If I my heart should to you break,
And then you to turn your mind from me   225

---

211 **jeopardy** peril, danger
212 **show . . . mind** share your thoughts;
cf. *TGV* 1.2.7–8: 'I'll show my mind /
According to my shallow simple skill.'
214 as a good companion should
216 **must needs** have to
  know understand (i.e. the reason
  for)
  heaviness sadness, grief (*OED* e)
218–20 Fellowship's pledge to aid
Everyman to the death increases the
irony of his refusal at 262ff.
221 **gramercy** thanks, thank you
(from French for 'great thanks'). A
somewhat folksy word, which begets
the similarly informal expressions of
Fellowship in the next line. Jonson will

have the puppets Damon and Pythias
exchange *gramercy* in *Bartholomew
Fair* (5.4.271–3), where it registers as
an archaism.
222 **Tush** an expression of impatience
  set . . . straw don't care at all. In
  homely language, Fellowship assures
  Everyman that no such thanks are
  needed between friends. Cf. Chaucer's
  'Nun's Priest's Tale': 'I sette nat a
  straw by thy dremynges' (3090).
224 **break** disclose, reveal
225 **And . . . me** and find you turning
  yourself away from me. Cf. *OED* turn
  v. 27 (*refl.*): 'To direct one's mind,
  will, attention, etc. to or from a person
  or thing'.

213 to] *Q3;* vnto *Q4*   215 was] *Q3;* is *Q4*   222 by] *Q3;* be *Q4*

And would not me comfort when ye hear me speak,
Then should I ten times sorrier be.

FELLOWSHIP

Sir, I say as I will do, indeed.

EVERYMAN

Then be you a good friend at need.
I have found you true herebefore.   230

FELLOWSHIP

And so ye shall evermore;
For in faith, an thou go to hell,
I will not forsake thee by the way.

EVERYMAN

Ye speak like a good friend; I believe you well.
I shall deserve it, an I may.   235

FELLOWSHIP

I speak of no deserving, by this day.
For he that will say and nothing do
Is not worthy with good company to go.
Therefore show me the grief of your mind
As to your friend most loving and kind.   240

EVERYMAN

I shall show you how it is:
Commanded I am to go a journey,
A long way, hard and dangerous,
And give a strait count, without delay,
Before the high Judge, Adonai.   245

---

227 **sorrier** more pained at heart, distressed
230 **herebefore** prior to this time
231 **so** i.e. find (Fellowship) *true* (230)
235 **deserve** become worthy of it (i.e. by virtue of my actions or qualities). See *R2* 3.3.199: 'As my true service shall deserve your love'.
it i.e. Fellowship's offer of companionship (232–3)
237 **say** i.e. promise (to do something)

240 **As** as one who is; *OED adv. (conj.,* and *rel. pron.)* 12a, b
244 **strait** strict, allowing no evasion; cf. *Mankind* 841 and n.
245 **high Judge** God is referred to as the ultimate judge in Genesis, 18.25; Isaiah, 33.22; and James, 4.12.
Adonai one of the names given in the Hebrew Bible to the Deity; *OED* cites the *Sarum Primer* (1557): 'O greate and marveilous Lord, Adonay' (i).

226 ye] *Q3;* you *Q4*

197

Wherefore, I pray you, bear me company,
As ye have promised, in this journey.
FELLOWSHIP
 That is matter indeed! Promise is duty,
 But, an I should take such a voyage on me,
 I know it well, it should be to my pain;   250
 Also it maketh me afeard, certain.
 But let us take counsel here as well as we can,
 For your words would fear a strong man.
EVERYMAN
 Why, ye said if I had need
 Ye would me never forsake, quick ne dead,   255
 Though it were to hell, truly.
FELLOWSHIP
 So I said, certainly,
 But such pleasures be set aside, the sooth to say;
 And also, if we took such a journey,
 When should we come again?   260
EVERYMAN
 Nay, never again, till the day of doom.
FELLOWSHIP
 In faith, then will not I come there!

248 **matter** i.e. something of importance (*OED sb.*[1] 3b)
 Promise is duty proverbial; cf. 'Promise is debt' (Dent, P603). Repeated in different form by Everyman at 822.
249 **take . . . me** commit myself to making the journey
250 **be to my pain** i.e. be painful to me; be to my detriment
251 **afeard** afraid (*ppl. a.*; not, at this time, dialectal or class-marked)
252 **counsel** Here and throughout *Everyman, counsel* is a serious form of advice implying direction and guidance based on judgement, deliberation and wisdom. See *OED sb.* 2a. With 'count'

and 'account', it is a keyword in the play; cf. its use at 400, 479, 490, 516, 579, 663 (*counsellors*), and 775 (*counselled*).
253 **fear** frighten (*OED v.* I.1)
254 **ye said** i.e. at 232–3
255 **quick ne dead** (neither) alive nor dead (see *OED* quick *a., sb.*[1], and *adv.* B.1a; cf. Acts, 10.42, and the Apostles' Creed)
258 **pleasures** Fellowship may use this word where we would expect 'pleasantries' – i.e. something that he has said largely to bring Everyman pleasure.
 be are (now)
 the sooth to say to speak truly
262 **come** go; for a similar usage, cf. 130 and n.

251 maketh] *Q4;* make *Q3* 252 well as] *Q3; om. Q4* 260 come again] *Q3;* againe come *Bevington*

Who hath you these tidings brought?

EVERYMAN

Indeed Death was with me here.

FELLOWSHIP

Now, by God that all hath bought,   265

If Death were the messenger,

For no man that is living today

I will not go that loathsome journey –

Not for the father that begat me!

EVERYMAN

Ye promised otherwise, pardie.   270

FELLOWSHIP

I wot well I said so, truly.

And yet, if thou wilt eat and drink and make good cheer,

Or haunt to women the lusty company,

I would not forsake you while the day is clear,

Trust me verily.   275

EVERYMAN

Yea, thereto ye would be ready.

To go to mirth, solace and play

Your mind to folly will sooner apply,

---

263 **tidings** news, information (*OED* tiding 2)

265 **God . . . bought** alluding to the belief that, through his sacrifice, Christ ransomed (sinful) humanity from God's wrath. See Acts, 20.2. For the phrasing here, cf. 1 Corinthians, 6.20: 'For ye are dearly bought: therefore glorifie God in your body and in your spirite, which are Gods.'

266 **were** i.e. was

267 **For** on behalf of

269 **begat** produced, was responsible for (i.e. my life)

270 **pardie** by God (from Middle French *par Dieu*)

272 **make good cheer** be merry (*OED sb.*¹ 4)

273 or lustfully seek out the company of women. See *OED* haunt *v.* 4: 'To frequent the company of (a person), to associate with habitually; to "run after"'; and cf. the medieval ballad 'The Clerk's Twa Sons o Owsenford' (*Ballads*, 72): 'haunt not wi the young women, / Wi them to play the fiel' (ll. 11–12).

274 **while . . . clear** i.e. while there is no trouble or hardship

276 **thereto** in that situation; cf. 274.

277 **go to** indulge in

278 **apply** bend, incline (i.e. your *mind* will turn itself to *folly*)

268 loathsome] *Q4;* lothe *Q3*   270 promised] *Q3;* promysed me *Q4*   271 said] *Q4;* say *Q3*   273 the] *Q3;* that *Q4*   278 to folly] *Q4; not in Q3*

Than to bear me company in my long journey.
FELLOWSHIP

Nay, in good faith, I will not that way.   280
But, an thou will murder or any man kill,
In that I will help thee with a good will.
EVERYMAN

Oh, that is a simple advice indeed!
Gentle fellow, help me in my necessity.
We have loved long, and now I need;   285
And now, gentle Fellowship, remember me!
FELLOWSHIP

Whether ye have loved me or no,
By Saint John, I will not with thee go.
EVERYMAN

Yet, I pray thee, take the labour and do so much for me
To bring me forward, for saint charity,   290
And comfort me till I come without the town.

---

280 **will not** i.e. will not go
281–2 Fellowship generously offers to help Everyman commit murder or manslaughter if such is required.
283 **simple** deficient in knowledge or learning
advice information (*OED* 8)
284 **Gentle** generous, noble (see *OED a.* and *sb.* 3a; entry 3b suggests it is used 'in polite or ingratiating address' from the early sixteenth century)
necessity need
286 **remember** bear in mind (*OED v.*[1] I.1a, perhaps also with a sense of 2b, bearing a person in mind as entitled to a gift or recompense. Cf. *Mac* 2.3.20–1: 'I pray you, remember the Porter')
287 **no** not
288 **Saint John** most likely John the Baptist, whose figure was remarkably popular in medieval England. It is also possible that Fellowship swears by John the Apostle (son of Zebedee,

brother to James and Peter), to whom is generally attributed authorship of the Gospel of John. A change from *Elck*, where Fellowship's counterpart (*Gheselscap*) swears by '*Tjacob!*', i.e. 'St James' (262).
289 **take the labour** take (upon yourself) the task, make the effort; cf. *Friar Rush*, 6: 'faire Mistresse, may it please you to take the labour and goe with me.'
do so much i.e. do this much. Cf. *MW* (Quarto): 'I pray you do so much as see if you can espie Doctor *Cayus* comming' (8.1–2).
290 **bring me forward** advance me on my way
291 **without** outside. Cf. *MND* 1.1.165: 'And in the wood, a league without the town'. The detail of leaving Everyman's village, town or city (the size of his community is unclear) comes from *Elck*: '*Tot voer di poerte*', 'up to the gates' (262).

280 Nay] *Q4;* Now *Q3*   281 will] *Q3;* wylte *Q4*   284 fellow] *Q3* (felawe*);* Felaw[ship]e *Bevington*

FELLOWSHIP

Nay, an thou would give me a new gown,

I will not a foot with thee go;

But, an thou had tarried, I would not have left thee so.

And, as now, God speed thee in thy journey,   295

For from thee I will depart as fast as I may.

EVERYMAN

Whither away, Fellowship? Will thou forsake me?

FELLOWSHIP

Yea, by my fay. To God I betake thee.

EVERYMAN

Farewell, good Fellowship. For thee my heart is sore.

Adieu forever; I shall see thee no more.   300

FELLOWSHIP

In faith, Everyman, farewell now at the end.

For you I will remember that parting is mourning.   [*Exit.*]

EVERYMAN

Alack! Shall we thus depart indeed –

Ah, Lady, help! – without any more comfort?

292 no, even if you were to give me a new gown

294 **tarried** remained, stayed

295 **as now** at this time, just now

God speed a conventional wish, paid to another, for a successful journey. Cf. 357, and *Mankind* 344 and n.

297 **Whither away** Where are you going?

298 **fay** faith

betake commend, commit; cf. 300n.

299–300 With 297 and these lines, the allegorical force of the drama asserts itself: Everyman finds himself literally and figuratively forsaken by 'Fellowship', whom/which he 'shall see . . . no more'.

299 **sore** pained, distressed (*OED a.*[1] 11a)

300 **Adieu** goodbye. Cf. 298, where Fellowship's valediction offers an English version of this French parting.

301 **at the end** at last

302 **For you** (1) because of (i.e. owing to the example of); (2) on account of my regard for

parting is mourning proverbial; cf. Dent, P82.1, and *RJ* 2.2.184: 'Parting is such sweet sorrow.'

303 **depart** part from each other, become separated

304 **Ah, Lady** Everyman hails the Virgin Mary, a figure often called upon for help by Christians in distress at this time.

more further

293 a] *Q3;* one *Q4*   294 have] *Q3;* a *Q4*   297 Will] *Q3;* wylt *Q4*   300] *Q3; assigned to Fellowship Q4*   forever; I shall] *Q3;* for I shall neuer *Q4*   301 SP] *Q3;* euery man *Q4*   end] *Q3;* ending *Cawley*   302 SD] *Adams*   303 SP] *Q3; om. Q4*   thus] *Q4;* this *Q3*   304 Ah] *Q3 (A);* O *Q4; om. Coldewey*

Lo, Fellowship forsaketh me in my most need.   305
For help in this world whither shall I resort?
Fellowship herebefore with me would merry make,
And now little sorrow for me doth he take.
It is said, 'In prosperity men friends may find,
Which in adversity be full unkind.'   310
Now whither for succour shall I flee,
Sith that Fellowship hath forsaken me?
To my kinsmen I will, truly,
Praying them to help me in my necessity.
I believe that they will do so,   315
For kind will creep where it may not go.
I will go say, for yonder I see them go. –
Where be ye now, my friends and kinsmen?

[*Enter* KINDRED *and* COUSIN.]

KINDRED

Here be we now at your commandment.
Cousin, I pray you show us your intent   320
In any wise, and not spare.

305 **most need** Everyman has used this expression with Death at 154.
308 And now he shows little sadness over me.
309–10 **In prosperity . . . unkind** proverbial; cf. Dent, P611: 'Prosperity gets friends but adversity tries them.'
309 **It is said** a conventional way of introducing a proverb or received opinion
311 **succour** help, aid
312 **Sith** seeing that
313 **kinsmen** those related by blood or marriage
will i.e. will go (with verb of motion understood)
314 **Praying** asking earnestly (*OED v.* 2a)

316 i.e. 'your kin will stick by you.' This proverb has the force of 'Blood is thicker than water.' Everyman has explained Fellowship's forsaking of him with one proverb, and now uses another to raise his hopes.
317 **say** try, put to the test; i.e. the truth of this maxim (316)
318 **Where be ye** Everyman calls across the playing space to attract their attention.
320 **Cousin** Kindred addresses Everyman (this word is used loosely for all relations).
show . . . intent Let us know your plan (*OED* intent *sb.* 6).
321 **any wise** any manner
spare hold back

305–428] *Q2, Q3, Q4; not in Q1; Q3 serves as control text*   311 flee] *Q3;* fly *Q2*   312 forsaken] *Q3;* forsake *Q2*   314 me] *Q3; not in Q2*   317 ²go] *Q3; om. Cawley*   318 ye] *Q3;* you *Q2*   SD] *Adams*   319 be we] *Q3;* we be *Q2*   321 and] *Q2, Q3;* and do *Q4*

COUSIN

    Yea, Everyman, and to us declare

    If ye be disposed to go any whither;

    For, wit you well, we will live and die together.

KINDRED

    In wealth and woe we will with you hold,   325

    For over his kin a man may be bold.

EVERYMAN

    Gramercy, my friends and kinsmen kind.

    Now shall I show you the grief of my mind:

    I was commanded by a messenger

    That is a high king's chief officer;   330

    He bade me go a pilgrimage, to my pain,

    And I know well I shall never come again.

    Also, I must give a reckoning strait,

    For I have a great enemy that hath me in wait,

    Which intendeth me for to hinder.   335

KINDRED

    What account is that which ye must render?

    That would I know.

EVERYMAN

    Of all my works I must show

---

323 **disposed** inclined; cf. *Son* 88.1: 'When thou shalt be disposed to set me light'.

326 proverbial: cf. Heywood, *1 If You Know*, 209: 'Lets meddle with our kindred; there we may be bold.' Hamlet plays with this expression in 'A little more than kin, and less than kind' (*Ham* 1.2.65).

329–30 Everyman uses euphemisms (*messenger* for 'Death'; *high king* for 'God'), perhaps to avoid frightening off Kindred and Cousin.

334 **great enemy** i.e. the devil. He is so called in the second part of *Nature*

(Medwall, 127): 'The last of all ys our great Enemy, / Whyche ever hath us in contynuall haterede' (ll. 22–3). This is the first mention of the devil in the play; he is referred to again at 599.

hath . . . wait lies in wait for me

335 who intends to hinder me

336 **account** Kindred's gloss of Everyman's *reckoning* (333)

338 **works** the first mention of a central topic: Everyman's 'moral actions considered in relation to justification' (*OED* work *sb*. 1b). Defined provisionally in the following four lines, these *works*

---

322 to us] *Q2, Q3;* vs to *Q4*   324 wit] *Q2, Q3* (wete*); wot *Q4*   you] *Q2, Q3;* ye *Q4*   we] *Q2; not in Q3*   325 hold] *Q2;* bolde *Q3*   326 be] *Q3;* be to *Q2*   bold] *Q2;* holde *Q3*   330 a] *Q2, Q3;* an *Q4*   chief] *Q3; not in Q2*   331 a] *Q3; not in Q2*   332 And] *Q2, Q3;* But *Q4*   333 a] *Q3; not in Q2, Q4*

How I have lived and my days spent;
Also of ill deeds that I have used   340
In my time, sith life was me lent,
And of all virtues that I have refused.
Therefore, I pray you, go thither with me
To help to make mine account, for saint charity.

COUSIN

What? To go thither? Is that the matter?   345
Nay, Everyman, I had liefer fast bread and water
All this five year and more.

EVERYMAN

Alas, that ever I was bore!
For now shall I never be merry,
If that you forsake me.   350

KINDRED

Ah, sir, what? Ye be a merry man;
Take good heart to you and make no moan.
But one thing I warn you, by Saint Anne:

---

will be folded into *deeds* at 503 – from
which point the figure of Good Deeds
will represent Everyman's *works* until
the last and only other explicit mention
at 622. The Dutch in *Elck* is '*wercken*'
(300). On good works see *Mankind*
25 and n., and pp. 55–6.
340 **used** done
341 **sith** since (that time)
342 **refused** renounced, abandoned
345 **matter** i.e. what is contemplated, at
    issue. See *OED sb.*[1] 5a, b; this passage
    antedates the examples there.
346–7 I'd rather go on a diet of (nothing
    but) bread and water for five years or
    more.
346 **liefer** rather. Often used in joking
    comparisons; cf. Infidelity to the title
    character in Wager, *Mary Magdalene*:
    'They had liefer haue you naked, be
    not afrayde, / Then with your best

holy day garment' (B2ᵛ).
348 **bore** born. Cf. *Fulgens* (Medwall, 74):
    'As ever I harde sith I was bore'.
349–50 Everyman may turn to Kindred
    with these lines.
350 **If that you** if you should
351 **Ah, sir, what** These words allow
    Kindred to distance himself from
    Everyman. Cf. the Nurse to Romeo
    in *RJ* 3.3.91: 'Ah sir, ah sir, death's the
    end of all.'
    Ye be you are
352 **Take . . . you** i.e. be of good cheer. Cf.
    Amphitryon in *Hercules*, 6: 'Conceiue
    in mynde some better thinges, and take
    good heart to thee.'
    moan complaint. Cf. Flute as Thisby
    in *MND* 5.1.321: '*Lovers, make moan.*'
353 **Saint Anne** mother of the Virgin
    Mary (commonly invoked in mild
    oaths: see *Mankind* 75 and n.)

348 bore] *Q2, Q3;* borne *Q4*   351+ Ah] *Q3 (A)*

As for me, ye shall go alone.

EVERYMAN

My Cousin, will you not with me go?   355

COUSIN

No, by our Lady, I have the cramp in my toe.

Trust not to me, for, so God me speed,

I will deceive you in your most need.

KINDRED

It availeth not us to tice.

Ye shall have my maid with all my heart;   360

She loveth to go to feasts, there to be nice,

And to dance and abroad to start.

I will give her leave to help you in that journey,

---

354 **As for me** both (1) as far as I'm concerned; and (2) as to the question of my accompanying you on this journey

356 **by our Lady** i.e. by the Virgin Mary, who was first invoked by Everyman at 304 and will be the object of the latter's special prayer beginning at 597. Kindred's is a mild oath; cf. the Prince in *1H4* 2.4.289–90: 'Now, sirs: by'r Lady, you fought fair.'
I . . . toe a patently ridiculous excuse; not in *Elck*, where Cousin speaks of having 'some business to settle' (327). In 'A matter touching the Iourney of Sir Humfrey Gilbarte Knight', Thomas Churchyard aligns 'the Cramp' with 'the Goute' and 'the cold' as three maladies of sedentary home life (*Discourse*, ll. 311–12).

357 **trust not to** do not place your trust in; cf. *AC* 3.7.62: 'Trust not to rotten planks.'
so . . . speed an ironic oath here: as at 295, one usually wishes 'God speed' to others, especially those undertaking a journey (Cousin is remaining in place). Perhaps with a recollection of 2 John, 1.11: 'For he that byddeth hym God

speede, is partaker of his euyll deedes.' Cf. *Mankind* 344 and n. Goods will deploy this exact phrase at 461.

358 **deceive** the first invocation of an important word and topic in *Everyman*. Death has already corrected Everyman on a key misunderstanding (cf. 161–7), and from Cousin's warning onward such misunderstanding will be referred to with forms of the verb *deceive*. See 372, 435, 449, 452, 829, 905, and cf. such biblical formulations as 'Let no man deccaue him selfe' (1 Corinthians, 3.18) and 'Let no man deccaue you with vayne wordes' (Ephesians, 5.6).

359 It won't help you to (try to) persuade us (*tice* = entice); cf. Tamora in *Tit* 2.2.92: 'These two have 'ticed me hither to this place.'

360 **maid** female servant
with . . . heart i.e. with my blessings, freely

361 **nice** finely dressed, elegant

362 **abroad to start** i.e. to abandon her duties. To 'start abroad' or 'astray' was to desert one's place; cf. *OED v.* 4c.

363 **give her leave** give her permission, allow her

355 you not] *Q3;* nat *Q2*   359 availeth] *Q3;* auayleth you *Q2*   362 And] *Q3;* For *Q2*

If that you and she may agree.

EVERYMAN

    Now show me the very affect of your mind: 365

    Will you go with me or abide behind?

KINDRED

    Abide behind? Yea, that will I, an I may.

    Therefore farewell till another day.   *[Exit.]*

EVERYMAN

    How should I be merry or glad?

    For fair promises men to me make,   370

    But, when I have most need, they me forsake.

    I am deceived; that maketh me sad.

COUSIN

    Cousin Everyman, farewell now,

    For, verily, I will not go with you.

    Also of mine own life an unready reckoning   375

    I have to account; therefore I make tarrying.

    Now God keep thee, for now I go.   *[Exit.]*

EVERYMAN

    Ah, Jesus, is all come hereto?

    Lo, fair words maketh fools fain;

---

364 **If . . . agree** Kindred's condition echoes a parent's intervention on the potential marriage of a daughter; cf. Capulet in *RJ* 1.2.17–19: 'My will to her consent is but a part, / And she agreed, within her scope of choice / Lies my consent.'

365 **very affect** true orientation, bent. Cf. *Palace*: 'I purpose to declare the effect of my mind' (26th Novel, 542).

366 **abide** remain, stay

369 **should** may (with implication of doubt that such is possible)

370 because men make me fair-sounding promises. Reference to attractive but empty words is made at 379, 466,

469, 534, 873.

372 **deceived** See 358n.

    sad sorrowful, mournful (*OED a.* and *adv.* 5a)

375–6 The *Everyman* author lends Cousin a wholly unexpected sobriety in these lines; in *Elck*, Cousin has apparently secular concerns to settle.

376 **make tarrying** i.e. stay behind. Cf. *Alphonsus*: 'Therefore good Laelius, make no tarrying' (2.2.603).

378 **is . . . hereto** i.e. has everything come to this pass?

379 **fair . . . fain** Flattering words easily make people foolish; proverbial: cf. Dent, W794.

---

366 abide] *Q3;* byde *Q2*   367 Abide] *Q3;* Byde *Q2*   368 SD] *Adams*   370 fair] *Q3;* feare *Q2*   promisses] *Q3;* promesse *Q2*   make] *Q2, Q3;* do make *Q4*   373 now] *Q3;* as nowe *Q2*   375 mine] *Q2, Q3;* my *Q4*   life] *Q2; not in Q3, Q4*   376 account] *Q3;* counte *Q2*   377 SD] *Adams*   379 maketh] *Q3;* make *Q2*

They promise and nothing will do, certain.   380
My kinsmen promised me faithfully
For to abide with me steadfastly,
And now fast away do they flee;
Even so Fellowship promised me.
What friend were best me of to provide?   385
I lose my time here longer to abide.
Yet in my mind a thing there is:
All my life I have loved riches;
If that my Good now help me might,
He would make my heart full light.   390
I will speak to him in this distress. —
Where art thou, my goods and riches?

[GOODS *calls out from a corner.*]

380 **certain** with certainty, surely
384 Fellowship made the very same promise (only to break it). See 213–14 and 232–3.
385 Which friend can best be counted on to help me?
386 **longer to abide** i.e. if I stay here any longer
388 God indicted the love of *worldly riches* at 60, and Death promised to strike down 'He that loveth richesse' at 76. Along with the amount of the bribe Everyman offers Death at 122 – *a thousand pound* – this line and Everyman's interaction with Goods characterizes him as more than ordinarily wealthy. See pp. 54, 58.
389 **my Good** Everyman will use the singular to refer to Goods here and in the latter's presence. Death has used the plural *worldly goods* (162), and Everyman will use the plural as well at 472 and 474, after he has been rejected by Goods. The singular *good* for the plural *goods* was beginning to be archaic at this time, but would survive in such proverbs as Tilley, G298 'As rises my good so rises my blood.' *OED a., adv.,*

and *sb.* 7b cites Berners, *Golden Boke of Marcus Aurelius* (*c.* 1533): 'The more goodde I hadde, the more couetous I was' (Ccb). The use of the singular from 389 to 453 suggests Everyman's misperception of material *goods* as an immaterial *good*; he temporarily reverses the movement from abstraction to specific discussed in 66n.
help me might i.e. is able to help me
390 **full light** entirely glad, joyful. Cf. *RJ* 4.2.46: 'My heart is wondrous light.'
391 **in this distress** i.e. in this distressful situation
392 SD Some flexibility of staging exists for the beginning of this sequence. Early productions like those of Ben Greet (1902) used an alcove for Goods's domain. He may also speak his initial lines hidden by properties representing the *chests, bags* and *packs* (395–7). Alternately, Goods could begin his lines offstage before entering. On staging, see Appendix 3. See Fletcher, 'Coveytyse', for discussion of an analogous sequence in *Perseverance.*
392 SD, 394 *corner . . . corners* a nook or recess in a room (see *MED* 6), with

380 promise] *Q3;* promes moche *Q2*   383 flee] *Q3;* flye *Q2*   386 lose] *Q3;* lese *Q2*   abide] *Q3;* byde *Q2*   390 He] *Q3;* It *Q2, Q4*   392 SD] *Cawley subst.; within* | *Adams*

GOODS

> Who calleth me? Everyman? What, hast thou haste?
> I lie here in corners, trussed and piled so high,
> And in chests I am locked so fast,   395
> Also sacked in bags. Thou mayst see with thine eye
> I cannot stir; in packs low I lie.
> What would ye have? Lightly me say.

EVERYMAN

> Come hither, Good, in all the haste thou may,
> For of counsel I must desire thee.   400

GOODS

> Sir, an ye i'the world have sorrow or adversity,
> That can I help you to remedy shortly.

EVERYMAN

> It is another disease that grieveth me;

the plural here lending an air of the proverbial. Cf. 'Beware of corners' (Whiting, C442), and *MM* 4.3.156: the 'duke of dark corners'.

394 Goods's implication is that he has been hoarded securely, and solely for Everyman's use. This is to the detriment not only of the 'poor', who could have benefited from Everyman's charity (cf. 432), but also – and crucially – of Everyman's *soul* (442). Throughout, this sequence depends on the idea that the Christian life is a treasure unto itself; see Colossians, 2.3, 9, and p. 53.
trussed packed, tied up

395–7 **chests . . . bags . . . packs** Goods's threefold description here is formulaic, yet may give an indication of the variety of stage properties that could be used to indicate Everyman's worldly wealth.

395 **so** exceedingly, very. Here and in the preceding line, Goods uses *so* as an intensifier in an affirmative clause. Cf. Chaucer's *The Parliament of Fowls*:

'The lyf so short, the craft so long to lerne' (1).
fast securely, without hope of escaping
397 **stir** move (a limb or member)
398 **ye** Goods changes pronouns here from *thou* (393) and *thine* (396) to the plural and polite form *ye*, perhaps indicating that Everyman has come closer onstage to Goods, who will temporarily (398, 401, 402, 426) use the more respectful pronoun. Such deference seems to contribute to Everyman's vain hopes.
Lightly swiftly, at once
me say tell me. Goods echoes Fellowship at 208.
399 **may** i.e. that you are able to exert
402 **remedy** cure, heal
403 **disease** Everyman's *distress* (217, 391) has become *disease*. Cf. Mark, 4.18–19: 'And ther ben othir that ben sowun in thornes; these it ben that heren the word, and disese of the world, and disseit of ritchessis, and othir charge of coueytise entrith, and stranglith the word, and it is maad with out fruyt' (Wycliffe).

394 trussed] *Q3;* trushed *Q2*   so high] *Q3;* nye *Q2*   395 so] *Q3;* full *Q2, Q4*   397 low] *Q3;* lowe where *Q2*   401, 414, 425 SP] *Q3;* good dedes *Q2*   401 an] *Q3 (&)*   sorrow] *Q2, Q3;* trouble *Q4*   402 That] *Q2, Q3;* Than *Q4*

In this world it is not, I tell thee so.
I am sent for another way to go,   405
To give a strait count general
Before the highest Jupiter of all.
And all my life I have had joy and pleasure in thee;
Therefore, I pray thee, go with me.
For, peradventure, thou mayst before God almighty   410
My reckoning help to clean and purify;
For it is said ever among
That 'Money maketh all right that is wrong.'
GOODS
Nay, Everyman, I sing another song;
I follow no man in such voyages.   415
For, an I went with thee,
Thou shouldest fare much the worse for me;

404 **it** i.e. the *disease* (403), which Goods has, according to his figuration, located *i'the world* (401)

405 **sent for** (1) summoned (recalling the play's full title); (2) sent in order that, so that

406 **count** account, reckoning of one's deeds in life. See *Perseverance*: 'Whanne Myhel his horn blowith at my dred dom, the count of here conscience schal putten hem in pres, & yelde a reknynge' (ll. 3618–20). See *give account* (0.2), 20 and n., and pp. 50–3.

407 **highest Jupiter** i.e. God. For Jupiter – known formally to the Romans as 'Jupiter Optimus Maximus' – as mightiest of the gods, see *Confessio Amantis*: 'O thou, almyhty Jupiter' (5.5741), and Lydgate, *Troy Book*: 'He [Jupiter] was lord of eyr, of lond, & see' (2.5636). Like his 'the high Judge, Adonai' (245), Everyman's elegant variation here seems undermotivated (neither phrase is in *Elck*); with its reference to an astronomical/astrological agency, perhaps the epithet is meant to indicate his stubborn belief

in multiple options for assistance.

410 **peradventure** perhaps, perchance

412 **ever among** in many places, everywhere. Cf. *MED* among *adv.*, *OED* among *adv. and prep.*, B. *adv.* 2. Cf. also *Arcadia*, 1593: 'And euer among shee woulde sawce her speeches with such Bastonados' (410, fol. 203).

413 **'Money . . . wrong'** proverbial: Dent, M1072. For Everyman's comic reliance on proverbs, see p. 54.

414 **I sing another song** i.e. I have another intent. Proverbial; cf. *Confessio Amantis*: 'Now schalt thou singe an other song' (2.3012). Cf. the modern 'sing a different tune'.

415 **no man** Goods, like Death and Fellowship before him, invokes the opposite of 'every man'; he will do so again at 426. Cf. 115–16, 267.

416 **thee** Here Goods returns to the less deferential 'thou' pronominal form. See 398n.

417 **for** because of, on account of. Goods's concentrated use of *for* (416, 417, 418, 421) seems to parody

404 thee] *Q2, Q3; om. Q4*   406 count] *Q2, Q3;* accounte *Q4*   408 joy and] *Q3;* my *Q2*   409 go] *Q3;* nowe go *Q2*   414 Nay] *Q3;* Nay nay *Q2*   417 shouldest] *Q2, Q4;* sholdes *Q3*

For because on me thou didst set thy mind,
Thy reckoning I have made blotted and blind,
That thine account thou cannot make truly,   420
And that hast thou for the love of me!

EVERYMAN

That would grieve me full sore
When I should come to that fearful answer.
Up, let us go thither together!

GOODS

Nay, not so. I am too brittle; I may not endure.   425
I will follow no man one foot, be ye sure.

EVERYMAN

Alas, I have thee loved, and had great pleasure

Everyman's frequent use of it in his preceding lines: see 400, 405, 410, 412, as well as *Before* (407, 410) and *Therefore* (409), which add to the cluster.

419 blotted smeared, as with ink. See *OED* blotted *ppl. a.*, citing Thynne: 'the blotted and rude wrytinge'. Cf. also *Mankind* 680–1 and n.

blind indistinct or illegible. Goods brags that he has blotted and thus obliterated Everyman's book of reckoning. See *MED adj.*, citing *Catholicon Anglicum* (*c.* 1475): 'To make Blynde . . . obliterare vt in libris' (15b).

420 That i.e. with the result that

421 And . . . . thou And (just) that is what you have received – i.e. the inability to make true *account* (420).

love of me Goods plays on the well-known passage from 1 Timothy, 6:10: 'For loue of money, is the roote of all euyll, whiche whyle some lusted after, they erred from the fayth, & pearced the selues through with many sorowes.' Goods's phrase may also ask us to understand not only those who

love goods, but the (negative) love Goods returns; a similar dual sense occurs at 430.

422 full sore very painfully. A common expression; see Mak in *Second Shepherds*': 'full sore am I and yll' (l. 231), and *MED* sore *adv.* 1a.

423 fearful inspiring or causing fear, terrible; having to give his *answer* terrifies Everyman.

answer i.e. his final *account* (420) before God. Cf. Death's 'For before God thou shalt answer' (107).

424 Up i.e. stand up! Everyman's imperative shows that Goods still *cannot* or will not *stir* (397).

thither there, in that direction

425 brittle fragile, feeble, with the suggestion, perhaps, of 'morally weak'. Often used (in alliterative phrases) to describe the body. See *MED* brotle *adj.*, and *OED* brittle *a.* 1b, citing Fisher, *Works 1*: 'These brytell bodyes of ours' (176). The reading here was perhaps influenced by the sound of *Elck*, which reads '*Neen, ick bin onbrangelijc*' (384), which might be translated as 'No, I am unbudgeable.'

---

418 didst] *Q2;* dyd *Q3*   421 the love of me] *Q3;* my loue trewely *Q2*   424 Up] *Q3;* Vp and *Q2*   425 brittle] *Q3;* brotell *Q2*   426 no man] *Q2;* man *Q3*   ye] *Q2, Q3;* thou *Q4*

All my life days on good and treasure.

GOODS

That is to thy damnation, without leasing,

For my love is contrary to the love everlasting.   430

But, if thou had me loved moderately during,

As to the poor give part of me,

Then shouldest thou not in this dolour be,

Nor in this great sorrow and care.

EVERYMAN

Lo, now was I deceived ere I was ware,   435

And all I may wit misspending of time!

GOODS

What, weenest thou that I am thine?

---

428 **life days** i.e. the days of my life. Cf. Malory: 'and soo haue kepte it my lyfe dayes' (Cap. 15, 104ʳ); and *Roister Doister*: 'all thy life days thou canst do me honestie' (4.3.63).

429 **to** resulting in, aimed towards
without leasing without lying, truly. According to *MED* this word was often used as a rhyme tag (see lesinge *ger.* 2, 1b). Cf. Jesus in the *Lord's Ascension*: 'ffor I go full securly / to my fader, heuyns kyng; / The which, without lesyng / is mekill more then I' (*Towneley*, ll. 110–11).

430 **my love** with the dual sense discussed in 421n.

431 **moderately** A noticeable qualification of Christ's direction to sell all that one has and give it to the poor, the word *moderately* here points towards the influence of Aristotle's *Nicomachean Ethics* and of humanism generally. For the biblical injunction, see Matthew, 19.21. Cf. also 699 and n.
during i.e. in your lifetime

433 **dolour** pain, suffering, painful disease

435 **Lo** Equivalent to our 'Oh!', this interjection suggests Everyman's growing consciousness of his predicament.

now just previously, lately
ere before
ware aware

436 **wit** (1) account, characterize as (*MED* witen *v.* 3b); (2) (as transitive) attribute to, blame on (witen *v.* 3.1b. a, b). For the former sense, cf. Malory, Vinaver: 'For this xiiij yere I neuer discouerd one thynge that I haue vsed / and that maye I now wyte my shame and my disauentur' (Bk 13, Cap. 20); for the latter, see the Prologue to 'Miller's Tale': 'therfore if that I mysspeke or seye, / Wyte it the ale of Southwerk, I you preye' (3139–40).
misspending a word used to denote 'improper spending of time' as well as 'squandering of treasure' (*MED* misspendinge *ger.*). *OED* misspending *sb.* cites Robert Barnes's *Works* (*c.* 1540): 'Mispending of goodes' (364).

437 the second time Everyman has been asked a form of this question; note Death's 'What, weenest thou thy life is given thee, / And thy worldly goods also?' (161–2). Here Everyman speaks to a figure representing just these *worldly goods*.

---

428 good] *Q3;* my good *Q2*   429–552] *Qq; Q1 serves as control text*   430 love] *Q1;* loue of *Q2*   432 give] *Q1;* to gyue *Q4* of] *Q1;* for the loue of *Q2;* for *Q4*   433 be] *Q1;* haue be *Q2*   435 was I] *Q1;* I was *Q4* ere] *Q1 (*or*)*   436 misspending] *Q1 (*myspendynge*);* my spendinge *Q3, Q4*

EVERYMAN

    I had weened so.

GOODS

    Nay, Everyman, I say no.

    As for a while I was lent thee,   440

    A season thou hast had me in prosperity.

    My condition is man's soul to kill;

    If I save one, a thousand I do spill.

    Weenest thou that I will follow thee?

    Nay, from this world not, verily.   445

EVERYMAN

    I had weened otherwise.

GOODS

    Therefore to thy soul Good is a thief,

    For when thou art dead, this is my guise:

    Another to deceive in this same wise

    As I have done thee, and all to his soul's reproof.   450

EVERYMAN

    O false Good, cursed thou be,

    Thou traitor to God, that hast deceived me

    And caught me in thy snare!

---

438 I . . . so Cf. Everyman's response to Death's earlier, and nearly identical question: 'I had weened so, verily' (163).

440 lent thee proverbial: 'Good is but a lent loan'; Whiting, G334, citing *Towneley*: 'Yis, all the good thou has in wone / Of godis grace is bot a loan' (13.116–17).

441 season (an indefinite) period of time. Cf. Luke, 4.13: 'He departed from hym for a season' (Tyndale).

442 condition nature, characteristic

443 spill destroy, vanquish, lead to damnation. Often used (as here) in contrast to 'save'; cf. *Mankind*: 'Ye may both save and spill your soul that is so

precious' (893).

445 this world i.e. the secular world of earthly existence. Cf. Matthew, 13.22: 'the bisynesse of this world' (Wycliffe).
verily in truth

448 guise practice, custom (*OED sb.* 2); cf. *Mac* 5.1.18: 'This is her very guise.'

449 wise way, manner

450 reproof shame, disgrace, trouble

453 snare trap. A biblical image: cf. Proverbs, 29.6: 'The synne of ye wicked is his owne snare, but ye righteous shal be glad and reioyse' (Coverdale). See also *Mankind*, where Titivillus enters holding a net (474 SD and n.).

438, 446 weened] *Q1* (wente)   442 condition] *Q1;* condycyons *Q4*   443 thousand] *Q1* (M.)   445 Nay, from] *Q1* (Nay fro); Nay nat fro *Q2;* Nay nat fro *Q2;* From *Q4*   not, verily] *Q1;* verely *Q2;* nay verely *Q4*   449 this] *Q1;* the *Q2, Q4*   450 done] *Q3;* do *Q1, Q2*   reproof] *Q1* (reprefe)   451 thou] *Q1;* may thou *Q2*   452 that] *Q1;* thou *Q4*   453 caught] *Q1;* caugh *Q3*

GOODS

    Marry, thou brought thyself in care,

    Whereof I am glad.   455

    I must needs laugh; I cannot be sad.

EVERYMAN

    Ah, Good, thou hast had long my heartly love!

    I gave thee that which should be the Lord's above.

    But wilt thou not go with me indeed?

    I pray thee truth to say.   460

GOODS

    No, so God me speed!

    Therefore farewell, have good day.   [*Exit.*]

EVERYMAN

    Oh, to whom shall I make my moan

    For to go with me in that heavy journey?

    First Fellowship said he would with me go –   465

    His words were very pleasant and gay –

    But afterward he left me alone.

    Then spake I to my kinsmen, all in despair,

---

454 **Marry** i.e. by the Virgin Mary (a mild oath)
care sin, distress (*MED* care *sb.*[1] 3c, a). Cf. Chaucer, 'Second Nun's Tale': 'mankynde . . . was ybounde in synne and cares colde' (346–7).

455 **Whereof** i.e. concerning the fact of which

457 **heartly** heartfelt, loyal

458 Cf. Christ's well-known directive in Luke, 20.25: 'And he sayde vnto them: Geve then vnto Cesar that which belongeth vnto Cesar: and to God that which pertayneth to God' (Tyndale).

460 **truth to say** i.e. to say truly

461 **so . . . speed** Cf. Cousin's identical, and similarly ironic, oath at 357.

462 **farewell . . . day** a clichéd expression,

then as now, that comes all the more painfully to Everyman in the context of Goods's refusal. One gets the sense of its trite nature from its repetition in Chaucer's works; cf. 'Knight's Tale': 'Ther was namoore but 'Fare wel, have good day!' (2740) and 'Nun's Priest's Tale': 'God woot, it reweth me; and have good day!' (3097).

463 **moan** request, entreaty

464 **heavy** difficult, hard to accomplish; with an implication of the task's troublesome nature and the sorrow it will bring them

466 **gay** pleasant sounding (*MED* gai *adj.* 3c). Cf. Lydgate, *Troy Book*: 'In his dites, that wer so fresche and gay / With sugred wordes vnder hony soote' (Prologue, 276–7).

---

455 glad] *Q1;* right gladde *Q2*   457 had long] *Q1;* had *Q4*   461 SP] *Q3;* Good *Q2; not in Q1*   462 have] *Q1;* and haue *Q2, Q3, Q4*   SD] *Adams*   464 in] *Q1;* om. *Q2*   465 said] *Q1;* he sayd *Q4*   go] *Q1 (gone)*

And also they gave me words fair.
They lacked no fair speaking,   470
But all forsook me in the ending.
Then went I to my Goods, that I loved best,
In hope to have comfort, but there had I least;
For my Goods sharply did me tell
That he bringeth many into hell.   475
Then of myself I was ashamed,
And so I am worthy to be blamed.
Thus may I well myself hate.
Of whom shall I now counsel take?
I think that I shall never speed   480
Till that I go to my Good Deed.
But, alas, she is so weak
That she can neither go ne speak.
Yet will I venture on her now. –
My Good Deeds, where be you?   485

[GOOD DEEDS *speaks from the ground.*]

GOOD DEEDS
Here I lie, cold on the ground;

473 **least** i.e. *comfort* or assistance
474 **sharply** reprovingly, sternly (*MED* sharpli *adv.* 3a; *OED* sharply *adv.* 1a, b, with implication of the painful effect of the words: cf. the similar resonance of *heavy* at 464)
480 **speed** achieve my goal, succeed
482 **she** Unlike the figures Everyman has met so far, Good Deeds is gendered female, in line with allegorical traditions regarding alms and charity.
483 **go** move; perhaps with a hint at how money or commodities can *go*, i.e. pass for or be valued at particular amounts

speak make a sound, talk; perhaps with a sense of the pleading involved in the phrase *speak for*: Good Deeds is currently too weak to help defend Everyman, but later she will regain her voice and *speak for* him (877).
484 **venture on** make a trial of (here, risk asking: *OED* venture *v.* 9a)
486 **cold . . . ground** Good Deeds, like Goods, is initially encountered prone or reclining. She does not rise until 619, and may be surrounded onstage not by moneybags (as Goods is, 394–7) but by the scattered, empty pages of Everyman's *works and deeds*

469 And] *Q1;* An *Q3*   470 fair] *Q1;* feare *Q2*   471 forsook] *Q1* (forsoke); forsake *Q3, Q4*   473 have] *Q1;* haue foūde *Q2*   474 my Goods] *Q1;* goodes *Q2*   475 into] *Q1;* in *Q4*   483 ne] *Q1;* nor *Q3, Q4*   485 SD] *Adams subst.*   486 on] *Q1;* in *Q3, Q4*

Thy sins hath me sore bound,
That I cannot stir.

EVERYMAN

Oh, Good Deeds, I stand in fear.
I must you pray of counsel, 490
For help now should come right well.

GOOD DEEDS

Everyman, I have understanding
That ye be summoned account to make
Before Messiahs, of Jerusalem king.
An you do by me, that journey with you will I take. 495

EVERYMAN

Therefore I come to you, my moan to make.
I pray you that ye will go with me.

GOOD DEEDS

I would full fain, but I cannot stand, verily.

EVERYMAN

Why, is there anything on you fall?

GOOD DEEDS

Yea, sir, I may thank you of all! 500

(see 503–7). In *Elck*, Virtue speaks of herself lying 'all withered in bed' (442–3). The phrase 'cold on the ground' hints at the grave Everyman journeys towards.

487 **sins . . . bound** Good Deeds may be represented as *bound* with cords or other symbols of restraint. Regardless of her appearance, this line introduces a crucial idea: people are bound by their sins unless and until released by the priesthood through the agency of the sacraments. Cf. 740–1.

489 **stand** remain (with pun on standing upright – in contrast to Good Deeds's position)

490 I must request your (supporting) advice.

491 **should . . . well** i.e. would be very welcome

492 **understanding** with pun, perhaps, on her position under the standing Everyman

493 **account to make** i.e. to give an account

494 **Messiahs . . . king** i.e. Jesus, the Messiah and King of Jerusalem; cf. 29–34, and List of Roles 2n.

495 **An . . . me** if you help me, act in accordance to my identity (the implication being that Everyman needs to attend to Good Deeds in order to secure her assistance). Cf. *Sages*, 62: 'But hit is skil, riyt and lawe, / To do bi me as bi thin awe.'

498 **full fain** very eagerly

499 **fall** fallen

500 **I . . . all** I may thank you in particular for my situation.

---

487 hath me] *Q1;* haue me so *Q4*   489 fear] *Q1;* great feare *Q2*   491 help . . . well] *Q3;* nowe helpe and well *Q1, Q2*   493 ye be] *Q1;* thou arte *Q4*   account] *Q1* (a counte)   497 you . . . will] *Q1;* the to *Q4*

215

If ye had perfectly cheered me,
Your book of account now full ready had be.
Look, the books of your works and deeds eke:
Ah, see how they lie here under the feet
To your soul's heaviness.   505

EVERYMAN

Our Lord Jesus help me,
For one letter herein can I not see.

GOOD DEEDS

There is a blind reckoning in time of distress.

EVERYMAN

Good Deeds, I pray you help me in this need,
Or else I am forever damned indeed.   510
Therefore help me to make my reckoning
Before the redeemer of all thing,
That king is, and was, and ever shall.

GOOD DEEDS

Everyman, I am sorry of your fall,

501 **perfectly** fully; with the suggestion of 'righteously', 'in a manner morally or religiously perfect' (see *OED adv.* 1, 2a) **cheered** encouraged, animated
503–4 Here a performance of *Everyman* would present a clear allegorical picture: Good Deeds indicates the lowly status of Everyman's *book of account* (502) by pointing out a volume or loose pages lying on the ground. Everyman might be cued to retrieve a book prior to 505–6.
503 **books** account, record (*OED* book *sb.* 2) **works and deeds** Everyman's actions in life. Cf. 338 and n.
505 **heaviness** sadness, sorrow (recalling Everyman's *heavy journey* at 464)
507 **For . . . see** For I cannot see anything written here.
508 **blind reckoning** illegible record (cf.

419n.), one that provides no help at such a juncture
510 **forever damned** Although God has lamented 'the seven deadly sins damnable' (36), Everyman first learns of damnation in the play from Goods at 429: 'That is to thy damnation'.
512 **the redeemer** i.e. Jesus Christ **thing** things
513 an echo of the Gloria Patri, the longstanding minor doxology of the Christian tradition: 'Glory be to the Father, and to the Son and to the Holy Ghost, As it was in the beginning, is now, and ever shall be, world without end.'
shall i.e. shall be
514 **fall** destruction, overthrow (*OED sb.*[1] 18a), with suggestions of the 'fall of man'; ironic reversal of Everyman's

502 account] *Q1* (a counte*)*; counte *Q3*   now full ready] *Q1*; full redy *Q3*; full redy now *Q4*   504 Ah, see] *this edn*; As e *Q1, Q2, Q3*; Beholde *Q4*; As *Lester*   here under the] *Q1*; here vnder *Q2*; vnder the *Q3, Q4*   507 herein can I] *Q1*; here I can *Q2, Q3*   508 There] *Q1*; Here *Q2*   510 forever] *Q1* (for euer*)*; for ouer *Q2*   511 my] *Q1*; om. *Q3*

And fain would I help you, an I were able.   515
EVERYMAN
Good Deeds, your counsel I pray you give me.
GOOD DEEDS
That shall I do verily.
Though that on my feet I may not go,
I have a sister that shall with you also,
Called Knowledge, which shall with you abide   520
To help you to make that dreadful reckoning.

[*Enter* KNOWLEDGE.]

KNOWLEDGE
Everyman, I will go with thee and be thy guide,
In thy most need to go by thy side.
EVERYMAN
In good condition I am now in everything,
And am wholly content with this good thing,   525
Thanked be God my creator.
GOOD DEEDS
And when she hath brought you there
Where thou shalt heal thee of thy smart,
Then go you with your reckoning and your Good Deeds
    together,
For to make you joyful at heart   530

question to her at 499: 'is there anything on you fall?'
518 **Though that** although
519 **sister** In the play's allegory, Good Deeds is the sister of Knowledge – the implication being that these two entities are as closely allied as possible.
shall i.e. shall go
521 **dreadful** inspiring dread
524 I am now well set (for my journey).
525 **this good thing** Knowledge's companionship
527–8 **there / Where** to the place where
528 **heal . . . smart** cure you of your suffering. The word *smart* here recalls with its rhyme Death's proverbial *dart* (see 76 and n.), the lance or spear with which he traditionally strikes down his victims.
530 **For to** in order to, so as to

519 with] *Q2; not in Q1*   521 SD] *Adams*   526 be] *Q1;* by *Q3*   creator] *Q1 (*creature*)*   527 she] *Bevington;* he *Qq*   you] *Q1;* the *Q4*   529 you . . . your . . . your] *Q1;* thou . . . thy . . . thy *Q4*   530 you joyful at] *Q1;* the ioyfull at the *Q4*

217

Before the blessed Trinity.

EVERYMAN

My Good Deeds, gramercy!

I am well content, certainly,

With your words sweet.

KNOWLEDGE

Now go we together lovingly   535

To Confession, that cleansing river.

EVERYMAN

For joy I weep! I would we there were.

But, I pray you, give me cognition

Where dwelleth that holy man, Confession?

KNOWLEDGE

In the house of salvation.   540

We shall find him in that place

That shall us comfort, by God's grace.

[CONFESSION *enters and* KNOWLEDGE *leads*
EVERYMAN *to him.*]

Lo, this is Confession. Kneel down and ask mercy,

For he is in good conceit with God almighty.

531 **Trinity** the unified-but-distinct Godhead of Father, Son and Holy Ghost; an idea central to Catholic teaching (cf. Matthew, 28.19)

536 Confession is part of the sacrament of penance in the Catholic Church; sins committed after baptism may be forgiven through the absolution offered by a priest once a repentant person confesses his or her sins and promises not to commit them again.
river Cf. *Elck*: 'She is a clear river, she will cleanse you' (487–8).

538 **cognition** knowledge (the Latinate register here in order to rhyme with *Confession*)

540 **house of salvation** perhaps drawing on the edifice of faith imagined in Psalms, 118.21–2: 'I wyll thanke thee for that thou hast heard me: and art become my saluation. The same stone which the buylders refused: is become the head stone of the corner.' Cf. Spenser's 'House of Holiness' in *FQ* (1.10). While productions may wish to employ a stage house here, and have Confession within it, the lines make it equally possible to have Confession enter (and subsequently exit).

544 **conceit** esteem

532 gramercy] *Q1*; I thanke the hartfully *Q4*   535 together] *Q1* (to gyder*)*; thether *Q4*   537 there were] *Q1*; were there *Q3, Q4*   538 you . . . cognition] *Q1*; yon to instructe me by intelleccyon *Q4*   539 man] *Q1*; vertue *Q4*   542 SD] *Adams subst.*

EVERYMAN [*Kneels.*]

O glorious fountain that all uncleanness doth clarify,   545
Wash from me the spots and vices clean,
That on me no sin may be seen.
I come with Knowledge for my redemption,
Repent with heart and full contrition;
For I am commanded a pilgrimage to take   550
And great accounts before God to make.
Now I pray you, Shrift, mother of salvation,
Help hither my Good Deeds for my piteous exclamation.

CONFESSION

I know your sorrow well, Everyman.
Because with Knowledge ye come to me,   555
I will you comfort as well as I can,
And a precious jewel I will give thee,
Called penance, voider of adversity.

---

545 **clarify** make pure and clear, or clean
546 i.e. wash clean from me the stains that vice has left
549 **Repent with heart** with a repentant heart. Cf. *Elizabetha*, 34: 'May now confesse with sore repenting heart'.
551 **great** i.e. greatly consequential
552 **Shrift** confession (*OED sb.* 5). Although 'shrift' was also used to describe the penance or absolution that followed upon the act of confession, Everyman has yet to be informed of penance (see 561ff.).
mother of salvation Like Good Deeds, and another saving figure, the Virgin Mary, *Shrift* as concept and character is gendered female in *Everyman*, while Confession is gendered male. In *Elck* Confession is female.
553 Help (raise) my Good Deeds so that

she may assist me in my sorrowful representations – i.e. of the *great accounts* (551), before my judge.
555–6 The implication is that a desperate resort to confession – one without *Knowledge* of what it truly means – would be unsuccessful.
558 **penance** The performance of a specific act signifying repentance after the commission of a sin or sins, penance was typically directed by a priest (understood to function as an agent of the Church) following the individual's confession, and usually involved the recitation of a familiar prayer or prayers. Penance is one of the seven sacraments of Christianity.
voider that which keeps off or drives away (*OED* 1, citing this passage, but see also *OED* 2: 'A piece of armour covering an exposed or unprotected

545 SD] *this edn*   546 and vices] *Q1;* of vyce *Q3;* of vyces *Q4*   clean] *Q1;* vnclene *Q3, Q4*   549 Repent] *Q1;* Redempte *Q3, Q4* (Redempe)   full] *Q1;* full of *Q4*   551 great accounts] *Q3;* a grete countes *Q1, Q2*   553–683] *Q2, Q3, Q4; not in Q1; Q3 serves as control text*   553 hither] *Q2; not in Q3, Q4*   558 voider] *Q2;* voyce voyder *Q3*

Therewith shall your body chastised be
With abstinence and perseverance in God's service.   560
Here shall you receive that scourge of me,
  [*Shows a whip.*]
Which is penance strong that ye must endure.
Remember thy saviour was scourged for thee
With sharp scourges and suffered it patiently;
So must thou, ere thou pass thy pilgrimage. –   565
Knowledge, keep him in this voyage,
  [*Gives the whip to Knowledge.*]
And by that time Good Deeds will be with thee.
[*to Everyman*] But, in any wise, be seeker of mercy,
For your time draweth fast; an ye will saved be,
Ask God mercy and he will grant truly.   570

place'). The word *voider* may also have suggested the receptacle used to carry away dirty utensils and food scraps from tables (*OED* 3), a sense that Richard Barnfield employed in analogizing life to a feast: 'Then with an earthen voyder (made of clay) / Comes Death, & takes the table clean away' ('A Comparison of the Life of Man', *Encomion*, ll. 6–7).

559 chastised disciplined, reformed (*OED* chastise *v.* 1, and *ppl. a.*)

560 abstinence forbearance from indulging the appetite, self-restraint; such could include restraint from sexual activity and fasting. See *OED* 2a, b.

perseverance steadfastness; with suggestion of the continuing or remaining in a state of grace, virtue or religious fidelity (*OED* 2). For the importance of *perseverance* to late medieval Christianity, see *Perseverance*.

561 scourge a whip or lash, sometimes

made with *knots* (576) to increase the pain. Everyman's *penance* (558, 562) includes punishing or 'mortifying' his flesh to diminish its hold on his attention. An ascetic strain in medieval Christianity would hold, with Mercy in *Mankind*, that 'Your body is your enemy; let him not have his will' (897).

563–4 recalling Christ's torment before the crucifixion; cf. Matthew, 27.26.

565 pass complete, bring to an end

566 voyage journey (i.e. the *pilgrimage*, 565), with implication of a more general enterprise or course of action (*OED sb.* 1c, 3)

568 seeker a seeker. But Q4's *sure* suggests the possibility also of Middle English *siker* (adj.), 'in assured possession of', 'bound to experience' (or 'obtain') – of which *seker* (Q2 and Q3) was a variant spelling (*MED* 4a).

569 draweth i.e. comes to an end
an . . . be if you wish to be saved

560 service] *Q3;* servyture *Coldewey*   561 you] *Q3;* ye *Q2*   SD] *Lester subst.*   563 Remember] *Q2;* To remembre *Q3, Q4*   565 pass thy] *Q2;* scape that paynful *Q3, Q4*   566 keep] *Q2, Q3;* hym and kepe *Q4*   SD] *this edn*   568 SD] *this edn*   568 seeker] *Q2, Q3* (seker); sure *Q4;* sicker *Lester*   570 truly] *Q3;* it the *Q2*

When with the scourge of penance man doth
him bind,
The oil of forgiveness then shall he find.   [*Exit.*]
EVERYMAN
Thanked be God for his gracious work,
For now I will my penance begin.
This hath rejoiced and lighted my heart,   575
Though the knots be painful and hard within.
KNOWLEDGE
Everyman, look your penance that ye fulfil,
What pain that ever it to you be,
And Knowledge shall give you counsel at will
How your account ye shall make clearly.   580
EVERYMAN
O eternal God, O heavenly figure,
O way of righteousness, O goodly vision –
Which descended down in a virgin pure
Because he would every man redeem,

571 **man** the universal sense: 'a man,
person'
bind tie fast; perhaps echoing
Matthew, 16.19: 'And whatsoeuer thou
byndest in earth, shalbe bounde in
heauen: and whatsoeuer thou loosest
in earth, shalbe loosed in heauen.'
572 **oil of forgiveness** the healing 'oil
of the tree of mercy' sought by Seth
for his father Adam in the apocryphal
gospel of Nicodemus, 3 (19). See
Quinn.
576 **within** (1) during the process of
(scourging myself) (*OED adv., prep.,
(a.)* 6c); (2) inwardly (i.e. in my body,
causing me *pain*, 578) (*OED* 3)
577 **your . . . fulfil** Be careful to complete
your penance.
579 **at will** at your command or pleasure

580 **clearly** distinct, with optical
clarity (*OED adv.* 2, with adverb
here functioning as an adjective).
Everyman's account is to be purged of
its *blotted and blind* (419) defects. He
has already expressed a desire to have
his book made clear at 136.
581 Everyman, still kneeling, begins a
prayer that addresses in turn God
(581–8); Jesus Christ (589–96); and the
Virgin Mary (597–604) before turning
to Knowledge at 605–7. As 583 makes
clear, each entity invoked in this trio
seamlessly involves the other two.
584 **redeem** For Christ as redeemer of
fallen humanity, see e.g. John, 6.51;
and Titus, 2.14: 'Which gaue hym
selfe for vs, that he myght redeeme vs
from all vnryghteousnesse.'

572 SD] *this edn*   573 his] *Q3;* this *Q2*   575 rejoiced] *Q3;* me reioysed *Q2*   577 look your penance]
Q2, Q3; your penaunce loke *Q4*   579 Knowledge] *Q3;* I *Q2*   shall] *Q2, Q3;* wyll *Q4*   584 redeem]
Q2, Q3; to redeme *Q4*

Which Adam forfeited by his disobedience – 585
O blessed Godhead elect and high divine,
Forgive me my grievous offence;
Here I cry thee mercy in this presence.
O ghostly treasure, O ransomer and redeemer,
Of all the world hope and conductor, 590
Mirror of joy, foundator of mercy,
Which enlumineth heaven and earth thereby,
Hear my clamorous complaint, though it late be;
Receive my prayers unworthy in this heavy life.
Though I be a sinner most abominable, 595

585 **disobedience** i.e. Adam's 'fall' as recounted in Genesis, 3. See also Romans, 5.19: 'For as by one mans disobedience many became sinners: so by the obedience of one, shall many be made ryghteous.'
586 **Godhead** 'the character or quality of being God' (*OED*). Cf. Huggarde: 'Of the blessed godhead most celestiall, / With the whiche godhead Christ was euer equal / So then where christ is, the godhead is alway' (ll. 256–8).
  elect chosen (here, by God) for an honour or function. Everyman has moved from an invocation of God, proper, to his *elect* son, Jesus Christ.
587 echoing the language of the Lord's Prayer; cf. Matthew, 6.12: 'And forgeue vs our dettes, as we forgeue our detters.'
  grievous offence detailed by God (for humanity collectively) at 22–62
588 **cry thee** beg from you, plead with you for
  this presence i.e. before my witnesses, in this special place and time. Cf. the Second King in *Shearmen*, 24: 'Now knele we downe here in this presence, / Be-sekyng that Lord of hy mangnefecens' (ll. 691–2).

589 **ghostly** spiritual
  ransomer one who ransoms another. Cf. Mark, 10.45: 'For the sonne of man also came not to be ministred vnto: but to minister, & to geue his lyfe, a raunsome for many.'
590 the hope and (spiritual) guide of the whole world. For *conductor*, cf. Psalms, 31.3: 'For thou art my strong rocke and fortresse: euen for thy name sake conduct me, and direct me.'
591 **Mirror of joy** example of gladness; cf. *Divine Weeks*, 429, of David: 'And so He rules on th'holy Mount (a mirror) / His Peoples Ioy, the Pagans only Terror' (ll. 823–4).
  foundator founder. Cf. *Weavers*, 39: 'The seylesteall Soferent, owre hy Gode eternall! / Wyche of this mervelus world ys the fowndatur' (ll. 177–8).
592 With this image of spiritual illumination, cf. Psalm, 18.28: 'Thou also hast lyghtened my candell: God my Lorde hath made my darknesse to be lyght.'
594 **prayers unworthy** unworthy prayers
  heavy the last use of a 'heavy'-form in the play (cf. 216, 464, 505); hereafter, the homonymic *heaven* (cf. 592) will supplant it in various forms.

586 Godhead] *Q4* (godhede)*;* godheed *Q2*, god heed *Q3*   587 me] *Q2; not in Q3*   589 ransomer and] *Q3;* mercyfull *Q2*   590 conductor] *Q4;* conduiter *Q2, Q3* (conduyter*)*   591 foundator] *Q3;* foundacion *Q2;* and founder *Q4*   592 enlumineth] *Q3;* illumyneth *Q2*   594 unworthy . . . life] *Q2, Q3;* of thy benygnytye *Q4*

Yet let my name be written in Moses' table.
O Mary, pray to the maker of all thing
Me for to help at my ending,
And save me from the power of my enemy,
For Death assaileth me strongly;   600
And, Lady, that I may by mean of thy prayer
Of your son's glory to be partner,
By the means of his passion, I it crave.
I beseech you help me my soul to save.   [*Rises.*]
Knowledge, give me the scourge of penance;   605
   [*Takes the whip.*]
My flesh therewith shall give a quittance.
I will now begin, if God give me grace.
KNOWLEDGE
   Everyman, God give you time and space.

596 **Moses' table** the Decalogue or ten
commandments, described in Exodus,
20.1–17; here invoked as a kind of
dual-purpose book that both conveys
the law and can record (like a book
of 'reckoning') Everyman's adherence
to it
598 to help me at my death
599 **my enemy** Satan; for the devil as
humanity's common enemy, see Christ
on the parable of the tares in Matthew,
13.39: 'and the enemy who sowed
them is the devil, and the harvest is
the end of the age; and the reapers
are angels.'
600 **assaileth** attacks, assaults
601–3 I greatly desire, Mary, that through
your prayer I might partake in the
glory that Christ earned by being
crucified.
601 **Lady** i.e. Mary (597)
   mean means
602 **partner** a sharer or partaker
606 The syntax here is ambiguous:

Everyman's line could mean,
alternately, (1) I will, with it (the
scourge), give my flesh a reprisal or
punishment (see *OED* quittance *sb*.
3; although this punitive sense is not
attested until 1590, cf. 612); or (2) My
flesh will, by being scourged, earn (i.e.
through its suffering) a discharge of
my debt (*OED* quittance *sb*. 2). The
OED gives, under a figurative cluster
in this last sub-entry, the example
of Robert Manning of Brunne's
Handlyng synne (*c*. 1303): 'the fourthe
sacrament ys penaunce, that ys for
synne a quytaunce' (10813).
607 **begin** i.e. scourging myself
608 **time and space** a conventional
phrase for denoting existence, often
rhyming with 'grace' (cf. 607). See
Like Will: 'Let vs call to God for his
mercie and grace: / And exhort that
all vice may be amended, / while we
in this world haue time and space' (ll.
1109–11).

596 be written] *Q2;* bewryten *Q3*   602 your] *Q2, Q3;* thy *Q4*   partner] *Q2, Q3* (partynere*);*
parte taker *Q4*   603 means] *Q3;* meane *Q2, Q4*   604 me] *Q2; not in Q3, Q4*   SD] *this edn*   605
SD] *Lester subst.*   606 give] *Q3;* haue *Q2*   a quittance] *Q4* (a quytaunce*);* aquaintaunce *Q2, Q3*
(acqueyntaunce*)*

Thus I bequeath you in the hands of our saviour;
Now may you make your reckoning sure.   610

EVERYMAN

In the name of the holy Trinity,
My body sore punished shall be.
Take this, body, for the sin of the flesh!   [*Whips himself.*]
Also thou delightest to go gay and fresh,
And in the way of damnation thou did me bring;   615
Therefore suffer now strokes of punishing.
Now of penance I will wade the water clear,
To save me from purgatory, that sharp fire.

GOOD DEEDS [*Stands.*]

I thank God, now I can walk and go,
And am delivered of my sickness and woe.   620

609 **bequeath you in** commit, entrust you to (*OED* bequeath *v.* 5)

610 **sure** (1) secure (i.e. full and trustworthy) (*OED a.* and *adv.* 13, in the phrase *make sure*); (2) certainly, with certainty (*OED a.* and *adv.* B.2)

613 **Take this** Everyman begins flagellating himself with the *scourge of penance* (571) he has received from Knowledge (who has handed it to Everyman at or after 605; to solidify the allegory, Confession has conveyed it to Knowledge at or after 566). Everyman appears to continue mortifying his flesh at least until 628.

sin . . . flesh wrongs committed by indulging the body. Cf. Romans, 8.3: 'For what the lawe coulde not do, in as much as it was weake through the fleshe, God sendyng his owne sonne, in the similitude of sinfull fleshe, euen by sinne, condempned sinne in the fleshe.'

614 **thou** Everyman addresses his body (by extension: bodies generally).

fresh finely attired. The phrase *gay and fresh* (or 'fresh and gay') was a conventional poetic tag; cf. 'Wife of Bath's Prologue': 'make me fressh and gay' (298).

615 **in . . . of** towards, in the path of (see *OED* way *sb.*[1] 35)

617 **water clear** Cf. Revelation, 22.1: 'And he shewed me a pure ryuer of water of lyfe, cleare as Cristall, proceadyng out of the throne of god, and of the lambe.'

618 **purgatory** the state, according to Catholic doctrine, 'in which souls who depart this life in the grace of God suffer for a time, because they still need to be cleansed from venial sins, or have still to pay the temporal punishment due to mortal sins, the guilt and the eternal punishment of which have been remitted' (*OED sb.*[1] 1a, citing the *Catholic Dictionary*)

619 Owing to Everyman's performance of penance (the flagellation beginning at 613), the personification of his *good*

610 Now] *Q2, Q3;* Thus *Q4*   611 of the holy] *Q3;* of all the hole *Q2*   612 sore punished] *Q3;* punnished sore *Q2*   613 SD] *Adams subst.*   614 delightest] *Q3;* delyted *Q2*   615 the] *Q2, Q3; om. Q4*   616 of] *Q2, Q3;* and *Q4*   618 purgatory, that sharp] *Q2, Q3;* hell and from the *Q4*   619 SD] *Adams subst.*   620 And] *Q2, Q3;* I *Q4*

Therefore with Everyman I will go and not spare;
His good works I will help him to declare.
KNOWLEDGE
Now, Everyman, be merry and glad.
Your Good Deeds cometh now; ye may not be sad.
Now is your Good Deeds whole and sound,　　625
Going upright upon the ground.
EVERYMAN
My heart is light and shall be evermore;
Now will I smite faster than I did before.
GOOD DEEDS
Everyman, pilgrim, my special friend,
Blessed be thou without end;　　630
For thee is preparate the eternal glory.
Ye have me made whole and sound;
Therefore I will bide by thee in every stound.
EVERYMAN
Welcome, my Good Deeds; now I hear thy voice,
I weep for very sweetness of love.　　635
KNOWLEDGE
Be no more sad, but ever rejoice.
God seeth thy living in his throne above.

works (622) is, in the figure of Good Deeds, at last able to stand and walk. This stage business would resonate with Christ's miraculous curing of the paralytic as told in Mark, 2.3–12.
628 **smite** i.e. strike myself with the scourge
629 **special friend** See 78 and n.
630 echoing the phrasing of Psalms, 106.48: 'Blessed be God the Lord of Israel fro world to world without end.'
631 **preparate** prepared; *OED*, citing Henry Bradshaw's *The life of saint*

Werburge of Chester (1513): 'All thynges were redy preparate' (1.3073).
632 **whole and sound** a conventional doublet, like *gay and fresh* (614); cf. 'Sir Degree', 25: 'the time was come that shee was vnbound, / & deliuered whole and sound' (ll. 153–4).
633 **stound** time (here: of trial or pain); see *OED sb.*[1] 2a.
634 **I . . . voice** For the importance of Good Deeds's voice, see 483 and n.
637 **in** from (i.e. while seated in). See pp. 68–9.

621 I will] *Q3;* will I *Q2* 622 good] *Q2, Q3;* god *Q4* 624 cometh now] *Q2, Q3;* do com *Q4* 626 upon] *Q3;* on *Q2* 629 pilgrim] *Q3;* pilgrimage *Q2* 631 preparate] *Q2, Q3;* prepared *Q4* 633 bide by] *Q2, Q3;* abyde with *Q4* thee in] *Q3;* the *Q2* 636 ever] *Q2, Q3;* euer more *Q4*

Put on this garment to thy behoof,
Which is wet with your tears,
Or else before God you may it miss   640
When ye to your journey's end come shall.

EVERYMAN

Gentle Knowledge, what do ye it call?

KNOWLEDGE

It is a garment of sorrow;   [*Offers a garment.*]
From pain it will you borrow.
Contrition it is,   645
That getteth forgiveness.
It pleaseth God passing well.

---

638 this garment This may have been either a white penitential sheet (often worn by public penitents) or a *cilice* or hairshirt, a penitential garment woven of rough cloth or hair (typically, goats' hair) and worn, by the seriously devout, to mortify the flesh. Craik proposes that a white sheet could double as a shroud for Everyman as he descends to the grave (Craik, 79). Scriptural mention of the haircloth garment comes in Psalms, 35.13 (sometimes translated 'sackcloth'): 'But as for me, when they were troublesome to me, I was clothed with haircloth. I humbled my soul with fasting; and my prayer shall be turned into my bosom' (Douay-Rheims).

behoof benefit, advantage; *OED*, citing Caxton's *Caton* (1483): 'Alle thynges shal come to your behoufe in habundaunce' (Eijb).

639 wet . . . tears Even though the performance may not have displayed Everyman crying upon the garment representing *Contrition* (645), allegorically true contrition would involve this conventional sign of genuine sorrow. Cf. *Very Woman*, 65: 'A few tears of his true contrition tender'd'.

640 you . . . miss i.e. feel the absence of it (the garment); also, lose the opportunity (*it*) for favourable judgement before God. Q4 reads, for this phrase, 'it be vnswete', suggesting that penitent *tears* (639) would work to cleanse the garment of stains or odours (cf. *OED* unsweet *a.*: unpleasant, distasteful).

644 borrow protect, save; *OED* $v.^1$ 4a, citing *Mundus et Infans*: 'Some good word that I may say / To borrow man's soul from blame' (ll. 761–2).

645 Contrition the condition of being bruised in heart; sorrow or affliction of mind for some fault or injury done (*OED*). Being contrite was the conventional first step towards forgiveness; cf. Psalms, 57.15: 'The sacrifices of God are a contrite spirit: a contrite and a broken heart, O God, thou wilt not despise' (Geneva). The king describes the power of 'contrition' in *Ham* (Q1, 1603) 10.8–9: 'Why, say thy sinnes were blacker than is jet – / Yet may contrition make them white as snow.'

646 getteth gains, obtains

647 passing well exceedingly. Cf. Polonius in *Ham* 2.2.347–8: 'I have a daughter that I love passing well.'

638 this] *Q3;* thy *Q2* 639 is . . . tears] *Q2, Q3;* with your teres is now all wete *Q4* 640 Or else] *Q2, Q3;* Lest *Q4* you may it miss] *Q3;* ye may it misse *Q2;* it be vnswete *Q4* 641 ye] *Q2, Q3;* you *Q4* 642 ye] *Q3;* you *Q2* 643 is] *Q3;* is called *Q2* a] *Q3;* the *Q2, Q4* SD] *this edn* 647 It] *Q4;* He *Q2, Q3*

GOOD DEEDS

Everyman, will you wear it for your heal?

EVERYMAN

Now blessed be Jesu, Mary's son,   [*Takes the garment.*]

For now have I on true contrition;   650

And let us go now without tarrying.

Good Deeds, have we clear our reckoning?

GOOD DEEDS

Yea, indeed, I have it here.   [*Points to the account book.*]

EVERYMAN

Then I trust we need not fear.

Now, friends, let us not part in twain.   655

KNOWLEDGE

Nay, Everyman, that will we not, certain.

GOOD DEEDS

Yet must thou lead with thee

Three persons of great might.

EVERYMAN

Who should they be?

GOOD DEEDS

Discretion and Strength they hight,   660

And thy Beauty may not abide behind.

KNOWLEDGE

Also, ye must call to mind

---

648 **heal** spiritual health, well-being, salvation (*OED* heal, hele *sb.*)

650 By willingly clothing himself in (the garment of) *contrition*, Everyman becomes – within the play's allegory – contrite.

652 **clear** Owing to the play's free hand with syntax, this word could be either a shortened form of 'cleared' or an adjective modifying *reckoning*.

655 **in twain** in two (Everyman is determined to stay with his new friends)

660–1 On *Discretion*, *Strength* and *Beauty*, see List of Roles 12n., 13n., 14n.

662 **call to mind** have in mind; the allegory suggests the wisdom of Everyman making full use of his five senses as he proceeds. That he is to lead, and not be led by them, is clear from 657.

648 you] *Q3;* ye *Q2*   649 SD] *this edn*   650 on] *Q3;* one *Q2*   653 have it] *Q4;* haue them *Q2;* haue *Q3*   SD] *this edn*   654 fear] *Q3;* to feare *Q2*   655 part in twain] *Q3;* departe atwayne *Q2*   656 SP] *Adams;* Kynrede *Q3*   661 abide] *Q3;* byde *Q2*

Your Five Wits as for your counsellors.

GOOD DEEDS

You must have them ready at all hours.

EVERYMAN

How shall I get them hither?   665

KNOWLEDGE

You must call them all together,

And they will hear you incontinent.

EVERYMAN

My friends, come hither and be present:

Discretion, Strength, my Five Wits and Beauty.

[*Enter* DISCRETION, STRENGTH, FIVE WITS *and* BEAUTY.]

BEAUTY

Here at your will we be all ready.   670

What would ye that we should do?

GOOD DEEDS

That ye would with Everyman go

And help him in his pilgrimage.

Advise you, will ye with him or not in that voyage?

STRENGTH

We will bring him all thither   675

To his help and comfort, ye may believe me.

DISCRETION

So will we go with him all together.

---

663 On the *Five Wits*, see List of Roles 15n.

664 **ready . . . hours** continually prepared (to assist you); playing on the phrase 'ready wit' (indicating quick, intelligent responsiveness)

665 **get them hither** assemble them here

667 **incontinent** immediately, without delay (*OED adv.* (*a.*) = incontinently *adv.*²)

670–93 Each of the companion figures speaks according to its identity: Beauty attractively (670–1, 688–9); Strength assertively (675–6, 684–5), Discretion judiciously (677, 690–3); and Five Wits with a sensory invocation (686–7).

674 **Advise you** consider, reflect upon (this) (*OED v.* 6 intr.)

---

665 them] *Q3;* them them *Q2*   666 SP] *Cawley;* Kynrede *Q3*   669 SD] *Adams*   670 all ready] *Q3;* redy *Q2, Q4*   671 would] *Q2;* wyll *Q3*   674 him] *Q3;* him go *Q2*   that] *Q3;* this *Q2*   676 his . . . comfort] *Q3;* helpe and comfort him *Q2*

EVERYMAN

> Almighty God, loved might thou be!
> I give thee laud that I have hither brought
> Strength, Discretion, Beauty and Five Wits –
>   lack I nought –   680
> And my Good Deeds, with Knowledge clear,
> All be in my company at my will here;
> I desire no more to my business.

STRENGTH

> And I, Strength, will by you stand in distress,
> Though thou would in battle fight on the ground.   685

FIVE WITS

> And though it were through the world round,
> We will not depart for sweet ne for sour.

BEAUTY

> No more will I unto Death's hour,
> Whatsoever thereof befall.

DISCRETION

> Everyman, advise you first of all;   690
> Go with a good advisement and deliberation.
> We all give you virtuous monition
> That all shall be well.

EVERYMAN

> My friends, hark what I will tell.
> I pray God reward you in his heavenly sphere.   695

---

679 **laud** praise

687 **for . . . sour** i.e. from (the effect of) any of life's pleasures or pains. Cf. Emilia in *Oth* 4.3.93–5, on wives: 'they see, and smell, / And have their palates both for sweet and sour / As husbands have.'

688 **Death's hour** i.e. the hour of death

689 whatever happens then

691 **advisement** plan (*OED* 2b); cf. Jeremiah, 26.13: 'Therfore amende your wayes, and your aduisementes, and be obedient vnto the voyce of the Lorde your God.'

692 **monition** intimation (i.e. a prophecy); cf. *OED* 3.

694 **hark** listen to

---

678 loved] *Q2, Q3;* lofed *Cawley*   might] *Q3;* may *Q2, Q4*   682 in my] *Q3;* in *Q2, Q4*   684–707] *Qq; Q1 serves as control text*   684 by you stand] *Q1;* stonde by you *Q4*   685 would] *Q1;* woldest *Q4*   687 ne for] *Q1;* ne *Q3;* nor *Q4*   691 deliberation] *Q2;* lyberacion *Q1*   692 virtuous] *Q1;* vertues *Q4*   694 hark] *Q1;* harken *Q3*   tell] *Q1;* you tell *Q2*   695 his] *Q2;* this *Q1*   heavenly] *Q1;* heuen *Q3*

Now hearken all that be here,
For I will make my testament
Here before you all present.
In alms, half my good I will give with my hands twain
In the way of charity with good intent,   700
And the other half still shall remain;
I it bequeath to be returned there it ought to be.
This I do in despite of the fiend of hell,
To go quite out of his peril
Ever after and this day.   705

KNOWLEDGE

Everyman, hearken what I say:
Go to Priesthood, I you advise,

697 **testament** will, orders to dispose
of (my) property (*OED sb.* 1; a use
surviving in the phrase 'last will and
testament')

699 With *alms* and *good* here, Everyman
returns, newly educated, to subjects
broached earlier in the play; see 78n.,
389n. His pledge to give *half* his *good*
(i.e. goods, wherewithal) moderates
Christ's injunction to sell what one has
and give it to the poor. This injunction
differs in the various gospels; cf.
Matthew, 19.21: 'sell that thou hast,
and geue to the poore, & thou shalt
haue treasure in heauen'; Mark, 10.21:
'sell whatsoeuer thou hast'; Luke,
18.22: 'Sell all that thou hast.' On the
play's investment in moderation, see
431 and n.

701–2 Where the *other half* of Everyman's
good (i.e. goods) will go is unclear.
Proposals include: (1) wealth to be
left for Everyman's family (De Vocht);
(2) payment of explicit (worldly)
debts (Cawley); (3) payment to those
(including the Church, and workers in
his employ) to whom Everyman may

be indebted owing to past practices
(Lester). *Elck* offers no clarity: 'the
other half thereafter / I assign to
where by right it should go' (657–
8). The ambiguity here may well be
intentional, designed (like 431) to
provide an escape from the sweeping
imperative of Luke, 18.22 (see 699 and
n.).

701 **still shall remain** i.e. that remains

702 **bequeath** leave to (formally, as in his
will or *testament*, 697)
there where

703 **in despite of** in contempt of,
scorning
fiend of hell Satan (euphemized
again at 884)

704 **quite out of** beyond
peril danger (posed by); cf. *OED sb.*
1b(c), citing *MND* 4.1.152: 'Without
the peril of the Athenian law'.

705 today and always

707 **Priesthood** 'the priestly office
personified'; *OED sb.* 1c, citing the
Lydgatian *Assembly*: 'Soo thedyr
went Presthod with benygnyte' (line
1426).

699 alms] *Q1*; almesse *Q2*   will give] *Q1*; gyue *Q2*   702 I it bequeath] *Q1*; In queth *Q3*; In quyet
Q4   704 quite] *Q1*; quit *Lester*   705 and this] *Q1*; this *Q2*   706 say] *Q1*; wyll saye *Q2*

230

And receive of him in any wise
The holy sacrament and ointment together;
Then shortly see ye turn again hither.   710
We will all abide you here.

FIVE WITS

Yea, Everyman, hie you that ye ready were.
There is no emperor, king, duke ne baron,
That of God hath commission
As hath the least priest in the world being.   715
For of the blessed sacraments pure and benign
He beareth the keys and thereof hath the cure
For man's redemption – it is ever sure –
Which God, for our soul's medicine,
Gave us out of his heart with great pain.   720
Here in this transitory life, for thee and me,

709 **holy sacrament** i.e. communion, in which a priest conveys bread and wine to an individual as a representation of Christ's flesh and blood. Cf. 724, 737n., 739n.
ointment the oil of *holy extreme unction* (725), the fifth of the seven sacraments in the Church at this time. Those who were sick or otherwise in danger of dying were administered the 'last rites', which included anointing the flesh with holy oil. This sacrament was based on an interpretation of Mark, 6.13 and James, 5.14–15.
710 **see ye** see that you
712 **hie** make haste
that . . . were so that you might be ready
713 Five Wits repeats much of Death's list of worldly authorities from 126, leaving out – because he is praising the priesthood – *pope*.
714–15 that has the authority from God which the lowliest priest in the world possesses; cf. *OED* commission *sb.*[1] 2a.

716 **blessed sacraments** the seven sacred rites manifesting inward grace, held by the Church to have been instituted by Christ for the sanctification of humanity. Listed from 723–5, these included baptism, confirmation, holy orders (*priesthood good*, 723), the holy Eucharist (i.e. communion), marriage, extreme unction and penance.
717 **keys** long a symbol of priesthood's efficacy, based on Christ's words to Peter in Matthew, 16.19: 'And I wyll geue vnto thee, the keyes of the kingdome of heauen.' Two crossed keys (one gold, one silver), bound by a cord, have been an icon of the Holy See since the fourteenth century.
718 **sure** certain, effective (i.e. as a *cure*)
719 **medicine** healing treatment
720 **with** i.e. as a result of (suffering)
721 **transitory life** a biblical commonplace; cf. Proverbs, 31.8: 'this transitorie worlde'; 1 James, 4.14: 'For what thyng is your lyfe? It is euen a vapour, that appeareth for a litle tyme, and then he vanisheth away.'

708–13] *Q2, Q3, Q4; not in Q1; Q3 serves as control text*   714–38] *Qq; Q1 serves as control text*   715 the least] *Q1;* at least *Lester*   717 the cure] *Q3;* cure *Q1, Q2;* he cure *Q4*   720 pain] *Q1;* pyne *Q4*

231

The blessed sacraments seven there be:
Baptism, confirmation, with priesthood good,
And the sacrament of God's precious flesh and blood,
Marriage, the holy extreme unction and penance;   725
These seven be good to have in remembrance,
Gracious sacraments of high divinity.

EVERYMAN

Fain would I receive that holy body,
And meekly to my ghostly father I will go.

FIVE WITS

Everyman, that is the best that ye can do.   730
God will you to salvation bring,
For priesthood exceedeth all other thing.
To us holy scripture they do teach,
And converteth man from sin, heaven to reach.
God hath to them more power given   735
Than to any angel that is in heaven.
With five words he may consecrate,
God's body in flesh and blood to take,

724 the sacrament of communion
726 **be** are
728 **that holy body** the body of Christ,
thought to be present in the communion
bread on the basis of Matthew, 26.26:
'When they were eatyng, Iesus toke
bread, and when he had geuen thankes,
he brake [it,] and gaue [it] to the
disciples, and saide: Take, eate, this is
my body.'
729 **meekly** with humility. In declaring
the manner of his approach to
Priesthood, Everyman echoes the
biblical phrasing of Psalms, 37.11:
'But the meeke spirited shall possesse
the earth', which Christ repeats as the
third Beatitude in the Sermon on the
Mount (Matthew, 5.5): 'Blessed (are)
the meke: for they shall inherite the
earth.'

ghostly father spiritual guide,
counsellor (cf. *Mankind* 208 and
n.)
732–3 The switch between singular
(*priesthood*) representing a collective
personification and the plural pronouns
they (733) and *them* (735) replicates
the shifting between *Every man* and
Everyman and *Good* and *Goods*. See
66n. and 389n.
732 **exceedeth** surpasses, excels beyond
734 **heaven to reach** so that he might
arrive at heaven
737 **five words** i.e. '*Hoc est enim corpus
meum*' (Latin): 'This is my body, which
is geuen for you' (Luke, 22.19). The
Latin here is the traditional form for
the priest's consecration of the Host
as recorded in the Roman missal, or
mass-book.

732 For] *Q1;* For good *Q4*   738 take] *Q1;* make *Q3, Q4*

And handleth his maker between his hands.
The priest bindeth and unbindeth all bands,   740
Both in earth and in heaven.
Thou ministers of all the sacraments seven,
Though we kissed thy feet, thou were worthy;
Thou art the surgeon that cureth sin deadly.
No remedy may we find under God,   745
But all only priesthood.
Everyman, God gave priests that dignity,
And setteth them in his stead among us to be;
Thus be they above angels in degree.   [*Exit Everyman.*]
KNOWLEDGE
If priests be good, it is so, surely.   750

739 **handleth his maker** a profoundly metaphysical image, one that emphasizes the awesome power of the priesthood upon earth and is based on the doctrine of the 'real presence'; see 728.

740 **bindeth . . . bands** ties and loosens all bonds. The Church authorized priests to 'bind' or 'unbind' sins, that is, to hold sinners responsible or grant them forgiveness, on the basis of Christ's words to Peter in Matthew, 16.19: 'what euer thou shalt bynde on erthe, schal be boundun also in heuenes; and what euer thou schalt vnbynde on erthe, schal be vnbounden also in heuenes' (Wycliffe; cf. also Matthew, 18.18), and to his disciples in John, 20.23.

741 **earth . . . heaven** echoing the Lord's Prayer, from Matthew, 6.10: 'Thy kingdome come. Thy will be done, in earth, as it is in heauen' (KJV).

744 **surgeon** healer, doctor; *OED* 1c, figurative uses, citing Exodus, 15.26: 'Then wyl I laye vpon ye none of the sicknesses, that I layed vpon Egipte,

for I am the Lorde thy surgione' (Coverdale).

746 **all only** exclusively, solely (through) (*OED* alonely *a.* and *adv.* 3c). See Mary Sidney's translation of Psalm 142: 'O Lord my safe abiding / Abides in thee: in thee all-only lieth / Lott of my life, and plott of my residing' (Sidney, *Psalms*, ll. 14–16).

748 **stead** place

749 **degree** dignity, rank (*OED sb.* 4a)

749 SD Everyman leaves the stage to take communion and receive extreme unction (cf. 709 and n.). His exit allows the play to avoid profaning these sacraments through their representation in a fiction, by actors.

750 'If the priests in question are good, what you say (i.e. concerning their exalted function and rank) is true.' With insight appropriate to the faculty she represents, Knowledge will qualify the enthusiasm of Five Wits by pointing out the potential for inadequate priests to sully the process of 'convert[ing] man from sin' (734).

739–44] *Q2, Q3, Q4; not in Q1; Q3 serves as control text*   739 hands] *Q2;* hande *Q3*   742 of] *Lester; not in Q2, Q3, Q4*   743 kissed] *Q2* (kyst*); kysse *Q3, Q4*   744 the] *Q2; not in Q3, Q4*   745–69] *Qq; Q1 serves as control text*   745 may] *Q1; om. Q3, Q4*   746 all only] *Q3;* alone on *Q1, Q2*   747 priests] *Bevington;* preest *Qq*   748 setteth] *Q3;* letteth *Q1, Q2*   to] *Q3; not in Q1, Q2*   749 SD] *Adams subst.*

But when Jesu hanged on the cross with great smart,
There gave he us out of his blessed heart
The same sacrament in great torment.
He sold them not to us, that Lord omnipotent;
Therefore Saint Peter the apostle doth say   755
That Jesu's curse hath all they
Which God their saviour do buy or sell,
Or they for any money do take or tell.
Sinful priests giveth the sinners example bad;
Their children sitteth by other men's fires,
                                I have heard,   760
And some haunteth women's company.
With unclean life, as lusts of lechery,
These be with sin made blind.

FIVE WITS

I trust to God no such may we find;
Therefore let us priesthood honour   765
And follow their doctrine for our soul's succour.
We be their sheep, and they shepherds be,

753 **same sacrament** i.e. his blood (cf. 738)
  in great torment through (and in spite of) his great suffering
754 **sold them not** Here Knowledge indicts the wrong of 'simony', the buying or selling of spiritual authority (involving giving or accepting money for such things as ecclesiastical office, confession, absolution, burial, marriage). Named after Simon Magus in Acts, 8.18–24, the offence of simony would be a perennial problem in the Church prior to the Reformation.
755–8 In Acts, 8.20–3, after Simon has offered money for the power of laying on of hands, Peter rebukes him as follows: 'Thy money perishe with thee, because thou hast thought that the gyfte of God may be obteyned with money. Thou hast neither part nor felowship in this busynesse: For thy hearte is not ryght in the syght of God.'
760 This line indicts miscreant clergy for both violating their pledge of celibacy and foisting illegitimate children on other men.
762 **as lusts of** as one who takes delight in (cf. *OED* lust *v.* 1, 1b)
763 Priests like this are blinded by sin.
764 **no such** i.e. no such priests
767 **sheep . . . shepherds** a common image in the Bible for describing the relation of spiritual guide to follower; cf. Mark, 6.34: 'And Iesus

751 hanged] *Q3;* henge *Q1, Q2, Q4*   752 gave he us] *Q1;* he gaue *Q3, Q4*   753 same sacrament] *Q1;* seven sacramentes *Bevington*   754 sold] *Q3;* helde *Q1, Q2*   to us] *Q3;* to *Q1, Q2*   755 doth] *Q3;* do *Q1;* do the *Q2*   756 hath] *Q1;* have *Q2*   763 with] *Q1;* without *Q2*   766 our] *Q2;* ours *Q1*

By whom we all be kept in surety.
Peace, for yonder I see Everyman come,
Which hath made true satisfaction.   770

GOOD DEEDS
Methink it is he indeed.

[*Enter* EVERYMAN *carrying a cross.*]

EVERYMAN
Now Jesu be our alder speed!
I have received the sacrament for my redemption
And then mine extreme unction.
Blessed be all they that counselled me to take it!   775
And now, friends, let us go without longer respite.
I thank God that ye have tarried so long.
Now set each of you on this rood his hand
And shortly follow me.
I go before; there I would be.   780
God be our guide.

went out, and sawe much people, and had compassion on them, because they were lyke sheepe, not hauyng a sheepheard: And he began to teache them many thynges.'
768 **surety** safety (*OED sb.* 1)
769 **Peace** quiet
770 **satisfaction** 'The performance by a penitent of the penal and meritorious acts enjoined by his confessor as payment of the temporal punishment due to his sin: the last of the constituent parts of the sacrament of penance' (*OED sb.* 2). By this time Everyman has expressed contrition (548–9) and made confession (545–53); we have already seen him perform *satisfaction* by scourging himself (613ff.). Offstage

he will receive communion and extreme unction (773–4).
772 **alder speed** best help; cf. *MED* alder– *(pref.)* and *OED* speed *sb.* 4a.
776 **without longer respite** echoing the words of Death: 'A reckoning he will needs have, / Without any longer respite' (99–100).
778 **rood** crucifix; a representation of the cross on which Christ was crucified, often used in oaths. Cf. *Ham* 3.4.13: 'by the rood, not so.' Called 'the rood of grace' by Strength at 813, Everyman's stage property is probably held out for his companions to swear upon – much as Hamlet may offer the cross-like pommel of his sword for Horatio and the soldiers to swear by at 1.5.145ff.

769 Peace] *Q2;* Passe *Q1*   770–5] *Q2, Q3, Q4; not in Q1; Q3 serves as control text*   771 Methink] *Q3;* Me thynketh *Q4*   SD *Enter* EVERYMAN] *Adams subst.   carrying a cross*] *this edn*   772 Jesu] *Q3;* Ihesu cryst *Q4*   our] *Q2;* your *Q3, Q4*   774 And then] *Q3;* And *Q2;* And thou *Q4*   776–800] *Qq; Q1 serves as control text*   778 his] *Q1;* your *Q3, Q4*   hand] *Q2 (*honde*);* houde *Q1*   780–1] *Q1; one line Q3*   781 our] *Q1;* your *Q3*

STRENGTH

    Everyman, we will not from you go

    Till ye have gone this voyage long.

DISCRETION

    I, Discretion, will bide by you also.

KNOWLEDGE

    And though this pilgrimage be never so strong,   785

    I will never part you fro.

STRENGTH

    Everyman, I will be as sure by thee

    As ever I was by Judas Maccabee.

    [They turn towards Everyman's grave.]

EVERYMAN

    Alas, I am so faint I may not stand.

    My limbs under me do fold.   790

    Friends, let us not turn again to this land,

    Not for all the world's gold;

    For into this cave must I creep,

    And turn to the earth, and there to sleep.

BEAUTY

    What? Into this grave? Alas!   795

785 and even if this journey should prove exceedingly difficult (*OED* strong *a.* 12a)

786 **you fro** from you

788 **Judas Maccabee** a mighty Jewish warrior of the second century BC whose story is told in the deuterocanonical book of 1 Maccabees. See Conley, 'Reference'.

788 SD Here Everyman's cohort begins escorting him to his grave. On implied movement in *Everyman*, see pp. 47–50, 67–8.

789 **faint** weak, feeble (*OED a.* 4, with the implication that he has been made so by fear; cf. *OED a.* 6)

791 **turn again** return, go back. Cf. *OED v.* 66, which, in addition to the physical senses of 'turning around' or 'returning', offers a spiritual sense, perhaps relevant here, of returning to a former condition (66e). Death has earlier told Everyman 'For turn again thou cannot by no way' (105).

793 **cave** i.e. Everyman's grave. Called a 'pit' (Dutch: '*put*') in *Elck* (750–1, 769). In John, 11.38, Lazarus's grave is located in a cave.

783 gone] *Q1;* done *Q3*   787 SP] *Q2 subst.; not in Q1, Q3, Q4*   788 was] *Q2;* dyde *Q1, Q3, Q4* (dyd)   SD] *Adams subst.*   789 so] *Q1;* om. *Q2*   790 do] *Q1;* doth *Q3*   794] *assigned to Beauty Q1*   the] *Q1; om. Q3*   to sleep] *Q1;* slepe *Q2*   795 SP] *Q2;* EVERYMAN *Q1 (*[ly mā*)*

EVERYMAN

Yea, there shall we consume, more and less.

BEAUTY

And what, should I smother here?

EVERYMAN

Yea, by my fay, and never more appear.

In this world live no more we shall,

But in heaven before the highest lord of all.   800

BEAUTY

I cross out all this. Adieu! By Saint John,

I take my tap in my lap and am gone.

EVERYMAN

What, Beauty? Whither will ye?

BEAUTY

Peace, I am deaf! I look not behind me,   804

Not an thou wouldst give me all the gold in thy chest. [*Exit.*]

EVERYMAN

Alas, whereto may I trust?

---

796 **consume** decay, rot (*OED* $v.^1$ 6a, intransitive)
more and less all of us, every one
797 **smother** be suffocated (*OED v.* 8, intransitive)
800 **in heaven** i.e. we shall live in heaven (the verb *live* understood from 799).
801 **cross out** cancel, erase (i.e. her earlier promise; cf. 688–9). See *OED* cross *v.* 4a: 'To cancel by marking with a cross or by drawing lines across'. Given the oaths sworn on Everyman's crucifix (cf. 782–8), the word *cross* is ironic here.
Saint John apparently used for the rhyme it offers with *gone* (802), though used earlier at 288 in place of

Elck's 'Jacob'; *Elck* has no oath at this moment.
802 Beauty's petulant farewell draws on a woman's *tap* – a name for the distaff used in weaving. See *OED* top $sb.^1$ 2a, citing John Jamieson's *An etymological dictionary of the Scottish language* (1808): '*Tap, To tak one's tap in one's lap, and set aff*, to turse up one's baggage, and be gone . . . from the practice of women accustomed to spin from a rock, who often carried their work with them to the house of some neighbour' (25).
804 **I am deaf** i.e. I will not listen to you. Cf. Falstaff's dodge in *2H4* 1.2.66: 'Boy, tell him I am deaf.'

---

796 SP] *Q2*; BEAUTY *Q1* (| |utye) we] *Q2*; ye *Q1, Q3*; you *Q4* 797 SP] *Q2*; EVERYMAN *Q1* (| | mã) 798 SP] *Q2*; before 797 *Q1* fay] *Q1*; fayth *Q3* 801–6] *Q2, Q3, Q4*; *not in Q1*; *Q3 serves as control text* 801 John] *Q2*; Iohan *Q3* 802 tap] *Q3*; cap *Q4* 805 wouldst] *Q3*; wolde *Q2, Q4* SD] *Adams* 806 trust] *Q3*; nowe trust *Q2*

Beauty goeth fast away and hie;
She promised with me to live and die.

STRENGTH

Everyman, I will thee also forsake and deny.
Thy game liketh me not at all.   810

EVERYMAN

Why, then, ye will forsake me all!
Sweet Strength, tarry a little space.

STRENGTH

Nay, sir, by the rood of grace,
I will hie me from thee fast,
Though thou weep till thy heart to–burst.   815

EVERYMAN

Ye would ever bide by me, ye said.

STRENGTH

Yea, I have you far enough conveyed.
Ye be old enough, I understand,
Your pilgrimage to take on hand.
I repent me that I hither came.   820

EVERYMAN

Strength, you too displease. I am to blame;
Yet promise is debt: this ye well wot.

---

807 Everyman's observation cements an allegorical truth: like Beauty, the figure onstage going *fast away*, beauty as a quality of creatures and plants is proverbially short-lived: cf. 'Beauty does fade like a flower' (Dent, B165).

810 **game** scheme, plan of action (*OED sb.* 5a, b). Strength distances himself from Everyman by suggesting it is all a trick.
liketh pleases, appeals to

812 **space** while
815 **to–burst** burst asunder, be shattered. For this construction cf. *Mankind* 249 and n., and 422 and n.
817 **conveyed** brought
820 **repent me** regret
821 **displease** are displeased (*OED v.* 2b, c; *MED* displesen *v.* 1a, b). Everyman could also be heard to suggest that Strength displeases *him*.
822 **promise is debt** proverbial; cf. 248n.

807–31] *Qq; Q1 serves as control text*   807 goeth] *Q1;* dothe *Q2*   and hie] *Q1;* hye *Q2;* fro me *Q3;* and from me *Q4*   808 She] *Q1;* He *Q2*   812 Sweet Strength, tarry] *Q1;* Strength tary I pray you *Q2*   815 till] *Q1;* to *Q3*   to–burst] *Q1;* brast *Q2, Q4*   816 bide] *Q1;* haue byde *Q2*   822] *Q2;* Wyll ye breke promyse that is dette *Q1, Q3;* wyll you breke promyse that is dette *Q4*

STRENGTH

    In faith, I care not.

    Thou art but a fool to complain;

    You spend your speech and waste your brain.   825

    Go thrust thee into the ground.   *[Exit.]*

EVERYMAN

    I had weened surer I should you have found.

    He that trusteth in his Strength

    She him deceiveth at the length.

    Both Strength and Beauty forsaketh me,   830

    Yet they promised me fair and lovingly.

DISCRETION

    Everyman, I will after Strength be gone;

    As for me, I will leave you alone.

EVERYMAN

    Why, Discretion, will ye forsake me?

DISCRETION

    Yea, in faith, I will go from thee.   835

    For when Strength goeth before,

    I follow after evermore.

EVERYMAN

    Yet, I pray thee, for the love of the Trinity,

---

827 I had thought I would have found you more reliable.

829 **She** perhaps so gendered in this line to avoid confusion with the masculine pronouns *He* (828) and *him* (829). On the gendered figures in the play, see pp. 55–6, 61. *Elck*'s 'Strength' is *Cracht* ('Power'), a feminine noun in Middle Dutch. The *She* in *Everyman* may also have been influenced by the beginning of the line in the Dutch original: '*Si*

vliet, als mist doet uuter gracht' (782, emphasis added), translated as 'It [i.e. Power] flees like mist from the ditch' (784).

831 **promised me fair** For the theme of attractive but empty words, see 379n.

836–7 The stage allegory copies the decay of one's faculties: just as one's beauty goes first, and strength next, so does one's discretion (in *Elck*, *Vroetscap* or 'Prudence') next depart.

---

823 I] *Q1;* as for that I *Q2*   825 You . . . your . . . your] *Q1;* Thou . . . thy . . . thy *Q2*   spend] *Q1;* spendeth *Q2*   waste] *Q1;* wastest *Q2*   826 thrust] *Q3;* thirste *Q1;* trusse *Q2*   SD] *Adams*   827 weened] *Q1 (went)*   828 He] *Q1;* But I se well he *Q2*   829 She him deceiveth] *Q1;* Is greatly disceyued *Q2*   830 Both] *Q1;* For *Q2*   forsaketh] *Q1;* hath forsaken *Q2*   831 fair and lovingly] *Q1;* stedfast to be *Q2*   832–7] *Q2, Q3, Q4; not in Q1; Q3 serves as control text*   835 faith] *Q3;* good fayth *Q2*   836 goeth] *Q3 (goth);* is gone *Q2*   837 I] *Q3;* Than I *Q2*   838–62] *Qq; Q1 serves as control text*   838 the love] *Q1;* loue *Q2*

Look in my grave once piteously.

DISCRETION

Nay, so nigh I will not come;   840

Farewell everyone.   *[Exit.]*

EVERYMAN

Oh, all thing faileth, save God alone –

Beauty, Strength and Discretion –

For when Death bloweth his blast,

They all run from me fast.   845

FIVE WITS

Everyman, of thee now my leave I take;

I will follow the other, for here I thee forsake.

EVERYMAN

Alas, then may I wail and weep,

For I took you for my best friend.

FIVE WITS

I will no longer thee keep.   850

---

839 **piteously** with pity, out of compassion

840 **so nigh** so close. Onstage Discretion declines to venture close enough to peek into the grave; allegorically, the line suggests that one's discretion will not be with one at the moment of death.

844 **when . . . blast** Death was sometimes represented as sounding a trumpet to signal the end time. Cf. Pleberio in *Spanish Bawd*, 169: 'Let not that cruell and dolefull sounding trumpet of death, summon vs away on the sudden and vnprouided.' For the iconography, see Davidson, *Guild*, Fig. 17 and Briesemeister, Figs 1, 3, 32, 34, 38.

849 **my best friend** The five wits, or senses, were proverbially invaluable. Everyman's compliment plays on a number of sayings, including those that hold wit 'better than force or strength' and 'more worthy than will' (Whiting, W418, W419), and the admonition 'Misspend not five, flee seven, keep well ten and come to heaven' (Whiting, F245), which refers to the five wits, seven deadly sins and ten commandments, respectively.

850–1 Five Wits's parting stages the proverb 'He is at his wit's end' (Dent, W558). Shakespeare describes this process in Jaques's Seven Ages of Man speech (*AYL* 2.7.166–7), where extreme age is likened to 'second childishness and mere oblivion, / *Sans* teeth, *sans* eyes, *sans* taste, *sans* everything.'

850 **keep** guard, protect (cf. 186)

839 once piteously] *Q1;* and thou shalt se *Q2* 840 I will] *Q1;* wyll I *Q3* 841 Farewell] *Q1* (Forwell)*;* Nowe farewell felowes *Q2* everyone] *Q1* (euerychone) SD] *Adams* 845 run] *Q1* (ronne)*;* ronne away *Q2* fast] *Q1;* full fast *Q3, Q4* 846 of . . . leave] *Q1;* my leue now of the *Q3* 848 I] *Q1;* I bothe *Q2* 849 took] *Q2;* take *Q1*

Now farewell and there an end.   [*Exit.*]

EVERYMAN

O Jesu, help! All hath forsaken me!

GOOD DEEDS

Nay, Everyman, I will bide with thee.

I will not forsake thee indeed;

Thou shalt find me a good friend at need.   855

EVERYMAN

Gramercy, Good Deeds. Now may I true friends see.

They have forsaken me every one;

I loved them better than my Good Deeds alone.

Knowledge, will ye forsake me also?

KNOWLEDGE

Yea, Everyman, when you to death do go,   860

But not yet, for no manner of danger.

EVERYMAN

Gramercy, Knowledge, with all my heart.

KNOWLEDGE

Nay, yet I will not from hence depart

Till I see where ye shall be come.

EVERYMAN

Methink, alas, that I must be gone,   865

To make my reckoning and my debts pay,

For I see my time is nigh spent away.

---

851 **there an end** i.e. that's that. Often used as an exit line in drama, as with Falstaff in *2H4* 3.2.327: 'let time shape, and there an end.'

855 **friend at need** repeating verbatim Everyman's (subsequently ironic) phrase to Fellowship at 229

860–1 Knowledge's promise suggests that, in distinction from the Five Wits and Discretion (practical judgement), Knowledge stands in part for the recognition of religious truths which will be Everyman's last possession. See *OED* knowledge *sb.* 9a, c.

861 **for . . . danger** no matter how dangerous things get

867 **nigh** nearly

851 there] *Q1*; here *Q2*   SD] *Adams*   852 O] *Q1*; Nowe *Q2*   853 bide] *Q1*; a byde *Q2*   855 good] *Q1*; god *Q4*   857 forsaken] *Q3*; forsake *Q1, Q2*   860 you] *Q1*; ye *Q3, Q4*   do *Q1*; shall *Q2, Q3*   863–8] *Q2, Q3, Q4*; *not in Q1*; *Q3 serves as control text*   864 be come] *Q3*; become *Q2, Q4*   865 Methink] *Q3*; Me thynketh *Q2, Q4*

Take example, all ye that this do hear or see,
How they that I loved best now forsake me,
Except my Good Deeds that bideth truly.   870

GOOD DEEDS

All earthly things is but vanity:
Beauty, Strength and Discretion do man forsake,
Foolish friends and kinsmen that fair spake;
All fleeth save Good Deeds, and that am I.

EVERYMAN

Have mercy on me, God most mighty,   875
And stand by me, thou mother and maid, holy Mary.

GOOD DEEDS

Fear not, I will speak for thee.

EVERYMAN

Here I cry God mercy.

GOOD DEEDS

Short our end and minish our pain;
Let us go and never come again.   880

868 **Take example** Learn this lesson. A common phrase in moral (i.e. exemplary) writings; cf. Ralph Roister in *Like Will*: 'But the time past cannot be called again this is no nay, / wherfore all you heere take example next by me' (ll. 959–60).

871 Good Deeds takes on the role of a preacher in quoting Ecclesiastes, 1.2: 'All is but most vayne vanitie saith the preacher, & all is most vayne [I say] and but playne vanitie.' In both passages 'vanity' stands for the empty pursuit and/or valuation of worthless things, and the mode of life that results from this. Cf. also the proverb 'Vanity is the mother of all evils' (Whiting, V7).

876 **mother and maid** alluding to the paradox of the virgin birth foretold in Matthew, 1.23: 'Behold, a virgin shalbe with childe, and shall bryng foorth a sonne.'

877 Good Deeds's robust promise to *speak for* Everyman casts her as his formal representative 'Before the high Judge, Adonai' (245), and contrasts with Everyman's earlier description of her as unable to speak (cf. 483 and n.). That her promise comes directly after Everyman's plea to *holy Mary* suggests that Good Deeds may symbolize Mary in her role as Everyman's helper.

879–80 Good Deeds's couplet prayer is a masterpiece of compression, even truncating its verbs: *Short* for 'Shorten' and *minish* for 'diminish'. The brevity here reinforces the rapidly approaching end of Everyman (and, consequently, the play) and calls up the proverb 'A short prayer penetrates heaven' (Tilley, P555; cf. *Mankind* 558 and n.).

868 example] *Q3;* ensample *Q2*   869–94] *Qq; Q1 serves as control text*   869 loved] *Q1;* loue *Q3*   now] *Q2;* do *Q1, Q3, Q4*   871 earthly things] *Q1;* ertly thynge *Q4*   874 fleeth] *Q1;* flyeth *Q2*   876 holy] *Q1; om. Q2*

EVERYMAN

Into thy hands, Lord, my soul I commend;
Receive it, Lord, that it be not lost.
As thou me boughtest, so me defend,
And save me from the fiend's boast,
That I may appear with that blessed host   885
That shall be saved at the doom.
In manus tuas, of mights most,
Forever, *commendo spiritum meum.*

      [*Everyman staggers into his grave, with Good Deeds.*]

KNOWLEDGE

Now hath he suffered that we shall endure.
The Good Deeds shall make all sure.   890
Now hath he made ending.
Methink that I hear angels sing

881 Everyman paraphrases Christ's last words on the cross from the gospel of Luke, 23.46: 'Father into thy handes I commende my spirite.' Repeated in their familiar Latin form at 887.

883 **thou me boughtest** Cf. 265 and n.

884 **fiend's boast** devil's threat. Cf. *MED* bost *sb.,* citing *In the name* (*c.* 1475): 'I make this to defende me / Fro myne enemyes and ther boost: Blesse me, lorde i*he*su, that I be not lost; / Thorgh vertu and grace of this holy syne' (1, p. 5, ll. 31–4).

885–6 Everyman hopes to be among those resurrected at the Last Judgement, when all will be judged. Cf. Acts, 17.31: 'he hath appoynted a day in the which he wyll iudge the worlde in ryghteousnesse.' In addition to this general reckoning, Catholic doctrine also maintained a particular judgement wherein God (knowing the individual's ultimate destination) would separate the saved from the damned, sending other souls to Purgatory for a while to be cleansed. It is this particular reckoning that the play seems to stage in the following lines.

887–8 the Latin version of Luke, 23.46, paraphrased in English at 881

888 SD Everyman's grave may be represented by an alcove or other space onstage. Greet's production in the early twentieth century sometimes employed a trap-door in a raised altar (see Fig. 17).

889 **that** i.e. what, that which. The sense is that Everyman's body has perished – something we all *endure.* Cf. *Elck*: 'He has undergone what we all have to pay' (843–4).

891 **made ending** come to his end

892 Knowledge's remark has led to much speculation on whether actual music is to be heard at this point in the play (and, if so, which song or songs might be appropriate). Cowling and Rastall have independently suggested the liturgical text '*Veni electa mea*'

881 Lord] *Q3;* lordes *Q1, Q2* 883 boughtest] *Q2;* broughtest *Q1* 886 doom] *Q1;* day of dome *Q2, Q3* 888 SD] *Adams subst.* 889 we] *Q1;* we all *Q3, Q4* 890 The] *Q1;* Thy *Q2* 892 Methink] *Q1;* Me thynketh *Q3, Q4*

And maketh great joy and melody
Where Everyman's soul shall received be.

[*Enter* ANGEL.]

ANGEL

Come excellent elect spouse, to Jesu.   895
Here above thou shalt go
Because of thy singular virtue.
Now the soul is taken the body fro,
Thy reckoning is crystal clear.
Now shalt thou into the heavenly sphere,   900
Unto the which all ye shall come
That liveth well before the day of doom.

[*Exeunt Angel and Knowledge.*]

('Come my elect one') owing to the Angel's line at 895 – which also translates Rastall's second suggestion, '*Veni sponsa Christi*'. Both of these songs appear in earlier medieval drama.

895 **elect spouse** chosen mate, beloved. The Angel refers to the election to salvation (i.e. eternal life) alluded to by God at 54, and discussed in 2 Thessalonians, 2.13 and Ephesians, 1.4, among other places. Marriage appears as a potent analogy in the Bible: at times God is represented as one's husband (cf. Hosea, 2.19); in the Christian Bible this is transferred to Christ (Matthew, 9.15; John, 3.29). Perhaps also with an allusion to the 'elect lady' and 'elect sister' of 2 John, 1.1 and 1.13, respectively. See 892n.

897 **singular** remarkable, eminent

899 **crystal clear** hence a complete contrast with its *blotted and blind* state after Goods's handling (cf. 419 and n.)

900 **shalt** i.e. shall go

901–2 The Angel switches address from Everyman to the audience; the verb *come* (901), contrasting with *go* (896), immediately implies the audience's separation from the *heavenly sphere* (900), and prepares for the Angel's exit.

902 **liveth well before** The sense intended here is most likely that of 'living well' (i.e. justly, morally) prior to doomsday – rather than suggesting that all who live 'well before' (i.e. many years prior to) doomsday shall be saved. But *Elck* generously stresses the possibility of widespread salvation: 'the plain of Heaven, where all together we may enter, great and small' (854–6). Q1 and Q2 less helpfully read 'well after'.

[*Enter* DOCTOR, *for the epilogue.*]

DOCTOR

This memorial men may have in mind.
Ye hearers, take it of worth, old and young,
And forsake Pride, for he deceives you in the end,   905
And remember Beauty, Five Wits, Strength and
                              Discretion:
They all at last do every man forsake,
Save his Good Deeds there doth he take.
But beware, for an they be small,
Before God he hath no help at all;   910
None excuse may be there for Everyman.
Alas, how shall he do then?
For after death amends may no man make,
For then mercy and pity doth him forsake.
If his reckoning be not clear when he do come,   915
God will say, '*Ite maledicti in ignem eternum.*'
And he that hath his account whole and sound,
High in heaven he shall be crowned;
Unto which place God bring us all thither,

902 SD2 DOCTOR See List of Roles 17n.
903 **memorial** (1) the play, considered like the title-page's *treatise*, as 'something by which the memory of a person, thing, or event is preserved' (*OED a.* and *sb.* B.2a); (2) memory (of *This*: with post-positive phrasing) (*OED* B.1a). Q3 reads 'moral', which repeats the Messenger-prologue's *moral play* (3).
904 **Ye hearers** repeating the Messenger-prologue's insistence on hearing at 1–2, 19, 21

of worth as a worthy thing
905 Cf. the proverb 'Pride will have a fall' (Dent, P581).
907 **at last** ultimately, in the end
908 **there** i.e. to heaven (cf. 900)
910 **he** i.e. *every man* (907)
912 **how** what
916 *Ite . . . eternum* Latin, from Matthew, 25.41: 'Depart from me ye cursed into euerlasting fire.'
919 The Doctor echoes the Angel's *Unto the which* (901), but his *thither* (= to there) indicates he shares the earthly space of the audience.

SD2| *Adams subst.*   903 memorial] *Q1*; morall *Q3*   904 of worth] *Q3*; aworthe *Q1*; a worthe *Q2*   905 deceives] *Q1*; disceyueth *Q2, Q3, Q4*   907 at] *Q1*; at the *Q3, Q4*   908 doth he] *Q3*; do he *Q1*; dothe *Q2*   909 for an] *Q1*; and *Q3*   915 do] *Q1*; doth *Q3*   916 *eternum*] *Q1*; eternam *Q4; aeternum* | *Bevington*   919 which] *Q1*; the whiche *Q4*   place] *Q2*; please *Q1*

That we may live body and soul together.   920
Thereto help the Trinity!
Amen, say ye, for saint charity!   [*Exit.*]

FINIS

920 **body . . . together** Although   is the resurrection of the dead. It
'the soul is taken the body fro' at   is sowen in corruption, it ryseth in
death (898), God may redeem and   incorruption.'
bodily resurrect the faithful. Cf.   921–2 The Doctor's brief close recalls
1 Corinthians, 15.35–49, esp. 42: 'So   Good Deeds's prayer at 879–80.

922 Amen] *Q1; om. Q4*   SD] *Lester*   finis] *Q1;* AME[N] *Q4 (the 'N' is torn in the unique copy)*

APPENDIX 1

CASTING *MANKIND*

Mankind can be performed efficiently by six actors. Given the play's gamesome dedication to the physical world, we are perhaps not surprised to find that five of its seven roles represent figures of sensual evil.

This first table shows the distribution of lines in *Mankind*. Because the Vices sometimes share lines (as does Mankind when under their influence), the total exceeds the actual lines in the play. Material on the missing leaf would of course add to the line counts of Mercy, Mischief and the Three Ns.

Role	Lines
Mercy	267
Mankind	163
New-Guise	119
Nowadays	105
Mischief	100
Nought	91
Titivillus	79

It has become traditional to double Mercy and Titivillus – the two most powerful figures played by the same actor – for actors and scholars alike have appreciated the ironic symmetry of such a choice: Good and Evil become two sides of the same coin.

Yet the text itself suggests that a doubling of Mischief and Titivillus is possible – even, perhaps, more likely. Support for this includes Mischief's otherwise unaccountable silence before,

247

during and briefly after Titivillus's appearance. A doubling of Mischief with Titivillus would explain this silence, and also better distribute lines in the play (see table above). Without the addition of Titivillus's lines, for instance, Mischief's part is smaller than every role save Nought's. Assigning Titivillus's lines to Mercy creates a significant imbalance of labour, for it makes Mercy's role over three times as large as four of the play's other roles. The following table contrasts these line distributions:

Mercy–Titivillus doubling	Lines	Mischief–Titivillus doubling	Lines
Mercy–Titivillus	346	Mercy	267
Mankind	163	Mischief–Titivillus	179
New-Guise	119	Mankind	163
Mischief	100	New-Guise	119
Nowadays	105	Nowadays	105
Nought	91	Nought	91

We should also consider the physical dexterity and showmanship called for in the Mischief and Titivillus roles. Compare Mischief's 'beheading' trick (413–50) and Titivillus's legerdemain with the audience and Mankind both (475–606). These episodes require similar kinds of bodily skill. When we contrast this with the oratorical skills implied in Mercy's role – oratory nowhere called for in Mischief's or Titivillus's roles – a Mischief–Titivillus doubling makes better theatrical sense than Mercy–Titivillus.

Yet while this arrangement accounts for several aspects of *Mankind*'s action, it has two drawbacks that need to be acknowledged. The first is the practical difficulty of Titivillus's offstage line, 'I come with my legs under me' at 454 while Mischief is still onstage. This could be solved, of course (and is so indicated in the casting chart, below), by having the Mercy actor, then out of sight, roar Titivillus's line; such offstage lines are common in *Mankind* (see below). The second drawback of a Mischief–Titivillus doubling is that the Mercy actor would be offstage from 309–726. While this absence may seem undesirable from an entertainment perspective (removing, that is, what may be the performance's primary actor for nearly half of its action), it facilitates the play's testing of Mankind and his (mistaken) feeling that Mercy is absent from his world. This absence could also provide a rest for the Mercy actor between two periods of sustained performance.

For more on performing *Mankind*, see Meredith, *Acting* and Heap.

The doubling chart on the following pages represents one possibility for casting *Mankind*. As mentioned above, this arrangement – which doubles Titivillus with Mischief rather than with Mercy – reflects a more equitable distribution of theatrical labour and accounts for Mischief's odd silence before, during and after Titivillus's appearance. Approximations for the manuscript's missing leaf have been added after 71. Although we cannot know what occurs during this lacuna, it seems likely that Mischief exits prior to the arrival of the Three Ns, leaving Mercy alone for a moment of direct address to the audience, as at 1–44, 162–85, 734–71 and 903–14.

Lines delivered 'offstage' – that is, from outside the view of the figures involved in the primary action (cf. 186–309, 424, 454, 783) – have been signalled here with square brackets. We have chosen not to record as separate sequences various 'quick exits' whereby an actor is likely to remain in full or partial view of the audience; cf. Titivillus's two quick trips with the corn and spade (541–55) and Mischief and the Three Ns' preparation of Mankind for hanging at 798–802.

Actor	1–44	45–71	missing leaf A	missing leaf B	72–161	162–85	186–309	310–22	323–30	331–400	401–12	413–25	426–57
1	Mercy	Mercy	Mercy	Mercy	Mercy	Mercy	Mercy						[as Titivillus]
2		Mischief	Mischief									Mischief	Mischief
3				New-Guise	New-Guise		[New-Guise]		New-Guise	New-Guise		[New-Guise]	New-Guise
4				Now-adays	Now-adays		[Now-adays]			Now-adays		[Now-adays]	Now-adays
5				Nought	Nought		[Nought]			Nought		[Nought]	Nought
6							Mankind	Mankind	Mankind	Mankind	Mankind		

Actor	458–74	475–524	525–40	541–64	565–80	581–606	607–11	612–30	631–5	636–7	638–78	679–95	696–701
1													
2		Titivillus	Titivil-lus	Titivillus	Titivil-lus	Titivillus					Mis-chief	Mis-chief	Mis-chief
3	New-Guise	New-Guise						New-Guise	New-Guise	New-Guise	New-Guise		New-Guise
4	Now-adays	Nowadays							Now-adays	Now-adays	Now-adays	Now-adays	Now-adays
5	Nought	Nought								Nought	Nought	Nought	Nought
6				Mankind			Man-kind	Man-kind	Man-kind	Man-kind	Man-kind	Man-kind	Man-kind

Actor	702–17	718–25	726–33	734–71	772–8	779–83	784–98	799–805	806–10	811–902	903–14
1			Mercy	Mercy					Mercy	Mercy	Mercy
2	Mischief	Mischief	Mischief		Mischief	Mischief	Mischief	Mischief	Mischief		
3	New-Guise	New-Guise	New-Guise		New-Guise	New-Guise	New-Guise	New-Guise	New-Guise		
4	Nowadays	Nowadays	Nowadays			Nowadays	Nowadays	Now-adays	Now-adays		
5		Nought	Nought			[Nought]	Nought	Nought	Nought		
6	Mankind	Mankind	Mankind					Mankind	Mankind	Mankind	

251

APPENDIX 2

ANALOGUES FOR *MANKIND*: *JACOB'S WELL*

Mankind borrows from many texts, though it does not seem dependent upon any single one. Several analogues have been suggested, including *Piers Plowman* (1380s) and the poem 'Mercy Passeth Righteousness' (1430s).[1] Like *Mankind*, the latter poem features a male Mercy, with the heartfelt refrain 'Mercy passeth righteousness.'

One of the most revealing analogues for *Mankind* comes in a fifteenth-century sermon collection entitled *Jacob's Well*. The passage reproduced below is based on the EETS text of Arthur Brandeis, with the spelling modernized and some punctuation and paragraphing added (ch. xli, pp. 255–7). In it, a figure of Mercy offers herself as the last court of 'appeal' for a sinner. Many of the themes and images of *Mankind* appear, though it is not necessary to imagine that the play was based on this work.

The excerpt involves a sinful scholar who dreams he is alone in a field in the midst of a 'horrible tempest of thunder and lightning'. He goes from house to house for shelter but, owing to his sinfulness, is turned down at the houses of Righteousness, Truth and Peace, respectively. Then:

> The clerk ran to the next house, and cried 'Help'. A woman answered, 'I am Mercy that dwelleth here. I forsake none that me loveth, me serveth, and to me clepeth[2] for help. Thou clepest now to me, but thou hast nought served me, nor loved herebefore in deeds and in service

1 See Keiller and MacKenzie. For texts, see *PP B-text*, *PP C-text* and 'Mercy'.
2 *clepeth*: calls.

of Mercy and of Meekness. But because thou clepest to me for help, I shall help thee. Go thy way safe from this tempest and serve me and love me in deeds of mercy and of meekness. Be merciful to thine enemies and to other[s] that done thee wrong, help thou poor, and then shalt thou have mercy that am mercy of God; for [unless] thou do mercy, no mercy shalt thou have.[1] "Judicium erit illi sine misericordia qui non fecerit misericordiam".[2]

In a passage here excised, the text offers the moral of the story, saying that the sinner stands guilty in the courts of Righteousness, Truth and Peace, and should take his case to Mercy's court for appeal:

Therefore, appeal from these three courts of Righteousness, of Truth, and of Peace, to the high arches of Mercy betimes ere[3] the sentence be given against thee, while thou art hale[4] in thy bodily life. This court of Mercy is penance, contrition, confession and satisfaction. Go to the judge of God, that is, to the priest and there appeal thyself and thy fellows, the Fiend, the World and the Flesh, of all the felony that thou, by thy fellows, hast done against God. Tell there how many persons thou hast slain in soul through thy sin and thy wicked example; and then art thou the king's child of heaven, then the justice, the priest, shall clothe thee in white leather, that is, armour of clean penance. Therewith fight, and slay them whom thou hast appealed, that is, the Fiend, the World and the Flesh.

And if there come a new quest,[5] afterward, in any new felony of sin to damn thee, if the ten commandments with

1   i.e. 'Unless you do merciful things, you shall not receive mercy.'
2   Latin version of James, 2.13: 'For he shall haue iudgement without mercie, that sheweth no mercie.'
3   before.
4   healthy.
5   i.e. inquest, trial.

the two commandments of the gospel[1] should endite[2] thee (for thou hast broken them all, yerne[3]) – ere this quest come in against thee afore the justice, the priest, give thee to thy salary and say thou art a clerk and canst read in thy psalter. Then shall the justice, thy priest, do the reading this Psalm of the psalter: '*Miserere mei, Deus, secundum magnam misericordiam tuam*',[4] 'Have mercy on me, lord, upon thy great mercy.' This is the psalm in the psalter. This is the psalm of grace as the year is the year of grace. If thou read well this verse of mercy, thou shalt be saved for thy clergy and be put to the bishops' prison of heaven, that is, into purgatory, and afterward be purged out with a quest of clerks, that is, with prayers of priests and with suffrages of all holy church.

1 The 'two commandments' referred to are (1) 'loue the Lorde thy God with all thy heart, and with all thy soule, and with all thy mynde' and (2) 'loue thy neyghbour as thy selfe' (Matthew, 22.37, 39).
2 i.e. indict; formally accuse or charge.
3 vigorously.
4 i.e read this psalm – Psalms, 50.3 (Vulgate), immediately translated.

APPENDIX 3

CASTING *EVERYMAN*

Everyman has seventeen roles, but can be played with fewer actors – seven, if the minimum number of performers is desired, with up to nine required if the production chooses to have God, Goods and Good Deeds within the spectators' view when the action begins. God has often been seated on a raised throne during performances, with Goods sequestered among moneybags or in an alcove upstage and Good Deeds prostrate next to the blank pages of Everyman's account book. It makes allegorical sense for God to survey the action; both Goods and Good Deeds also have reason for being already onstage when Everyman encounters them: in each case, his inability to get them to move (Goods because, being selfish, he does not wish to, Good Deeds because, being undernourished, she cannot) is an important part of the play's theme.

The table below shows the distribution of lines and calculates the number of actors needed for three possible casting arrangements: the first with all actors entering and exiting; the second with God continually present (perhaps, as is traditional, on a raised seat or throne); the third with God, Goods and Good Deeds all present onstage when the action begins. The numerals in these final three columns signify the total number of actors needed up through the appearance of each figure listed.

Role	Lines	No actors continually present	God continually present	God, Goods, Good Deeds continually present
Messenger	21	1	2	4
God	48	2	2	4
Death	78	2	2	4
Everyman	378	2	3	5
Fellowship	58	2	3	5
Kindred	19	3	4	7
Cousin	14	3	4	7
Goods	41	3	4	7
Good Deeds	55	3	4	7
Knowledge	68	3	4	7
Confession	19	4	5	7
Beauty	10	4	5	9
Strength	21	5	6	9
Discretion	13	6	7	9
Five Wits	49	7	8	9
Angel	8	7	8	9
Doctor	20	7	8	9

The 'most crowded' sequence of the play occurs when Everyman's faculties (Beauty, Strength, Discretion and Five Wits) join him, Knowledge and Good Deeds onstage. This makes for a total of seven performers visible between lines 670 and 805 when Everyman begins the last stage of his journey to the grave. John Wasson notes that, save for this unusually populated sequence, *Everyman* (as well as *Elckerlijc*) can be performed by three actors. Acknowledging that this group is referred to at 871 and 905, he nonetheless speculates that the suddenly full stage at 670 may be the product of a later phase of the original play's composition (Wasson, 20).

Wasson suggests the following, seven-actor casting: (1) Messenger, Death, Kindred, Goods, Knowledge; (2) God, Fellowship, Cousin, Good Deeds, Angel, Confession; (3) Everyman, Doctor; (4) Discretion; (5) Five Wits; (6) Beauty; (7) Strength (Wasson, 18). While seven actors can indeed play this text, Wasson's distribution works imperfectly, as Everyman kneels before Confession in the presence of Good Deeds at 545ff. – hence the same actor cannot play Good Deeds and Confession. Frost envisions a ten-actor casting, with (1) Everyman, (2) Good Deeds and (3) Knowledge, played by single actors, and the other parts as follows: (4) Messenger, Discretion; (5) God, Confession; (6) Death, Strength; (7) Kindred, Angel; (8) Goods, Doctor; (9) Fellowship, Five Wits; (10) Cousin, Beauty (Frost, 42).

The doubling chart on the following pages represents only one possibility for casting *Everyman*. Even this seven-actor arrangement includes flexibility. A director or company could choose, for instance, to have the Angel played by almost any of the seven actors in the production, and the Doctor played by any but the actor portraying the Angel.

Actor	1–21	22–63	64–79	80–6	87–183	184–202	203–302	303–18	319–68	369–77	378–92	393–462	463–85
1	Messenger		Death	Death	Death				Kindred			Goods	
2		God	God				Fellowship		Cousin	Cousin			
3					Everyman	Everyman	Everyman	Everyman	Everyman	Everyman	Everyman	Everyman	Everyman
4													
5													
6													
7													

Actor	486–521	522–42	543–72	573–669	670–749	750–71	772–805	806–26	827–41	842–51	852–88	889–94	895–902	903–22
1		Knowl-edge	Knowl-edge	Knowl-edge	Knowl-edge	Knowl-edge	Knowl-edge	Knowl-edge	Knowl-edge	Knowl-edge	Knowl-edge	Knowl-edge	Knowl-edge	
2	Good Deeds	Good Deeds	Good Deeds	Good Deeds	Good Deeds	Good Deeds	Good Deeds	Good Deeds	Good Deeds	Good Deeds	Good Deeds			
3	Every-man	Every-man	Every-man	Every-man	Every-man		Every-man	Every-man	Every-man	Every-man	Every-man			
4			Con-fession		Discre-tion	Discre-tion	Discre-tion	Discre-tion	Discre-tion					Doctor
5					Five Wits	Five Wits	Five Wits	Five Wits	Five Wits	Five Wits				
6					Strength	Strength	Strength	Strength						
7					Beauty	Beauty	Beauty						Angel	

259

APPENDIX 4

ANALOGUES FOR *EVERYMAN*: THE TALE OF THE FAITHFUL FRIEND

Both *Everyman* and its source, the Dutch play *Elckerlijc*, dramatize the story of a man abandoned by those whom he had assumed would help him, and surprised to be assisted by a faithful friend. This story of the 'faithful friend' draws on a parable found in Buddhist literature as early as the third century BCE, and which appears in the literature of many Eastern and Western nations. It was available to the *Elckerlijc* author in various European versions.

The core of this parable involves a man with a set number of companions or friends who abandon him in a time of need. In almost all versions, this tale is explained by an authoritative teacher, someone who suggests the lessons it teaches us. The analogy with *Everyman* and *Elckerlijc* is instructive. In *Everyman*, the group of Fellowship, Kindred and Cousin, and Goods parallels the false friends of the traditional tale, while Good Deeds stands for the faithful friend who will go with one all the way to the grave.

Our first excerpt comes from the Buddhist tradition in a text from before the Christian era. It is translated from the *Miscellaneous Agama* by Genji Takahashi.[1] The false friends are four 'wives' who stand for part of the Buddhist monks' (the Bhiksu's) own bodies. Only when one purifies one's intention (the fourth 'wife' here), Buddha suggests, can one enter Nirvana:

> Hereupon Buddha paused, and then began explaining
> the parable saying, 'The first wife stands for man's body.

---

1 Text from Takahashi, 33–8.

Every man loves his body, but when the close of his life approaches him, he will not be able to do with his body as he desires. The second wife represents man's wealth. Every man is rejoiced when accompanied by wealth, otherwise he is troubled. In case of death, however, he must go, leaving it all behind, howsoever he has cherished it.

The third wife is man's knowledge, parents, wife, children, brothers, sisters, maids, and everyone and everything connected with him. They make much of him, and will follow him sobbing, as far as the burial place beside the Castle Wall, but only that far. Then they must stop following him and leave his body alone amongst other graves and return. It will perhaps not be more than ten days that they will mourn for the dead, then their memory of him will totally disappear from their minds and they will enjoy themselves in merrymaking as before.

The fourth wife symbolizes man's intention. Very few persons on earth hold fast to their intention. They liberate and spoil it and become dissipated. Their avarice, their intemperance will ignore righteousness. When Death calls for them, it is only their intention that follows them, and in this case, to an evil world.

Therefore Bhiksu, you should keep your mind straight, and your intention right. Cast off your discontent. Without your evil deeds, you will never be punished. Without your punishment, you will not be born. Without your birth, you will not get old. Without your old age, you will never fall ill. Without your illness, you will never die. Without your death, you will never enter Nirvana.' Buddha explained thus and the Bhiksu received the parable with great joy.

Our second excerpt shows the story's shape in the Christian tradition. In a manuscript version of a story from the popular collection, *Gesta Romanorum*, a father orders his son to appeal to three of his friends for help.[1] Each of these friends declines to help the son. When he tells his father what has happened, the father in the story interprets the narrative; the text itself offers yet another layer of interpretation labelled 'Declaracio' (late Latin for 'Explanation'):

> The father said 'Son, thou hast no friend; for the first friend is a friend of name, the second is a friend at meat, the third is an enemy at need.' Then said the father: 'Son, go to my friend alone that I have, that is, the Son of God, Jesu Christ, and tell him thy cause.' The son did so. Then his father's friend said, 'If thou have any theft, bring it to me, and if it be treason, put it to me; and I shall die for thee.' Then this was deemed a friend alone, among all other.

> **Explanation.** The first friend is the world, or else money, for the which man consumes himself night and day in labour and business. The second friend is the flesh, and fleshly friends, that receiven[2] largely feeding and clothing; but they lead him unto the prison, that is, the grave, and cast him into the pit. The third friend is the devil, that leads him unto the doom, there to accuse him, and to hang him with him in hell. But the fourth friend, that is Christ, the which is a sicker[3] friend alone, that for his friends suffered death. He is a true friend alone, among all other, and none so true as he. Amen etc.

For discussion of this story in medieval literature, see Ross, 345 and Fletcher, '*Everyman*'.

---

1 Text from additional MS 9066, in *Gesta Romanorum*, 127–32. The spelling and some punctuation have been modernized.
2 Receive, i.e. make use of; cf. *OED v.* 15a.
3 Sure, certain.

ABBREVIATIONS AND REFERENCES

Quotations from and references to Shakespeare are keyed to the most recent Arden edition. Unless otherwise noted, all references to the Bible in English are to the Bishops' Bible (1568). Quotations from the Vulgate Bible refer to Bonifatius Fischer et al. (eds), *Biblia sacra iuxta vulgatam versionem*, 4th edn, rev. Robert Weber (Stuttgart, 1994). In all references, place of publication is London unless otherwise stated. All online works are quoted and cited in the form in which they were consulted in or before January 2009.

ABBREVIATIONS

ABBREVIATIONS USED IN NOTES

a.	adjective
adv.	adverb
anon.	anonymous
Bk	Book
c.	around, approximately (used for dates)
cf.	compare, see in comparison
ed., eds	editor, editors
edn	edition
e.s.	extra series
facs.	facsimile
ger.	gerund, gerundive
ll.	lines
MS, MSS	manuscript, manuscripts
n., nn.	note, notes
n.s.	new series
om.	omitted
opp.	opposite
o.s.	original series
prep.	preposition
rev.	revised
RSC	Royal Shakespeare Company
sb.	substantive (used for 'noun' in *OED* entries)
SD	stage direction

SP	speech prefix
s.s.	special series
subst.	substantially
this edn	a reading introduced in this edition
v.	verb
vol., vols	volume, volumes

ABBREVIATIONS FOR SHAKESPEARE PLAYS

AC	*Antony and Cleopatra*
AW	*All's Well That Ends Well*
AYL	*As You Like It*
CE	*The Comedy of Errors*
Cor	*Coriolanus*
Cym	*Cymbeline*
E3	*King Edward III*
Ham	*Hamlet*
1H4	*King Henry IV, Part 1*
2H4	*King Henry IV, Part 2*
H5	*King Henry V*
1H6	*King Henry VI, Part 1*
2H6	*King Henry VI, Part 2*
3H6	*King Henry VI, Part 3*
H8	*King Henry VIII*
JC	*Julius Caesar*
KJ	*King John*
KL	*King Lear*
LC	*A Lover's Complaint*
LLL	*Love's Labour's Lost*
Luc	*The Rape of Lucrece*
MA	*Much Ado about Nothing*
Mac	*Macbeth*
MM	*Measure for Measure*
MND	*A Midsummer Night's Dream*
MV	*The Merchant of Venice*
MW	*The Merry Wives of Windsor*
Oth	*Othello*
Per	*Pericles*
PP	*The Passionate Pilgrim*
PT	*The Phoenix and Turtle*
R2	*King Richard II*
R3	*King Richard III*
RJ	*Romeo and Juliet*

Son	*Sonnets*
STM	*Sir Thomas More*
TC	*Troilus and Cressida*
Tem	*The Tempest*
TGV	*The Two Gentlemen of Verona*
Tim	*Timon of Athens*
Tit	*Titus Andronicus*
TN	*Twelfth Night*
TNK	*The Two Noble Kinsmen*
TS	*The Taming of the Shrew*
VA	*Venus and Adonis*
WT	*The Winter's Tale*

REFERENCES

EDITIONS OF *MANKIND* AND *EVERYMAN* COLLATED

Adams	*Chief Pre-Shakespearean Dramas*, ed. J.Q. Adams (Boston, 1924)
Brandl	*Quellen des weltlichen Dramas in England vor Shakespeare*, ed. Alois Brandl (Strassburg, 1898)
Bevington	*Medieval Drama*, ed. David Bevington (Boston, 1975)
Cawley	*Everyman, and Medieval Miracle Plays*, ed. A.C. Cawley (1956)
Coldewey	*Early English Drama: An Anthology*, ed. John C. Coldewey (New York, 1993)
Cooper & Wortham	*The Summoning of Everyman*, ed. Geoffrey Cooper and Christopher Wortham (Nedlands, W.A., 1980)
Eccles	*The Macro Plays: The Castle of Perseverance, Wisdom, Mankind*, ed. Mark Eccles, EETS, o.s. 262 (Oxford, 1969)
Furnivall & Pollard	*The Macro Plays*, ed. F.J. Furnivall and Alfred W. Pollard (1904)
Hawkins	*The Origins of the English Drama*, ed. Thomas Hawkins (Oxford, 1773)
Knittel & Fattic	*A Critical Edition of the Medieval Play 'Mankind'*, ed. Frank Knittel and Grosvenor Fattic (Lewiston, N.Y., 1995)
Lester	*Three Late Medieval Morality Plays*, ed. G.A. Lester (1981)
Macro, Bevington	*The Macro Plays: The Castle of Perseverance, Wisdom, Mankind*, ed. David Bevington (New York, 1972)

Manly	*Specimens of the Pre-Shakspearean Drama*, ed. John M. Manly (Boston, 1897)
MS	*Mankind.* The Macro Manuscript (Folger Shakespeare Library, MS V.a.354)
Q1	[*The Summoning of Everyman*] The First Quarto. Exists in two fragments: one containing two leaves of sheet B (the Bandinel Fragment) and one containing four leaves of sheet C (the Douce Fragment). Printed by Richard Pynson [*c.* 1518–19]. STC 10604
Q2	[*The Summoning of Everyman*] The Second Quarto. Fragment containing ten leaves, sheets B–C, only. Printed by Richard Pynson [*c.* 1525–8]. STC 10604.5
Q3	*The Summoning of Everyman.* The Third Quarto. Printed by John Skot [*c.* 1521–8]. STC 10606
Q4	*The Summoning of Everyman.* The Fourth Quarto. Printed by John Skot [*c.* 1528–31]. STC 10606.5

OTHER WORKS CITED

Alexander-Cassamus	[*Alexander-Cassamus fragment*] *Editio princeps des mittelenglischen Cassamus (Alexanderfragments) der Universitätsbibliothek Cambridge*, ed. Karl Rosskopf (Erlangen, 1910)
Alford	John Alford, 'The role of quotation in *Piers Plowman*', *Speculum*, 52 (1977), 80–99
Alliterative *Morte*	*Alliterative Morte Arthure*, in *King Arthur's Death: The Middle English Stanzaic Morte Arthur and Alliterative Morte Arthure*, ed. Larry D. Benson, rev. Edward E. Foster (Kalamazoo, Mich., 1994)
Alphonsus	Robert Greene, *Alphonsus, King of Arragon*, in *The Plays and Poems of Robert Greene*, ed. J. Churton Collins, 2 vols (Oxford, 1905), vol. 1
Alton	R.E. Alton, review of *Macro*, Bevington, *Review of English Studies*, 28 (1977), 328–30
Anderson	M.D. Anderson, *Drama and Imagery in English Medieval Churches* (Cambridge, 1963)
Antichrist	*Antichrist*, in *Chester*, vol. 1, 491–516
Apius	*Apius and Virginia*, in Robert Dodsley (ed.), *A Select Collection of Old English Plays*, 4th edn, 15 vols (New York, 1964)
Arcadia, 1590	Philip Sidney, *The Countess of Pembroke's Arcadia* (1590), STC 22539a
Arcadia, 1593	Philip Sidney, *The Countess of Pembroke's Arcadia* (1593), STC 22540

Art and Crafte	*The Art and Crafte to Knowe Well to Dye* (1495?), STC 790
Ashley	Kathleen M. Ashley, 'Titivillus and the battle of words in *Mankind*', *Annuale Mediaevale*, 16 (1975), 128–50
Assembly	*The Assembly of Gods*, ed. O.L. Triggs, EETS, e.s. 69 (1896)
Aylett	Robert Aylett, *The Bride's Ornaments* (1625), STC 1000.5
Bacquet	Paul Bacquet, '*Everyman* et l'orthodoxie catholique médiévale', *Études Anglaises*, 35 (1982), 296–310
Baker	Donald C. Baker, 'The date of *Mankind*', *PQ*, 42 (1963), 90–1
Ballads	*English and Scottish Popular Ballads*, 5 vols (New York, 1882–98)
Bartholomew Fair	Ben Jonson, *Bartholomew Fair*, in *Ben Jonson*
Beadle, *Cambridge*	Richard Beadle (ed.), *The Cambridge Companion to Medieval English Theatre* (Cambridge, 1994)
Beadle, 'Monk'	Richard Beadle, 'Monk Thomas Hyngham's hand in the Macro manuscript', in Richard Beadle and A.J. Piper (eds), *New Science Out of Old Books: Studies in Manuscripts and Early Printed Books in Honour of A.I. Doyle* (Aldershot, 1995), 315–41
Beadle, 'Prolegomena'	Richard Beadle, 'Prolegomena to a literary geography of later medieval Norfolk', in Felicity Riddy (ed.), *Regionalism in Late Medieval Manuscripts and Texts: Essays Celebrating the Publication of 'A Linguistic Atlas of Late Mediaeval English'* (Cambridge, 1991)
Beaty	Nancy Lee Beaty, *The Craft of Dying: A Study in the Literary Tradition of the Ars Moriendi in England* (New Haven, 1970)
Beene	LynnDiane Beene, 'Language patterns in *Mankind*', *Language Quarterly*, 21 (1983), 25–9
Ben Jonson	*Ben Jonson*, ed. C.H. Herford and Percy and Evelyn Simpson, 11 vols (Oxford, 1925–52)
Best	Thomas W. Best, '*Everyman* and Protestantism in the Netherlands and Germany', *Daphnis*, 16 (1987), 13–32
Bevington, 'Popular'	David Bevington, 'Popular and courtly traditions on the early Tudor stage', in Neville Denny (ed.), *Medieval Drama*, Stratford-Upon-Avon Studies 16 (New York, 1973), 91–107
Bevington, 'Castles'	David Bevington, 'Castles in the air: the morality plays', in Eckehard Simon (ed.), *The Theatre of Medieval Europe: New Research in Early Drama* (Cambridge, 1991), 97–116

Billington	Michael Billington, review of RSC production of *Everyman*, *Guardian*, 16 November 1996.
Bowers	John M. Bowers, '*Mankind* and the political interests of Bury St Edmunds', *Æstel*, 2 (1994), 77–103
Brannen	Anne Brannen, '100 years of *Mankind* criticism: how a very bad play became good', *Medieval Perspectives*, 15 (2000), 11–20
Brantley & Fulton	Jessica Brantley and Thomas Fulton, '*Mankind* in a year without kings', *JMEMS*, 36 (2006), 321–54
Briesemeister	Dietrich Briesemeister, *Bilder des Todes* (Unterschneidheim, 1970)
Briscoe & Coldewey	Marianne G. Briscoe and John C. Coldewey (eds), *Contexts for Early English Drama* (Bloomington, 1989)
Brody	Alan Brody, *The English Mummers and their Plays: Traces of Ancient Mystery* (Philadelphia, 1969)
Brome Play	*The Brome Play of Abraham and Isaac*, in *Non-cycle Plays and Fragments*, ed. Norman Davis, EETS, s.s. 1 (Oxford, 1970)
Bunny	Edmund Bunny, *A Book of Christian Exercise* (1584), STC 19355
Bush	W. Stephen Bush, '*Everyman* (Kinemacolor)', *Moving Picture World*, 23 August 1913
Bynum	Caroline Walker Bynum, *Jesus as Mother: Studies in the Spirituality of the High Middle Ages* (Berkeley, 1982)
Carpenter	Sarah Carpenter, 'Morality-play characters', *METh*, 5 (1983), 18–28
Cass	Eddie Cass, Michael J. Preston and Paul Smith, *The English Mumming Play: An Introductory Bibliography* (2000)
Castle, *Game*	Dorothy R. Castle, *The Diabolical Game to Win Man's Soul: A Rhetorical and Structural Approach to* Mankind (New York, 1990)
Cawsey	Kathy Cawsey, 'Tutivillus and the "kyrkchaterars": strategies of control in the Middle Ages', *SP*, 102 (2005), 434–51
CD	*Comparative Drama*
Chambers, E.K., *Close*	E.K. Chambers, *English Literature at the Close of the Middle Ages* (Oxford, 1945)
Chambers, E.K., *Medieval*	E.K. Chambers, *The Medieval Stage*, 2 vols (Oxford, 1903)
Chambers, M.	Mark Chambers, 'Weapons of conversion: *Mankind* and medieval stage properties', *PQ*, 83 (2004), 1–11
Chaucer	*The Riverside Chaucer*, ed. Larry D. Benson, 3rd edn (Boston, 1987)

Chester	*The Chester Mystery Cycle*, ed. R.M. Lumiansky and David Mills, EETS, s.s. 3, 2 vols (Oxford, 1974)
Churchyard	Thomas Churchyard, *Churchyards Challenge* (1593), STC 5220
CL	*College Literature*
Clark	James M. Clark, *The Dance of Death in the Middle Ages and Renaissance* (Glasgow, 1950)
Clopper, 'Audience'	Lawrence M. Clopper, '*Mankind* and its audience', *CD*, 8 (1974), 347–55
Clopper, *Drama*	Lawrence M. Clopper, *Drama, Play, and Game: English Festive Culture in the Medieval and Early Modern Period* (Chicago, 2001)
Cobbler's Prophecy	Robert Wilson, *The Cobbler's Prophecy* (1594), STC 25781
Confessio Amantis	In *The English Works of John Gower*, ed. G.C. Macaulay, EETS, e.s. 81–2 (Oxford, 1900–1)
Conflict	Nathaniel Woodes, *The Conflict of Conscience* (1581), STC 25966
Conley, 'Aural'	John Conley, 'Aural error in *Everyman*', *NQ*, 22 (1975), 244–5
Conley, 'Doctrine'	John Conley, 'The doctrine of friendship in *Everyman*', *Speculum*, 44 (1969), 374–82
Conley, 'Garbling'	John Conley, 'The garbling in *Everyman* of the deadly sins specified in *Elckerlijc*', *NQ*, 39 (1982), 159–60
Conley, 'Identity'	John Conley, 'The identity of Discretion in *Everyman*', *NQ*, 30 (1983), 394–6
Conley, 'Phrase'	John Conley, 'The phrase "The oyle of forgyuenes" in *Everyman*: a reference to Extreme Unction?', *NQ*, 22 (1975), 105–6
Conley, 'Reference'	John Conley, 'The reference to Judas Maccabeus in *Everyman*', *NQ*, 14 (1967), 50–1
Conversion	*The Conversion of St Paul*, in *Religious Plays*, 1–23
Coogan	Mary Philippa Coogan, *An Interpretation of the Moral Play*, Mankind (Washington, D.C., 1947)
Cornelia	Robert Garnier, *Cornelie*, trans. Thomas Kyd (1594), STC 11622
Country Justice	Michael Dalton, *The Country Justice* (1618), STC 6205, facs. (New York, 1975)
Coventry	*Two Coventry Corpus Christi Plays*, ed. Hardin Craig, EETS, e.s. 87, 2nd edn (Oxford, 1957)
Coverdale	*Biblia the Bible*, trans. Miles Coverdale (Cologne?, 1535)
Cowling	Douglas Cowling, 'The Angels' song in *Everyman*', *NQ*, 35 (1988), 301–3

Craik	T.W. Craik, *The Tudor Interlude: Stage, Costume, and Acting* (Leicester, 1958)
Cuda	Margaret Curtis Cuda, 'The challenge of *Everyman*: the summoner and the summoned', *Bulletin of the West Virginia Association of College English Teachers*, 15 (1993), 21–30
Cunningham	John Cunningham, 'Comedic and liturgical restoration in *Everyman*', *CD*, 22 (1988), 162–73
Davidson, *Guild*	Clifford Davidson, *The Guild Chapel Wall Paintings at Stratford-upon-Avon* (New York, 1988)
Davidson, *Visualizing*	Clifford Davidson, *Visualizing the Moral Life: Medieval Iconography and the Macro Morality Plays* (New York, 1989)
Davidson, 'Woodcut'	Clifford Davidson, 'Of woodcut and play', *EDAM Newsletter*, 3 (1981), 14–17
Davidson & Stroupe	Clifford Davidson and J.H. Stroupe (eds), *Drama in the Middle Ages: Comparative and Critical Essays (Second Series)* (New York, 1991)
Davis	Norman Davis, review of *Macro*, Bevington, *NQ*, 220 (1975), 78–9
De Vocht	Henry de Vocht, *Everyman: A Comparative Study of Texts and Sources* (Louvain, 1947)
Denny	Neville Denny, 'Aspects of the staging of *Mankind*', *Medium Ævum*, 43 (1974), 252–63
Dent	R.W. Dent, *Shakespeare's Proverbial Language: An Index* (Berkeley, 1981)
Devil Conjured	Thomas Lodge, *The Devil Conjured* (1596), STC 16655
Dietrich	Julia Dietrich, '*Everyman*, lines 346–7', *Explicator*, 40 (1982), 5
Dillon, *Early*	Janette Dillon, *The Cambridge Introduction to Early English Theatre* (Cambridge, 2006)
Dillon, *Language*	Janette Dillon, *Language and Stage in Medieval and Renaissance England* (Cambridge, 1998)
Dillon, '*Mankind*'	Janette Dillon, '*Mankind* and the politics of "Englysch Laten"', *M&H*, 20 (1994), 41–64
Discourse	Thomas Churchyard, *A Discourse of the Queen's Majesty's Entertainment* (1578), STC 5226
Divett	Anthony W. Divett, 'An early reference to devil's-masks in the Nottingham records', *METh*, 6 (1984), 28–30
Divine Weeks	Joshua Sylvester (trans.), *Du Bartas His Divine Weeks and Works* (1621), STC 21653
Doctors	*The Play of the Doctors*, in *Towneley*
Douay-Rheims	*The Holie Bible*, Douay-Rheims Version (1609–10)

Douglas & MacLean Audrey Douglas and Sally-Beth MacLean (eds), *REED in Review: Essays in Celebration of the First Twenty-Five Years* (Toronto, 2006)

Driver Martha W. Driver, *The Image in Print: Book Illustration in Late Medieval England and Its Sources* (2004)

Duclow Donald F. Duclow, '*Everyman* and the *ars moriendi*: fifteenth-century ceremonies of dying', *FCS*, 6 (1983), 93–113

Dunbar William Dunbar, *The Complete Works*, ed. John Conlee (Kalamazoo, Mich., 2004)

Edmund Saint Abbo of Fleury, *Life of Saint Edmund*, in *Three Lives of English Saints*, ed. Michael Winterbottom (Toronto, 1972)

EETS Early English Text Society

Elck '*Everyman' and Its Dutch Original, 'Elckerlijc'*, ed. Clifford Davidson, Martin W. Walsh and Ton J. Broos (Kalamazoo, Mich., 2007)

Elizabetha James Aske, *Elizabetha triumphans* (1588), STC 847, facs. (New York, 1969)

Elliott John Elliott, *Playing God: Medieval Mysteries on the Modern Stage* (Toronto, 1989)

EMD *European Medieval Drama*

Emmerson, 'Eliding' Richard K. Emmerson, 'Eliding the "medieval": Renaissance "New Historicism" and sixteenth-century drama', in James J. Paxson, Lawrence M. Clopper and Sylvia Tomasch (eds), *The Performance of Middle English Culture: Essays on Chaucer and the Drama in Honor of Martin Steevens* (Cambridge, 1998), 25–41

Emmerson, 'History' Richard K. Emmerson, 'Dramatic history: on the diachronic and synchronic in the study of early English drama', *JMEMS*, 35 (2005), 39–66

Encomion Richard Barnfield, *The Encomion of Lady Pecunia* (1598), STC 1485

Enough William Wager, *Enough is as Good as a Feast* (1570?), STC 24933

Epitaphes George Turberville, *Epitaphes, Epigrams, Songs and Sonets* (1567/76), STC 24326, facs. (Delmar, N.Y., 1977)

ES *English Studies*

Evans Bertrand Evans, *Shakespeare's Comedies* (Oxford, 1960)

Fair Maid *The Fair Maid of the Inn*, in *Comedies and Tragedies Written by Beaumont and Fletcher* (1647), Wing B1581

Faustus *Doctor Faustus*, in Marlowe

FCS *Fifteenth-Century Studies*

Feldman	Sylvia D. Feldman, *The Morality-Patterned Comedy of the Renaissance* (The Hague, 1970)
Fifield, 'Community'	Merle Fifield, 'The community of morality plays', *CD*, 9 (1975–6), 332–49
Fifield, *Rhetoric*	Merle Jane Fifield, *The Rhetoric of Free Will: The Five-Act Structure of the Medieval Morality Play* (Leeds, 1974)
First Shepherds'	*The First Shepherds' Play*, in *Towneley*
Fletcher, 'Coveytyse'	Alan Fletcher, '"Coveytyse copbord schal be at the ende of the castel by the beddys feet"', *ES*, 68 (1987), 305–12
Fletcher, '*Everyman*'	Alan J. Fletcher, '*Everyman*: an unrecorded sermon analogue', *ES*, 66 (1985), 296–9
Fletcher, 'Meaning'	Alan J. Fletcher, 'The meaning of "gostly to owr purpos" in *Mankind*', *NQ*, 229 (1984), 301–2
Flower	John Reynolds, *The Flower of Fidelity* (1650), Wing R1304
Forest-Hill	Lynn Forest-Hill, '*Mankind* and the fifteenth-century preaching controversy', *MRDE*, 15 (2003), 17–42
FQ	Edmund Spenser, *The Faerie Queene*, ed. A.C. Hamilton, 2nd edn (2001)
Freeman	Arthur Freeman, '*Everyman* and others: the Bandinel fragments', *Library* 9 (2008), 397–427
Freewyl	Francesco Negri, *Freewyl* (1573?), STC 18419
Friar Rush	*The History of Friar Rush* (1620), STC 21451
Frost	Cheryl Frost, '*Everyman* in performance', *Literature in North Queensland*, 6 (1978), 39–48
Fukuyama	Francis Fukuyama, 'The end of history?', *The National Interest*, 16 (1989), 3–18
Fulgens	*Fulgens and Lucrece*, in Medwall
Garner	Stanton B. Garner, 'Theatricality in *Mankind* and *Everyman*', *SP*, 84 (1987), 272–85
Geneva	*The Holy Bible* (Geneva, 1560)
Gesta Romanorum	*Early English Variants of the 'Gesta Romanorum'*, ed. Sidney J.H. Herrtag, EETS, e.s. 33 (1879)
Gibson, 'Bury'	Gail McMurray Gibson, 'Bury St. Edmunds, Lydgate, and the N-Town Cycle', *Speculum*, 56 (1981), 56–90
Gibson, *Theater*	Gail M. Gibson, *The Theater of Devotion: East Anglian Drama and Society in the Late Middle Ages* (Chicago, 1989)
Gibson, '*Wisdom*'	Gail McMurray Gibson, 'The play of *Wisdom* and the abbey of St. Edmund', *CD*, 19 (1985), 117–35
Gilman	Donald Gilman (ed.), *Everyman and Company: Essays on the Theme and Structure of the European Moral Play* (New York, 1989)

Godfrey, '*Everyman*' Bob Godfrey, '*Everyman* (re)considered', *EMD*, 2 (1998), 113–30

Godfrey, 'Forms' Bob Godfrey, '"I saie not, as by plaine storie, / But as yt were in figure by an allegorie": a re-examination of dramatic forms in the early Tudor period', in *Tudor Theatre: Allegory in the Theatre/L'Allégorie au théâtre* (Bern, 2001), 39–54

Goldhammer Alan D. Goldhammer, '*Everyman*: a dramatization of death', *Classica et Mediaevalia*, 30 (1966), 596–616

Golding Arthur Golding (trans.), *Metamorphosis* (1567), STC 18956

Gower *The English Works of John Gower*, ed. G.C. Macaulay, EETS, e.s. 81–2 (Oxford, 1900–1)

Grantley Daryll Grantley, *English Dramatic Interludes, 1300–1580: A Reference Guide* (Cambridge, 2004)

Gray Douglas Gray, 'The Five Wounds of Our Lord', *NQ*, 10 (1963), 50–1, 82–9, 127–34, 163–8

Greene, 'Poem' R.L. Greene, 'A Middle English love poem and the "O-and-I" refrain-phrase', *Medium Ævum*, 30 (1961), 130–5

Greg W.W. Greg, *Materialien zur Kunde des älteren englischen Dramas*, 28 (Louvain, 1910)

Griffiths Jeremy Griffiths, 'Thomas Hyngham, monk of Bury and the Macro plays manuscript', in Peter Beal and Jeremy Griffiths (eds), *English Manuscript Studies 1100–1700*, vol. 5 (1995), 214–19

Guisers' *The Guisers' Play*, in *English Ritual Drama: A Geographical Index*, ed. E.C. Cawte, Alex Helm and N. Peacock (1967)

Gwydonius Robert Greene, *Gwydonius* (1584), STC 12262

Harkness Janet Harkness, 'Departure and irony in *Everyman*', in Richard Matthew and Joachim Schmole-Rostosky (eds), *Papers on Language and Medieval Studies Presented to Alfred Schopf* (Bern, 1988), 59–67

Harper & Mize Elizabeth Harper and Britt Mize, 'Material economy, spiritual economy, and social critique in *Everyman*', *CD*, 40 (2006), 263–311

Harty Kevin J. Harty, *The Reel Middle Ages: American, Western and Eastern European, Middle Eastern and Asian Films about Medieval Europe* (Jefferson, N.C., 1999)

Heap Carl Heap, 'On performing *Mankind*', *METh*, 4 (1982), 93–103

Hercules	Seneca, *Hercules Furens*, trans. Jasper Heywood (1561), STC 22223
Heywood, *Pardoner*	John Heywood, *The Pardoner and the Friar*, Malone Society Reprints (Oxford, 1984)
Heywood, *Proverbs*	John Heywood, *The Proverbs and Epigrams of John Heywood* (Manchester, 1867)
Heywood, *Weather*	John Heywood, *The Play of the Weather*, in Bevington
Hickscorner	*Hickscorner*, in *Two Tudor Interludes*, ed. Ian Lancashire (Manchester, 1980)
Hillman	Richard Hillman, '*Everyman* and the energies of stasis', *Florilegium*, 7 (1985), 206–26
Historical Poems	*Historical Poems of the XIVth and XVth Centuries*, ed. Rossell Hope Robbins (New York, 1959)
Holland	Peter Holland, 'Theatre without drama: reading *REED*', in Holland & Orgel, 43–67
Holland & Orgel	Peter Holland and Stephen Orgel (eds), *From Script to Stage in Early Modern England* (Houndmills, Basingstoke, 2004)
Holthausen	Ferdinand Holthausen, 'Zu *Everyman*', *Archiv*, 92 (1894), 411–12
Honest Lawyer	S.S., *The Honest Lawyer* (1616), STC 21509a
2 Honest Whore	Thomas Dekker, *The Honest Whore, Part 2* (1630), STC 6506
Huggarde	Miles Huggarde, *The Assault of the Sacrament of the Altar* (1554), STC 13556
Hummelen, 'Boundaries'	W.M.H. Hummelen, 'The boundaries of the rhetoricians' stage', *CD*, 28 (1994), 235–51
Hummelen, 'Drama'	W.M.H. Hummelen, 'The drama of the Dutch rhetoricians', in Gilman, 169–92
1 If You Know	Thomas Heywood, *If You Know Not Me, You Know Nobody*, Part 1, in *The Dramatic Works of Thomas Heywood*, 6 vols (New York, 1964), vol. 1
Interlude	*Interlude of the Four Elements: An Early Morality Play*, ed. James Orchard Halliwell (1848)
Isaac	Winifred F.E.C. Isaac, *Ben Greet and the Old Vic: A Biography of Sir Philip Ben Greet* (1964/5)
Jacob and Esau	*Jacob and Esau* (1568), STC 14327
Jacob's Well	'*Jacob's Well*', an Englisht Treatise on the Cleansing of Man's Conscience, ed. Arthur Brandeis, EETS, o.s. 115 (1900)

Jambeck	Thomas J. Jambeck, '*Everyman* and the implications of Bernardine humanism in the character "Knowledge"', *M&H*, n.s. 8 (1977), 103–23
Jambeck & Lee	Thomas J. Jambeck and Reuben R. Lee, '"Pope Pokett" and the date of *Mankind*', *MS*, 39 (1977), 511–13
Jennings	Margaret Jennings, 'Tutivillus: the literary career of the recording demon', *SP*, 74 (1977), 1–95
Jew of Malta	*The Jew of Malta*, in Marlowe
JMEMS	*Journal of Medieval and Early Modern Studies*
Johan Johan	[John Heywood], *Johan Johan the Husband*, Malone Society Reprints (Oxford, 1972), STC 13298
Johnson	Wallace H. Johnson, 'The double desertion of Everyman', *American Notes and Queries*, 6 (1968), 85–7
Jones	Robert C. Jones, 'Dangerous sport: the audience's engagement with the Vice in the moral interludes', *Renaissance Drama*, n.s. 6 (1973), 45–64
Kahrl	George M. Kahrl, *The Garrick Collection of Old English Plays* (1982)
Keiller	Mabel M. Keiller, 'The influence of *Piers Plowman* on the Macro play of *Mankind*', *PMLA*, 26 (1911), 339–55
Kelly	Michael R. Kelly, *Flamboyant Drama: A Study of 'The Castle of Perseverance', 'Mankind', and 'Wisdom'* (Carbondale, Ill., 1979)
Killing of Children	*The Killing of the Children*, in *Religious Plays*, 96–115
Killing of Abel	*The Killing of Abel*, in *Towneley*
King	Pamela King, 'Morality plays', in Beadle, *Cambridge*, 240–64
KJV	*The Holy Bible*, King James Version (1611)
Klausner & Marsalek	David N. Klausner and Karen S. Marsalek (eds), '*Bring furth the pagants*': *Essays in Early English Drama Presented to Alexandra F. Johnston* (Toronto, 2007)
Knack to Know	*A Knack to Know a Knave* (1594), STC 15027
Knyghthode	*Knyghthode and Bataile*, ed. R. Dyboski and Z.M. Arend, EETS, o.s. 201 (1935)
Kölbing	Eugen Kölbing, 'Kleine Beiträge zur Erklärung und Textkritik vor-Shakespeare'scher Dramen', *Englische Studien*, 21 (1895), 170–2
Kolve	V.A. Kolve, '*Everyman* and the parable of the talents', in Sandro Sticca (ed.), *The Medieval Drama* (Albany, 1972), 69–98
Ladd	Roger A. Ladd, '"My condicion is mannes soule to kill" – Everyman's mercantile salvation', *CD*, 41 (2007), 57–78

Legendys	Osbern Bokenham, *Legendys of Hooly Wummen*, ed. Mary S. Serjeantson, EETS, o.s. 206 (Oxford, 1938)
Like Will	Ulpian Fulwell, *Like Will to Like* (1587), STC 11474
Lydgate, *Dance*	John Lydgate, *Dance of Death*, ed. Florence Warren and Beatrice White, EETS, o.s. 181 (Oxford, 1931)
Lydgate, *Fall of Princes*	*Lydgate's Fall of Princes*, ed. H. Bergen, EETS, e.s. 121–3, 3 vols (1924)
Lydgate, *Minor Poems*	*The Minor Poems of John Lydgate*, ed. Henry Noble MacCracken and Merriam Sherwood, EETS, o.s. 192 and e.s. 107, 2 vols (Oxford, 1911 & 1934)
Lydgate, *Troy Book*	John Lydgate, *Troy Book*, Part 1, ed. Henry Bergen, EETS, e.s. 97 (1906)
M&H	*Medievalia et Humanistica*
MacKenzie	W. Roy MacKenzie, 'A new source for *Mankind*', *PMLA*, 27 (1912), 98–105
McKinnell	John McKinnell, 'Modern productions of medieval English drama', in Richard Beadle and Alan J. Fletcher (eds), *The Cambridge Companion to Medieval English Theatre*, 2nd edn (Cambridge, 2008), 287–325
McRae	Murdo William McRae, 'Everyman's last rites and the digression on priesthood', *CL*, 13 (1986), 305–9
MÆ	*Medium Ævum*
Magnificence, Neuss	John Skelton, *Magnificence*, ed. Paula Neuss, Revels Plays (Manchester, 1980)
Magnyfycence, EETS	John Skelton, *Magnyfycence* (1530?), ed. R.L. Ramsay, EETS, e.s. 98 (Oxford, 1908)
Malory	Thomas Malory, *Caxton's Malory*, ed. James W. Spisak, 2 vols (Berkeley, 1983)
Malory, Vinaver	*The Works of Sir Thomas Malory*, ed. Eugene Vinaver, rev. P.J.C. Field, 3 vols (Oxford, 1990)
Manly	John Matthews Manly, '*Elckerlijc-Everyman*: the question of priority', *MP*, 8 (1910), 269–77
Marlowe	Christopher Marlowe, *'Doctor Faustus' and Other Plays*, ed. David Bevington and Eric Rasmussen (Oxford, 1995)
Marshall	John Marshall, '"O ȝe souerens þat sytt and ȝe brothern þat stonde ryght wppe": addressing the audience of *Mankind*', *EMD*, 1 (1996), 105–19
Mary Magdalene	*Mary Magdalene*, in *Religious Plays*, 24–95
Mateer	Megan Mateer, 'The woman in *Everyman*', *EMD*, 2 (1998), 23–35
May	Steven W. May, 'A medieval stage property: the spade', *METh*, 4 (1982), 77–93

MED	*The Middle English Dictionary*, ed. Frances McSparran, http://quod.lib.umich.edu/m/med/ (Ann Arbor, Mich., 2006)
Medwall	*The Plays of Henry Medwall*, ed. Alan H. Nelson (Cambridge, 1980)
Meier	Hans H. Meier, 'Middle English styles in translation: a note on *Everyman* and Caxton's Reynard', in Jacques B.H. Alblas, Richard Todd and August J. Fry, *From Caxton to Beckett: Essays Presented to W.H. Toppen on the Occasion of His Seventieth Birthday* (Amsterdam, 1979), 13–30
'Mercy'	'Mercy Passith Rightwisnes' in *Hymns to the Virgin and Christ, The Parliament of Devils, and Other Religious Poems*, ed. Frederick J. Furnivall, EETS, o.s. 24 (1867), 95–100
Meredith, *Acting*	Peter Meredith (ed.), *'Mankind': An Acting Edition* (Leeds, 1997)
Meredith, 'Professional'	Peter Meredith, 'The professional travelling players of the fifteenth century: myth or reality?', *EMD*, 2 (1998), 21–34
Mertens	Thom Mertens, 'The Modern Devotion and innovation in Middle Dutch literature', in Erik Kooper (ed.), *Medieval Dutch Literature in Its European Context*, Cambridge Studies in Medieval Literature, 21 (Cambridge, 1994), 226–41
METh	*Medieval English Theatre*
Metrical	*The Metrical Life of Christ: ed. from MS BM Add. 39996*, ed. Walter Sauer, Middle English Texts, 5 (Heidelberg, 1977)
Mills, 'Anglo-Dutch'	David Mills, 'Anglo-Dutch theatres: problems and possibilities', *METh*, 18 (1996), 85–98
Mills, 'Theaters'	David Mills, 'The theaters of *Everyman*', in John A. Alford (ed.), *From Page to Performance: Essays on Early English Drama* (East Lansing, Mich., 1995), 127–49
Mirror of Salvation	John Conley, Guido de Baere, H.J.C. Schaap and W.H. Toppen, *The Mirror of Everyman's Salvation: A Prose Translation of the Original 'Everyman'* (Amsterdam, 1985)
Monarche	Sir David Lindsay, *Monarche*, in *The Works of Sir David Lindsay of the Mount, 1490–1555*, ed. Douglas Hamer, 4 vols (Edinburgh, 1931–6)
Monologue	*A Dramatic Monologue by Law*, in *Secular Lyrics of the XIVth and XVth Centuries*, ed. Rossell Hope Robbins, 2nd edn (Oxford, 1961)

Moran	Dennis V. Moran, 'The life of Everyman', *Neophilologus*, 56 (1972), 324–30
More	Thomas More, *The Works of Sir Thomas More* (1557), STC 18076
MP	*Modern Philology*
MRDE	*Medieval and Renaissance Drama in England*
MS	*Mediaeval Studies*
Mundus et Infans	*Mundus et Infans*, in G.A. Lester (ed.), *Three Late Medieval Morality Plays: 'Mankind', 'Everyman', 'Mundus et Infans'* (London and New York, 1981)
Murray	John J. Murray, 'The cultural impact of the Flemish Low Countries on sixteenth- and seventeenth-century England', *The American Historical Review*, 62 (1957), 837–54
Natale	Richard Natale, 'British Everyman caught Oscar's eye', *Daily Variety*, 287.16 (25 April 2005)
Nature	*Nature*, in Medwall
Neuss	Paula Neuss, 'Active and idle language: dramatic images in *Mankind*', in Neville Denny (ed.), *Medieval Drama*, Stratford-Upon-Avon Studies 16 (New York, 1973), 40–67
Nichols	Ann Eljenholm Nichols, 'Costume in the moralities: the evidence of East Anglian art', *CD*, 20 (1986–7), 305–14
NQ	*Notes and Queries*
N-Town	*The N-Town Play Cotton MS Vespasian D. 8*, ed. Stephen Spector, EETS, s.s. 12, 2 vols (Oxford, 1991)
O'Connor	Marion O'Connor, '*Everyman, The Creation* and *The Passion*: the Royal Shakespeare Company Medieval Season 1996–1997', *MRDE*, 11 (1999), 19–32
ODEP	*The Oxford Dictionary of English Proverbs*, ed. W.G. Smith, rev. F.P. Wilson, 3rd edn (Oxford, 1970)
OED	*The Oxford English Dictionary*, ed. J.A. Simpson and E.S.C. Weiner, 2nd edn, <http://www.oed.com> (Oxford, 1989)
Oosterwijk	Sophie Oosterwijk, 'Lessons in "hopping": the Dance of Death and the Chester Mystery Cycle', *CD*, 36 (2002–3), 249–87
Palace	William Painter, *Palace of Pleasure*, vol. 2 (1567), STC 19124
Pammelia	Thomas Ravenscroft, *Pammelia* (1609), STC 20759
Paraphrase of Erasmus	Desiderius Erasmus, *The Seconde Tome or Volume of the Paraphrase of Erasmus upon the New Testament*, trans. Miles Coverdale and John Old (1549), STC 2854.7

Parker	John J. Parker, *The Development of the Everyman Drama from 'Elckerlyc' to Hofmannsthal's 'Jedermann'* (Doetinchem, 1970)
Parsons	Ben Parsons, 'Dutch influences on English literary culture in the early Renaissance, 1470–1650', *Literature Compass*, 4 (2007), 1–20
Pearsall	Derek Pearsall, *John Lydgate* (1970)
Pecock	Reginald Pecock, *The Repressor of Over Much Blaming of the Clergy*, ed. Churchill Babington, 2 vols (1860)
Pedlers	*The pedlers prophecie* (1595), STC 25782
Peek	George S. Peek, 'Sermon themes and sermon structure in *Everyman*', *South Central Bulletin*, 40 (1980), 159–60
Peele	*The Old Wives Tale*, ed. F.S. Hook, in *The Life and Works of George Peele*, ed. Charles Tyler Prouty, 3 vols (New Haven, 1952), vol. 3
Perkins	William Perkins, *An Exposition of the Lords Prayer* (1595), STC 19702a
Perseverance	*The Castle of Perseverance*, in *Macro*, Bevington, 2–153
Pettitt, 'Early English'	Thomas Pettitt, 'Early English traditional drama: approaches and perspectives', *RORD*, 25 (1982), 1–30
Pettitt, 'Pyramus'	Thomas Pettitt, '"This man is Pyramus": a pre-history of the English Mummers' Plays', *METh*, 22 (2000), 70–99
Pierce Penniless	*Pierce Penniless*, in Thomas Nashe, *Strange Newes* (1592), STC 18377
PMLA	*Publications of the Modern Language Association*
Post	R.R. Post, *The Modern Devotion: Confrontation with Reformation and Humanism*, Studies in Medieval and Reformation Thought, 3 (Leiden, 1968)
Potter	Robert A. Potter, *The English Morality Play: Origins, History, and Influence of a Dramatic Tradition* (1975)
PP B-text	William Langland, *Piers Plowman*, ed. George Kane and E. Talbot Donaldson, 2nd edn (1988)
PP C-text	William Langland, *Piers Plowman: the C-text*, ed. Derek Pearsall (Exeter, 1994)
PQ	*Philological Quarterly*
Price	Amanda Price, 'Dramatizing the Word', *Leeds Studies in English*, 29 (1998), 293–303
Primer	[*The Salisbury Primer*] (1532), STC 15976
Processus Talentorum	*Processus Talentorum*, in *The Towneley Plays*, ed. George England and Alfred W. Pollard (1897)
Puddephat	Wilfrid Puddephat, 'The mural paintings of the Dance of Death in the Guild Chapel of Stratford-upon-Avon', *Birmingham Archaeological Society Transactions*, 76

	(1960), 29–35
Puttenham	George Puttenham, *The Art of English Poesy: A Critical Edition*, ed. Frank Whigham and Wayne A. Rebhorn (Ithaca, 2007)
Quinn	Esther Casier Quinn, *The Quest of Seth for the Oil of Life* (Chicago, 1962)
Raftery	Margaret Mary Raftery, '*Mankind* for Africa', *RORD*, 41 (2002), 168–98
Rastall	Richard Rastall, 'Music and liturgy in *Everyman*: some aspects of production', *Leeds Studies in English*, n.s. 29 (1998), 305–14
Register	*The English Register of Godstow Nunnery*, ed. Andrew Clark, 3 vols (1911)
Religious Lyrics	*Religious Lyrics of the XVth Century*, ed. Carleton Brown (Oxford, 1939)
Religious Plays	*The Late Medieval Religious Plays of Bodleian MSS Digby 133 and E. Mus. 160*, ed. Donald C. Baker, John L. Murphy and Louis B. Hall, Jr, EETS, o.s. 283 (Oxford, 1982)
Reliques	*Reliques of Ancient English Poetry*, ed. Henry B. Wheatley (New York, 1966)
Rendall	Thomas Rendall, 'The times of mercy and judgement in *Mankind*, *Everyman*, and *The Castle of Perseverance*', *English Studies in Canada*, 7 (1981), 255–69
Riggio	Milla Cozart Riggio (ed.), *The Play of Wisdom: Its Texts and Contexts* (New York, 1998)
Robin Conscience	*Robin Conscience*, in *Remains of the Early Popular Poetry of England*, ed. W. Carew Hazlitt, 4 vols (1864)
Roister Doister	Nicholas Udall, *Ralph Roister Doister* (1566?), STC 24508
RORD	*Research Opportunities in Renaissance Drama*
Ross	W.O. Ross (ed.), *Middle English Sermons*, EETS, o.s. 209 (1940)
Roston	Murray Roston, *Biblical Drama in England: From the Middle Ages to the Present Day* (Evanston, Ill., 1968)
Ryan	Denise Ryan, '"If ye had parfytely chered me": the nurturing of Good Deeds in *Everyman*', *NQ*, 42 (1995), 165–8
Saddlers	*The Saddlers: The Harrowing of Hell*, in *York Plays*
Sages	*The Seven Sages of Rome*, ed. Karl Brunner, EETS, o.s. 191 (Oxford, 1933)
Salisbury	John of Salisbury, Bishop of Chartres, *Letters*, ed. W.J. Millor and H.E. Butler, rev. C.N.L. Brooke ([1955]–

	1979)
Samuel	William Samuel, *An Abridgement of All the Canonical Books of the Old Testament* (1569), STC 21690
Scale	Walter Hilton, *The Scale of Perfection*, ed. Thomas H. Bestul (Kalamazoo, Mich., 2000)
Schenkeveld	Maria A. Schenkeveld, *Dutch Literature in the Age of Rembrandt: Themes and Ideas* (Amsterdam, 1991)
Schmidt	A.V.C. Schmidt, *The Clerkly Maker: Langland's Poetic Art* (Cambridge, 1987)
Schmitt	Natalie Crohn Schmitt, 'The idea of a person in medieval morality plays', *CD*, 12 (1978), 23–34
Schreiber	Earl G. Schreiber, '*Everyman* in America', *CD*, 9 (1975), 99–115
Schwartz	John Schwartz, 'Here comes comedy's Everyman', *New York Times*, special section 44–68 (9 September 2007)
Second Shepherds'	*The Second Shepherds' Play*, in Bevington
SG	Suzanne Gossett, private communication
Shearmen	*The Shearmen and Taylors' Pageant*, in *Coventry*
Sidney, *Psalms*	*The Psalms of Sir Philip Sidney and the Countess of Pembroke*, ed. J.C.A. Rathmell (New York, 1963)
'Sir Degree'	'Sir Degree', in *Bishop Percy's Folio Manuscript: Ballads and Romances*, ed. John W. Hales and Frederick J. Furnivall, 3 vols (1867–8)
Skelton, *Bowge*	*The Bowge of Courte*, in *John Skelton, the Complete English Poems*, ed. John Scattergood (New Haven, 1983)
Skelton, Dyce	*The Poetical Works of John Skelton*, ed. Alexander Dyce, 3 vols (Boston, 1864)
Skelton, Henderson	*The Complete Poems of John Skelton, Laureate*, ed. Philip Henderson, 2nd edn (1948)
Skelton, Kinsman	John Skelton, *Poems*, ed. Robert S. Kinsman (Oxford, 1969)
Smart, 'Concluded'	W.K. Smart, 'Some notes on *Mankind* (concluded)', *MP*, 14 (1916), 293–313
Smart, 'Continued'	W.K. Smart, 'Some notes on *Mankind* (continued)', *MP*, 14 (1916), 45–58
Smart, '*Mankind*'	W. K. Smart, '*Mankind* and the mumming plays', *Modern Language Notes*, 32 (1917), 21–5
Southern	Richard Southern, *The Staging of Plays before Shakespeare* (1973)
SP	*Studies in Philology*
Spanish Bawd	James Mabbe (trans.), Fernando de Rojas, *The Spanish Bawd, Represented in Celestina* (1631), STC 4911
Speaight	Robert Speaight, *William Poel and the Elizabethan*

	Revival (1954)
Spinrad	Phoebe S. Spinrad, 'The last temptation of Everyman', *PQ*, 64 (1985), 185–94
Sponsler, 'Archives'	Claire Sponsler, 'Drama in the archives: recognizing medieval plays', in Holland & Orgel, 111–30
Sponsler, *Drama*	Claire Sponsler, *Drama and Resistance: Bodies, Goods, and Theatricality in Late Medieval England* (Minneapolis, 1997)
Sponsler, *Ritual*	Claire Sponsler, *Ritual Imports: Performing Medieval Drama in America* (Ithaca, 2004)
Stanyhurst	*Thee first foure bookes of Virgil his Aeneis*, trans. Richard Stanyhurst (1582), STC 24806
Stanzaic *Morte*	*Stanzaic Morte Arthur*, in *King Arthur's Death: The Middle English Stanzaic Morte Arthur and Alliterative Morte Arthure*, ed. Larry D. Benson, rev. Edward E. Foster (Kalamazoo, Mich., 1994)
Stanzaic *Morte*, EETS	*Le Morte Arthur: A Romance in Stanzas of Eight Lines*, ed. J. Douglas Bruce, EETS, e.s. 88 (1903)
STC	Short-Title Catalogue. *A Short-Title Catalogue of Books Printed in England, Scotland, & Ireland, and of English Books Printed Abroad, 1475–1640*, 2nd edn, begun by W.A. Jackson and F.S. Ferguson, completed by Katherine F. Pantzer, 3 vols (1976)
Sternhold, *Psalms*	*The Whole Book of Psalms*, trans. Thomas Sternhold et al. (1633), STC 2645.7
Stock	Lorraine Kochanske Stock, 'The thematic and structural unity of *Mankind*', *SP*, 72 (1975), 386–407
Streitman	Elsa Streitman, 'The Middle Dutch *Elckerlijc* and the English *Everyman*', *MÆ*, 52 (1983), 111–14
Szittya	Penn R. Szittya, *The Antifraternal Tradition in Medieval Literature* (Princeton, 1986)
Takahashi	Genji Takahashi, *A Study of 'Everyman' with Special Reference to the Source of Its Plot* (Tokyo, 1953)
Tanner	Ron Tanner, 'Humor in *Everyman* and the Middle English morality play', *PQ*, 70 (1991), 149–61
Tapiteres	*The Tapiteres and the Couchers: Dream of Pilate's Wife; Jesus Before Pilate*, in *York Plays*
Thomas	Helen S. Thomas, 'The meaning of the character Knowledge in *Everyman*', *Mystics Quarterly*, 14 (1961), 3–13
Thompson	Elbert N.S. Thompson, *The English Moral Plays*, *Transactions of the Connecticut Academy of Arts and Sciences*, 14 (1910), 291–414

Thundy	Zacharias P. Thundy, 'Good Deeds rediviva: *Everyman* and the doctrine of revivisence', *FCS*, 17 (1990), 421–37
Tide	George Wapull, *The Tide Tarrieth No Man* (1575), STC 25018
Tigg	E.R. Tigg, 'Is *Elckerlijc* prior to *Everyman?*', *Journal of English and Germanic Philology*, 38 (1939), 568–96
Tilley	Morris P. Tilley, *A Dictionary of Proverbs in England in the Sixteenth and Seventeenth Centuries* (Ann Arbor, Mich., 1950)
Towneley	*The Towneley Plays*, ed. Martin Stevens and A.C. Cawley, EETS, s.s. 13, 2 vols (Oxford, 1994)
Twycross & Carpenter	Meg Twycross and Sarah Carpenter, *Masks and Masking in Medieval and Early Tudor England* (Aldershot, 2002)
Tydeman	William Tydeman, *English Medieval Theatre, 1400–1500* (1986)
Tyndale	[*The New Testament*], trans. William Tyndale (Cologne, 1525)
Van Bruaene	Anne-Laure Van Bruaene, '"A wonderfull tryumfe, for the wynnyng of a pryse": guilds, ritual, theater, and the urban network in the southern Low Countries, ca. 1450–1650', *Renaissance Quarterly*, 59 (2006), 374–405
van Dixhoorn	Arjan van Dixhoorn, 'Writing poetry as intellectual training: chambers of rhetoric and the development of vernacular intellectual life in the Low Countries between 1480 and 1600', in Koen Goudriaan, Jaap van Moolenbroek and Ad Tervoort (eds), *Education and Learning in the Netherlands, 1400–1600: Essays in Honour of Hilde de Ridder-Symoens* (Leiden, 2004), 201–22
Van Dyke	Carolynn Van Dyke, 'The intangible and its image: allegorical discourse and the cast of *Everyman*', in Mary J. Carruthers and Elizabeth D. Kirk (eds), *Acts of Interpretation: The Text and its Contexts, 700–1600: Essays on Medieval and Renaissance Literature in Honor of E. Talbot Donaldson* (Norman, Okla., 1982), 311–24
Van Laan	Thomas Van Laan, '*Everyman*: a structural analysis', *PMLA*, 78 (1963), 465–75
Van Oostrom	Frits Pieter Van Oostrom, *Court and Culture: Dutch Literature, 1350–1450*, trans. Arnold J. Pomerans (Berkeley, 1992)
Vanhoutte	Jacqueline Vanhoutte, 'When *Elckerlijc* becomes *Everyman*: translating Dutch to English, performance to print', *Studies in the Humanities*, 22 (1995), 100–16

Very Woman	Philip Massinger, *A Very Woman*, in *Three New Plays* (1655), Wing M1050
Volpone	Ben Jonson, *Volpone*, in *Ben Jonson*
Vos	R. Vos (ed.), *Den Spieghel der Salicheit van Elckerlijc* (Groningen, 1967)
Wager, *Mary Magdalene*	Lewis Wager, *The Life and Repentance of Mary Magdalene* (1566), STC 24932
Waite	Gary K. Waite, *Reformers on Stage: Popular Drama and Religious Propaganda in the Low Countries of Charles V, 1515–1556* (Toronto, 2000)
Walker	Greg Walker (ed.), *Medieval Drama: An Anthology*, Blackwell Anthologies (Oxford, 2000)
Warren	Michael J. Warren, 'Everyman, Knowledge once more', *Dalhousie Review*, 54 (1974), 136–46
Wasson	John M. Wasson, 'Interpolation in the text of "Everyman"', *Theatre Notebook*, 27 (1972), 14–20
Weavers	*The Weavers' Pageant*, in *Coventry*
Wedgwood	Josiah C. Wedgwood, *History of Parliament*, 2 vols (1936)
Weiler	A.G. Weiler, 'Recent historiography on the Modern Devotion: some debated questions', *Archief voor de Geschiedenis van de Katholieke Kerk in Nederland*, 26 (1984), 161–79
Wenzel, 'Enemies'	Siegfried Wenzel, 'The three enemies of man', *MS*, 29 (1967), 47–66
Wenzel, *Sloth*	Siegfried Wenzel, *The Sin of Sloth: Acedia in Medieval Thought and Literature* (Chapel Hill, N.C., 1967)
Wertz	Dorothy Wertz, 'Mankind as a type-figure on the popular religious stage: an analysis of the fifteenth-century English morality plays', *Comparative Studies in Society and History*, 12 (1970), 83–91
Westfall	Suzanne R. Westfall, *Patrons and Performance: Early Tudor Household Revels* (Oxford, 1990)
Whipping	[John Weever?], *The Whipping of the Satyre* (1601), STC 25352
White	Paul Whitfield White, *Drama and Religion in English Provincial Society, 1485–1660* (Cambridge, 2008)
Whiting	Bartlett Jere Whiting, *Proverbs in the Earlier English Drama* (Cambridge, Mass., 1938)
Wing	Wing Short-Title Catalogue. *A Short-Title Catalogue of Books Printed in England, Scotland, Ireland, Wales, and British America, and of English Books Printed in Other Countries, 1641–1700*, compiled by Donald Wing, 2nd edn, rev. and enl., 4 vols (New York, 1972–98)

Wojciehowski	Hannah Wojciehowski, 'The merchant's emporium: Thomas More's Antwerp, 1515', unpublished essay
Wood	Francis A. Wood, '*Elckerlijc–Everyman*: the question of priority', *MP*, 8 (1910), 279–302
Wortham	C.J. Wortham, '*Everyman* and the Reformation', *Parergon*, 29 (1981), 23–31
Wounds	Thomas Lodge, *The Wounds of Civil War* (1594), STC 16678
Wright, L.	Laura Wright, 'Some morphological features of the Norfolk Guild certificates of 1388/9: an exercise in variation', in Peter Trudgill and Jacek Fisiak (eds), *East Anglian English* (Woodbridge, 2001), 79–162
Wright, R.	Robert Wright, 'Community theatre in late medieval East Anglia', *Theatre Notebook*, 28 (1974), 24–39
Wycliffe	Josiah Forshall and Frederic Madden (eds), *The Holy Bible: Wycliffite Versions*, 4 vols (Oxford, 1850)
York Plays	*York Plays: The Plays Performed by the Crafts or Mysteries of York on the Day of Corpus Christi in the 14th, 15th, and 16th Centuries*, ed. Lucy Toulmin Smith (Oxford, 1885)
Ypocresye	*The Image of Ypocresye*, in *Ballads from Manuscripts* [...], ed. Frederick J. Furnivall, 2 vols (1872)
Zandvoort	R.W. Zandvoort, '*Elckerlijc-Everyman*', *ES*, 23 (1941), 1–9

INDEX

Printed in Great Britain
by Amazon